PROPERTY INVESTMENT APPRA

By the same authors

Statutory Valuations (*Andrew Baum*)

The Income Approach to Property Valuation
(*Andrew Baum and David Mackmin*)

Andrew Baum & Neil Crosby

PROPERTY INVESTMENT APPRAISAL

Routledge

LONDON

First published 1988 by Routledge
New in paperback 1989
11 New Fetter Lane, London EC4P 4EE
29 West 35th Street, New York, NY 10001

© 1988, 1989 Andrew Baum and Neil Crosby

Printed in Great Britain by T.J. Press (Padstow) Ltd., Padstow, Cornwall

British Library Cataloguing in Publication Data

Baum, Andrew, *1953–*
    Property investment appraisal.
    1. Great Britain. Real property.
    Investment. Analysis
    I. Title II. Crosby, Neil
    332.63'24'0941

ISBN 0–415–04367–0

Valuation is a human process in which foresight enters. Coming events cast their shadows before. Our valuations are always anticipations.

Irving Fisher (*The Theory of Interest*, 1930)

CONTENTS

PART TWO   MODELS

PART THREE   APPLICATIONS

FIGURES

TABLES

PREFACE

The debate regarding property investment valuation techniques has raged in earnest since the property crash of the early 1970s. Techniques used in appraising the value of investment properties, seemingly beyond debate, have come under the scrutiny of many observers and commentators, not all of them property valuers.

We have set out in this text to investigate many of the questions raised by this debate. One of the most important questions is the role of the valuer, which must be defined before any technique utilised in his or her work can be properly examined. The distinction between valuation (exchange value) and analysis (appraisal of worth) is therefore a continuing theme throughout the text.

We see property investment appraisal in crisis. The initial manifestation of this crisis is the apparent divergence of market value and investment worth, an indication of an inefficient market. As valuers perform their natural role of making the market more efficient, the distinction will reduce. We hope this text represents a philosophy which will help the acceleration of this very process.

We set out to investigate conventional techniques in both their historical and present-day contexts. We attempt to identify their logical base, and consider whether they remain logical in today's market. We then proceed to examine new alternatives, which are also investigated with a logical basis as the paramount criterion.

The text has been organised in an attempt to put both sides of the argument concerning *valuation* in an objective way. This has proved extremely difficult: each of us is convinced that modern alternatives do represent a significant step forward and should be adopted by the valuation profession without delay. As regards *anaiysis* techniques, we feel there is no debate. The rationale of this book is that the same basis may be used for both valuation and analysis, that is for all appraisals, and in this respect it is difficult to disguise our preferences.

We base our conclusions not only on the theoretical foundation of logic. We make use of considerable empirical research in tracing the fall from grace of conventional valuation techniques. We believe that progress will only be made by the adoption of a logical technical base and a continuing effort to examine the behaviour of the market: in other words, it is probably time to shift the emphasis of the last decade away from theoretical, and towards empirical, research. We expect to see the fruits of this type of work increasingly revealed in the quarterly *Journal of Valuation*.

To a limited extent this text is complementary to RKP texts *The Income Approach to Property Valuation* and *Statutory Valuations*: it is intended as an undergraduate and postgraduate text which presumes an understanding of financial mathematics, some statistics and basic conventional valuation techniques. Equally importantly, we would like this book to change the approach of practitioners and to found a platform for research in property investment appraisal. At the very least, it must make a contribution to a continuing and vital debate.

The use of the male gender throughout is not meant to imply that property ownership and analysis is restricted to males.

ACKNOWLEDGMENTS

The genesis of this book was the coincidence of Crosby's PhD research (chapter 3, parts of 4, 5, 6 and 7) and Baum's development of property investment appraisal models (chapters 1, 2, parts of 4, and 8). We would therefore like to thank all who helped with the former, listed in full in Crosby's thesis (Crosby, 1985); the students and staff who helped us to develop and refine the contents of this work at Trent Polytechnic, the University of Reading, City University, the National University of Singapore and Texas A & M University; various audiences hoping to continue their own professional development but probably contributing more to Baum's in the Far East and Australia; and employers and colleagues at PMA and Richard Ellis, particularly Martin Newell (now of the City University) for his development of a simulation program for use in chapter 8.

The seminal theoretical researches of Ernest Wood, Michael Greaves and Roy Mason were an inspiration. We are also grateful to Gerald Brown and Andrew Adams of the City University and Jon Robinson of the University of Melbourne for their helpful insights and criticisms. Yu Shi Ming of the National University of Singapore contributed to parts of chapter 4.

We are in enormous debt to our typist, Sue Williams, whose efforts went far beyond the expected, and to Gerald Harlow and the partners of Harlow Shelton and Co., Chartered Surveyors, Nottingham, for providing access to much of the original Nottingham property market data. We would also like to thank Chris Radford and Ian Sibley of the City University for additional help.

Finally, while we have done our best to eliminate factual inaccuracies and mathematical errors within these pages, we cannot accept any responsibility for losses which result from application of techniques recommended herein: we cannot afford the insurance premiums.

Andrew Baum
Prudential Portfolio Managers Ltd

Neil Crosby
The University of Reading

NOTE TO READERS

With a few noted exceptions, we have performed all calculations with perfect accuracy, rounding answers to the nearest pound. However, we have adopted a policy of showing multipliers to four decimal places only, which may sometimes result in the apparent solution varying slightly from the given answer.

For example, where a rent of £100,000 is multiplied by the year's purchase in perpetuity at 7 per cent, the calculation would be presented as follows:

Rent	£100,000	
YP in perp. @ 7%	14.2857	
Valuation		£1,428,571

The correct solution is found by £100,000/0.07. We regret any confusion which might be caused in the pursuit of accuracy. We prefer, however, to risk this confusion in order to prove that certain solutions equate without the ubiquitious reservation '(rounding errors apart)'.

Where we have used examples found in other textbooks to illustrate the historical application of technique, these have also been recalculated in the above manner, even though some of the solutions were rounded in the original texts.

Part One

INTRODUCTION

Chapter One

PROPERTY INVESTMENT APPRAISAL
IN ITS CONTEXT

1.1 WHAT IS APPRAISAL?

The subject of this book is the appraisal of property investments. In choosing the term 'appraisal' we have two distinct applications in mind, which happens to follow the *Shorter Oxford Dictionary* rather than the massed jargonists of the US 'appraisal' and UK 'valuation' professions. By appraise we mean:

(1) to fix a price for;
(2) to estimate the amount, or worth of.

The first of these meanings implies what is known in the UK as the valuation process or, in the US, the appraisal process: the estimation of open market value or the prediction of the most likely selling price. This is (AIREA, 1984, 194):

> The most probable price in cash, terms equivalent to cash, or in other precisely revealed terms, for which the appraised property will sell in a competitive market under all conditions requisite to fair sale, with the buyer and seller each acting prudently, knowledgeably, and for self-interest and assuming that neither is under undue duress.

or (RICS, 1981, 230)

> The best price at which an interest in a property might reasonably be expected to be sold by private treaty at the date of valuation assuming:
>
> (a) a willing seller;

    (b) a reasonable period within which to negotiate the sale taking into account the nature of the property and the state of the market;
    (c) values will remain static throughout the period;
    (d) the property will be freely exposed to the market;
    (e) no account is to be taken of an additional bid by a special purchaser.

The second of the two meanings, the estimation of worth, is not necessarily market-based. It is conceived in this book as the estimation of worth to an individual, given his/her subjective estimates of relevant factors. 'Worth' may be a value expressed as a price; it may alternatively be a rate of return expressed as a percentage of the outlay necessary to secure the acquisition of an investment property.

We cannot continue to use the term 'appraisal' to cover either meaning. We therefore view this as a source term from which the two specific applications are derived. We use the term *valuation* for the former (prediction of the most likely selling price); we use *analysis* for the latter (the estimation of worth). Figure 1.1 illustrates this.

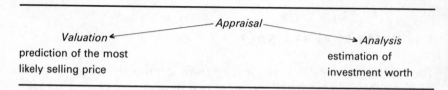

Figure 1.1   Appraisal, valuation and analysis

Appraisals of property investments should be accurate: that is, they should closely predict selling price, or they should assess worth to an individual correctly. They should also be rational, in order to facilitate decision-making.

It has been concluded many times (see, for example, Trott, 1980) that the conventional method of appraising property investments is irrational. We examine the basis of this suggestion and the consequent possibilities of inaccuracy in part 2 of this book. Nonetheless, charges of appraisal inaccuracy are much less common. Is it not true (as is often stated) that, if a market uses irrational or illogical methods in the fixing of price, appraisal techniques must mirror such irrationality in order to be accurate? Is it not also true that the accuracy of conventional property investment appraisals is proven by the lack of conclusive evidence to the contrary?

We answer both questions in the negative, and it is our response to these common beliefs that prompts us to produce this book. Firstly, appraisals can rarely be proved to be inaccurate. Secondly, even if they were to be, a rational foundation is essential in the exercise of professional expertise.

Appraisals can rarely be proved inaccurate for many reasons. All valuations are hedged by a series of assumptions. Special purchasers are excluded from consideration; a full exposure to the market, which is not defined, is assumed; no price movements over the marketing period are contemplated, even though full exposure may require a lengthy marketing period in an era of changing prices; and so on.

Predictions of the most likely selling price will only be shown to be wrong when prices achieved are revealed, and this is rarely the case. Over-valuations are often justified in time in a rising market, and in any event vendors will rarely sell significantly below valuation avoiding proof of an over-estimate. Estimations of individual worth – analysis, in our terminology – would be impossible to prove inaccurate (by what criteria?); and in the fixing of a price in order to attract a sale (a variation on the valuation theme) the valuer is protected from criticism except where an auction is conducted formally or informally between a vendor and eager potential buyers and a high price results. An undersell is rare (reserve pricing ensures this in auctions); private treaty sales rarely permit an oversell (and in any case the purchaser may have been special).

It is no accident that there have been relatively few reports of litigation related to valuation negligence. It is even common to quote an acceptable margin of error of up to 15% in valuations (see *Singer and Friedlander v. John D. Wood*, 1977, 212 EG 243). Reports of variations in valuations between valuers (for example, Hager and Lord, 1985; Miles, 1987) are interesting: there may be wide errors in samples of valuations but none are suggested as being inaccurate.

Finally, the valuation process is not, as is usually supposed, divorced from the operation of the market in fixing the price of an investment. Valuers often influence price rather than attempt an independent and objective prediction. This is a result of the process by which properties are valued (priced) for sale. Valuations of this type are, within the larger practices, carried out by those actively involved in marketing (agents). This results in the confluence of the valuation process and the market price mechanism. It is no justification of valuation accuracy that prices paid are close to valuations when negotiations are carried out by valuers. This invalidates tests of valuation accuracy and seriously questions beliefs in market efficiency (see, for example, Brown, 1985) based on an apparently objective comparison of valuations and prices paid.

Even if a proof of appraisal accuracy were to be possible, irrational techniques which produced such accuracy should not necessarily be defended. It should be the aim of an appraisal to achieve accuracy by means of rational techniques. If buyers or sellers were to become aware of an inefficient sub-sector of the property market, prices will inevitably change and valuations based on irrational techniques will immediately become capable of dangerous inaccuracy. The short leasehold market (see Baum and Butler, 1986) is an example of the breakdown of conventional techniques, lack of confidence in valuations for pricing leading to the use of tender sales, and the gradual, continuing adoption of an explicitly rational cash flow model for short leasehold appraisals.

Valuation follows analysis in the appraisal process. Fraser's suggestion (Fraser, 1985a) that 'if the market is irrational, the last type of model appropriate for market valuation is a rational model' appears to ignore this fact. It presumes a separation of the valuer from the market. It also appears to presume that an irrational (sub-)market will continue to be irrational, that is inefficient in the extreme, and that with its continuation goes the protection of irrational valuations. But surely any semblance of market efficiency will produce a shift in prices, so that irrational valuations will always be outdated and potentially inaccurate.

Rational analysis does not necessarily imply a questioning of market price, but instead allows changes in observed prices to be reflected in changes in meaningful variables, permitting the accurate revaluation of other assets. We hope to show that conventional appraisal models do not permit this to happen.

Lack of rationality is increasingly inappropriate in today's de-regulated and international capital markets. A change to rational analysis and valuation will facilitate increased market efficiency and the rapid assimilation of any observable changes in equilibrium price into appraisals.

1.2 INVESTMENT

We are concerned with the appraisal of real property investments. More specifically, we are concerned with the prediction of the most likely selling price of a real property investment in the market, or with the estimation of the worth of such an investment to a prospective purchaser.

What is it that distinguishes a real property investment from other types of real property? The most useful distinction we can employ is that between property acquired for occupation and that acquired for investment. The desire for shelter or a place to do business or to enjoy recreation may be contrasted with the desire for 'a vehicle into which funds can be placed with the expectation that they will be preserved or increase in value and/or generate positive returns' (Gitman and Joehnk, 1984).

Investment is 'the sacrifice of something now for the prospect of later benefits' (Greer and Farrell, 1984). How does an investment 'generate positive returns' or 'later benefits'? It can do this in three ways:

(a) by generating a flow of income (or reducing income tax);
(b) by generating a return of capital (or reducing capital tax), whether it be less than, equal to or in excess of the initial sacrifice; or
(c) by producing a psychic income, a positive feeling induced by investment ownership.

Investment return is therefore a function of income, capital return, and psychic income.

Appraisal of the latter is neither vital nor straightforward and will not concern us greatly (but see 2.1.4 below). Consideration of the first two factors is the essence of investment valuation and analysis.

1.3 INVESTMENTS

Property investments cannot be appraised in isolation, although the education and development of the valuation profession in many countries may suggest that this is so. By its nature, appraisal is a comparative or relative process, and property investments must at some stage be appraised in comparison with alternative investment vehicles (see 1.4 below). It is necessary in property investment appraisal to understand something of the nature of alternative outlets and their relative strengths and weaknesses.

Four broad investment types will be briefly considered and analysed in comparison with property investment vehicles. These are:

(a) bank deposits;
(b) fixed interest securities;
(c) index-linked gilts; and
(d) equities, or ordinary shares.

The following analysis is rudimentary: further detail is provided by Rutterford (1983).

1.3.1 Bank deposits

While not usually regarded as an alternative outlet for investment funds divided between fixed interest securities, equities and property, bank deposits are a useful starting point for a basic comparative investment analysis. The common distinction between savings and investment does not help. As Sharpe (1985) puts it:

A distinction is often made between investment and savings. The latter is defined as foregone consumption, with the former restricted to 'real' investment of the sort that increases national output in the future. While this distinction may prove useful in other contexts, it is not especially helpful for analysing the specifics of particular investments or even large classes of investment media. A deposit in a 'savings' account at a bank is investment in the eyes of a depositor.

In the UK, and for our purposes, bank deposits are identical in principle to building society accounts of the more common type. Each are characterised by the setting aside of cash in return for regular interest. This may be annual, six-monthly (as is typical with many building society accounts) or more regular. While the capital invested may appear to grow in such an account, it is important to note that what is really happening is the addition of compound interest to a fixed (in monetary terms) capital sum.

Rates of interest are typically not guaranteed for any substantial period and may vary with no specified limits. Consequently, a summary of the means of generation of return in a bank deposit investment (see 1.2 above) can be stated as follows.

(1) Capital: the investment provides a return of capital of an amount exactly equal in money terms to the original investment.

(2) Income: the investment provides a return in the form of interest which may vary upwards or downwards over time.

1.3.2   Fixed interest securities

Conventional gilts and other fixed interest securities which are not index-linked are typically a major component of the portfolios of major investors (for our purposes this means insurance companies or pension funds (institutions)). Conventional fixed interest securities may be divided into gilt-edged securities (gilts), which are UK government fixed interest securities, and others, typically corporate fixed interest securities (debentures, loan stocks and preference shares, the latter strictly being fixed *income* securities providing dividends rather than interest). Our discussion and generalisations focus upon the particular characteristics of the much more common gilt, although the majority of comments made relate to all fixed interest securities. A suitable generic term for this type of investment is 'bonds'; the term 'stocks' is increasingly used for ordinary shares (see 1.3.3 below).

Bonds are a means of borrowing cash. The UK government has in the past issued gilts for specific nationalisation programmes and named the gilt accordingly. Currently, gilts are issued for general financing of government responsibilities; the modern names are Treasury, Exchequer and Funding.

Gilts are usually issued in amounts of £100 nominal value and will normally sell upon issue at a price close to this figure. By this means, the issuer assumes immediate use of the capital which changes hands in return for a commitment to pay interest in two equal six-monthly instalments on two pre-specified dates, and to repay the nominal value at a specific date in the future (except in the case of undated gilts, which carry no commitment to repay the capital invested).

The amount of interest is fixed and determined by the coupon, decided before the time of issue of the gilt. The coupon is a rate of interest; the amount of interest per annum is the product of the coupon and the nominal value of, usually, £100. The amount of interest per 6 months is therefore given by:

$$\text{Interest per 6 months} = \frac{\text{coupon} \times \text{nominal value}}{2}$$

For example, Exchequer 12½% 1994 pays interest of $\dfrac{12\frac{1}{2} \times £100}{2}$

$$= £6.25, \text{ per 6 months.}$$

The payment of interest continues until redemption of the gilt. Short dated gilts are identified by a redemption date within 5 years; mediums by redemption within 5 to 15 years; longs by redemption over 15 years away; and undateds by unspecified redemption. For other than the latter types the redemption date is specified, like the coupon, at the date of issue; Exchequer 12½% 1994, for example, is redeemed at a specified date in 1994. As time goes by, longs become mediums, mediums become shorts, and shorts disappear as they are redeemed. Undateds continue unchanged, and are likely to remain so. While the government has the option to redeem after a given date, the six undated gilts which remain unredeemed all have coupons of between 2½% and 4%: and no government will choose to replace these loans unless interest rates fall to very low levels.

Thus for redeemable fixed interest gilts held until the redemption date the cash flow to be produced by the investment can be predicted with certainty. Market prices will not, however, remain constant. Immediately after issue the stock market price-fixing mechanism will begin to operate, and market prices will fluctuate. Simplistically, if interest rates rise immediately after issue, the coupon is likely to become low in relation to new issues, the payment of interest will be comparatively less and the price of the bond will fall. The opposite would occur if interest rates fall as they did in 1982, giving large capital gains for many bondholders.

The market value of a gilt (as quoted in the financial press on a daily basis) represents a midpoint price around which gilts can be bought and sold. Given this readily available information and the certain income flow, the *internal rate of return* on fixed interest securities held to redemption can be accurately computed.

Take, for example, Exchequer 12½% 1990. This has a redemption date of 22nd March. Let us assume that at 1st October 1987 £100 nominal value of this stock can be bought for £104.59. The timing and amount of expected cash flows are shown overleaf. (Note that tax deductions are ignored; in addition, this example ignores accrued interest, which must be considered when the date of purchase does not coincide with an interest payment date.)

This cash flow produces a half yearly rate of return of 5.18%; annualised, this represents a before-tax internal rate of return or *gross redemption yield* of 10.64%. Note, however, that this would normally be quoted in nominal terms, that is 2 × 5.18%: see Figure 1.2.

This certainty is removed by the possibility of sale before redemption. As

Date	£
1st October 1987	(104.59)
22nd March 1988	6.25
20th September 1988	6.25
22nd March 1989	6.25
20th September 1989	6.25
22nd March 1990	6.25 + 100 = 106.25

values move up and down, the prospect of selling the gilt to make a capital gain or loss arises. Given that future prices cannot be predicted, no certain calculation of internal rates of return can be made without an assumption that the gilt is held to redemption. It is, however, possible to be a little more positive by concluding that while future prices (and therefore gains and losses) cannot be predicted, there is a tendency for the value of the gilt to approach £100 plus the last interest payment as the redemption date approaches. Over time, interest payments become less important; and the redemption value becomes more important. The value of a gilt with 6 months to run should thus be close to £100 plus the final interest payment.

The financial pages of national newspapers quote gross redemption yields on the nominal basis noted above. They also quote *interest yields* expressing the relationship between the current price and the annual interest payments. For irredeemable gilts only the latter is, of course, presented. Figure 1.2 shows a typical (mythical) extract.

BRITISH FUNDS

1987							Yield	
High	Low	Stock			Price £	+ or −	int.	red.
				'Shorts' (lives up to five years)				
108½	101¼	Exch.	12½ pc	1990	104	+¾	11.96	10.36
Highest trading price in 1987	Lowest trading price in 1987	Stock	Coupon	Redemption year	Price	Price movement since last quote	Interest only yield	Nominal gross redemption yield

Figure 1.2 Typical gilt price information

The generation of return from government bonds can therefore be summarised as follows:

(1) Capital: the investment provides a return of capital in an amount

which may be more or less than the original investment. If
held to redemption, the return will be the nominal value of
£100; in any case, as the redemption date approaches the
return of capital will tend towards this price.

(2) Income: the investment produces an income in the form of interest,
paid half yearly in arrears. Being determined by the coupon
and the nominal value, this never varies: a bond is a fixed
interest investment.

1.3.3   Index-linked gilts

Index-linked government bonds are a relatively recent innovation and their
effect on the market is limited by their availability. Broadly speaking, they
offer an income which is fixed in real, rather than monetary, terms and a
redemption payment which is again fixed in real terms.

Parity with real values is attempted by tying interest payments and the
redemption to the retail price index, albeit lagged by eight months. (This is
to cope with the problem of accrued interest, which is included in the price
of all gilts. Without lagging the interest payment, given that it could never
be predicted the price could not be calculated.) The coupon is the nominal
interest, around 2–3% to date.

The return on index-linked gilts is therefore the product of a nominal
interest rate, an inflation-linked interest payment and an inflation-linked
return of capital, normally a gain. While the calculation of the gross
redemption yield is complex (see Rutterford, 1983), it can be broadly
estimated as $(1 + d)(1 + i) - 1$, where d = inflation rate and i = real return.
Thus Treasury 2% I.L.1988 unless resold within a short period has an
unknown redemption yield, as this will depend upon the inflation rate
between the time 8 months prior to purchase and 8 months prior to sale or
redemption; but if inflation is expected to average 6%, if the stock is held to
redemption and if it is purchased at close to its nominal value of £100 then
the expected redemption yield will be around $(1 + 0.06)(1 + 0.02) - 1, =$
0.08120 or 8.12%. If compared to fixed interest gilts producing a known 10
or 11% when held to redemption, these index-linked gilts would not be
purchased in these conditions unless purchasers were greatly concerned
with inflation risk (see chapter two).

The return generated by index-linked gilts is summarised below.

(1) Capital: the investment provides a return of capital in an amount
which may be more or less than the original investment.
However, given positive inflation, a monetary capital gain
would be expected. The return of capital depends on the rate
of inflation intervening between dates 8 months prior to
purchase and 8 months prior to redemption. Assuming that

the gilt is purchased at par on issue, the capital gain matches inflation, so that the price is maintained in real terms.

(2) Income: the investment provides a varying income equal to the nominal interest rate plus (minus) the lagged inflation (deflation) rate.

1.3.4 Ordinary shares

Ordinary shares, or equities, represent a share of ownership in a company. While they may or may not carry voting rights, all imply a fractional share in the equity value (total assets less debt) of a company. They are commonly issued with a nominal or par value of 25p.

Income is normally paid twice-yearly and is in the form of dividends (interim and final), which are determined by the company's profits and management policy, each of which may change from year to year. The income from shares, therefore, while it may have some relationship to the last declared dividend, is unpredictable.

An equity is 'irredeemable' in normal circumstances, other than by sale. The resale price is market determined and may be higher or lower than the purchase price. Again, therefore, capital return is unpredictable. Experience shows that the volatility of profits and dividend policy (among other factors) is reflected in the volatility of share prices. It should be borne in mind that there is no safety net as there is in the case of gilts with a guaranteed redemption; on the other hand, capital gain prospects are similarly unlimited.

Yield measures for ordinary shares are, as a consequence, largely unhelpful (although they are used a great deal by analysts). An internal rate of return, always the most complete return measure, can only be estimated given a prediction of resale date, resale price and all intervening interim and final dividends, or by projecting dividends to infinity (see below, page 13). This is so hazardous that it is rarely attempted. The only yield measure in common use is the relationship of *last* year's interim and final dividend to the current quoted price. Even next year's dividend yield can only be an estimate.

Dividend yield is no measure of total return. Low dividend yields may imply expected increases in dividends, expected capital gains or both. They are relatively volatile and do not form the basis of sound investment decision-making without the addition of a considerable volume of extra information. The price-earnings ratio, a comparison of price per share with earnings per share, is a standard additional measure of the quality of the share, where a high P/E ratio may imply anticipated growth in earnings and therefore in share values. It can be used in the estimate of resale price in attempts to forecast holding period return, or IRR. Resale price is a product of earnings per share and the P/E ratio at the resale point, which may show cyclical fluctuation and be capable of some qualified estimation. More usually, however, the predicted IRR of an ordinary shareholding reflects the rationality that the value and therefore sale price of a share must ultimately reflect all future anticipated dividends. Assuming annual dividends,

$$Po = \frac{D1}{1 + e} + \frac{D2}{(1 + e)^2} + \frac{D3}{(1 + e)^3} ....$$

where Po is the price in year 0; $D1$, $D2$ and $D3$ are expected dividends in years 1, 2 and 3; and e is the overall required return (target rate). If dividends are expected to increase in a common ratio (g), the series becomes

$$Po = \frac{D1}{1 + e} + \frac{D1(1 + g)}{(1 + e)^2} + \frac{D1(1 + g)^2}{(1 + e)^3} ....$$

Summating this geometric progression gives

$$Po = \frac{D1}{e-g}$$

(Those familiar with common presentations of property valuation mathematics (see, for example, Baum and Mackmin, 1981) may recognise '$e-g$' as a capitalisation rate and the above formula as the income approach or investment method: of that, considerably more will follow.)

Such a model may be employed for valuation (estimation of a likely selling price for a share which has never traded on the stock market, for example) or analysis (estimation of anticipated return, e). In either case it is instructive to note the effect of anticipated dividend or income growth.

For example, shares available at £1.25, last year's total dividend being 8p and expected to increase at a rate of 7% pa, would produce an estimated IRR of 13.4%.

$$1.25 = \frac{0.08}{e - 0.07}$$

$$e - 0.07 = \frac{0.08}{1.25} \; ; \quad e = \underline{13.4\%}$$

Such a model is naive, to say the least. It does, however, reveal a vital factor in property investment appraisal: anticipated growth in income and capital, g, and its effect upon initial yield. The initial or dividend yield in the example is low in comparison to the overall yield:

$$\frac{0.08}{1.25} = \underline{6.4\%} \text{ compared to } \underline{13.4\%}.$$

This is fundamental and provides a central point of reference in this book.

The return from ordinary shares is generated as follows.

(1) Capital: the investment may produce a return of capital which may exceed or be less than the original investment. All capital may be lost, however: at the same time, there is no limit on the possible amount or timing of redemption.

(2) Income: the investment provides a varying income dependent upon earnings and management policy.

1.3.5 Property

Property (in the UK and many commonwealth countries), or real estate (in North America, Australia and elsewhere) may be acquired for many purposes other than investment. Broadly speaking, a distinction may be made between property owned for occupation (although there may be a simultaneous investment service performed by that property) and property owned for investment *per se*.

Property owned as an investment may be either freehold, connoting effective superior ownership, or leasehold, connoting an inferior form of ownership subject to a superior landlord, either leaseholder(s) or leaseholder(s) and freeholder. (For fuller details of UK land tenure, see Gray and Symes, 1981.) The distinction between freehold and leasehold property considerably complicates a generalised view of property investment returns. While ownership of a freehold interest indicates perpetual ownership of indestructible land together with the more transient structure built upon it, ownership of a leasehold indicates a wasting asset. Yet this is too simplistic: some leases retain their value after the lease end due to the phenomenon of key money (see Fraser, 1984a; Baum, 1985) and the automatic renewal ensured by the operation of the 1954 Landlord and Tenant Act, and some freeholds exhibit a declining quality. Nonetheless, it is fair to generalise the permanent nature of a freehold and the temporary nature of a leasehold. It is in these two forms that property investments are almost universally held in the UK, especially by larger scale investors. Figures 1.3 and 1.4 show the general relationship of the capital values over time of freehold and leasehold investments in a period of inflation.

It can be seen from Figure 1.3 that in a period of inflation a freehold property investment may be expected to show a profit upon resale. Obsolescence may contribute to a declining (although difficult to measure) building component value, so that refurbishment or redevelopment may be necessary to maintain performance, but the general trend of value is upward. Freehold house owners will verify this: a town house not unknown to one of the authors acquired in 1975 for £10 600 now sells for £49 500 despite the fact that its heating system requires renewal, its windows are rotten and its roof is now halfway through its estimated economic life.

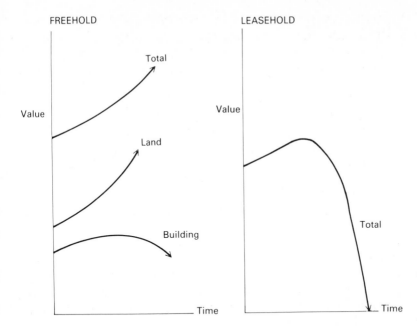

Figure 1.3 and 1.4 Term structure of property investment values

A 25 year lease in the same property, on the other hand, would by now almost certainly have peaked in value and would be entering a period of rapid decline to zero by the year 2000. The same is broadly true of an investment in leasehold commercial property.

Nonetheless, the problem of building depreciation or obsolescence of freehold buildings should not, as has usually been the case in the property world, be understated. Poorly designed buildings located in low land value areas will produce a more rapid fall off in performance than carefully restored and refurbished buildings in the City of London. Not to distinguish between these vastly different investment types would be most dangerous, and in this text we suggest approaches to the problems.

The income produced by a property investment is in the form of rent reduced by operating expenses of various types. While operating expenses will be incurred both regularly (management, service provision) and infrequently (repairs), rent will normally be received at regular intervals, quarterly in advance being typical in the UK. Analogous to the stock market and its differentiation between cum-dividend and ex-dividend investments is the apportionment procedure applied to rents received in advance in respect of a full rent period during which the property is sold. Apportionment of the rent which relates to the period between completion and the next rent date is in the favour of the purchaser and is in effect deducted from the purchase price (see Bornand, 1985).

The payment of rent is governed by the provisions of the lease. There is no standard arrangement in the English speaking world: US leases are of varying types but rarely for longer than 10 years and often for 3 year periods; Australian leases of offices are typically for 9 years; Singapore and Hong Kong leases are usually for 3 year periods; and the UK has a standard (although increasingly questioned) 25 year lease which appears to favour UK landlords and to suggest their peculiar strength in the market.

It is apparent there is little conformity. The regularity with which rents may be increased is, however, more standard. While the US, Hong Kong and Singapore 3 year lease is usually at a fixed rent and the Australian 9 year lease incorporates 3 yearly reviews, the UK lease usually fixes rents for 5 year intervals with upward only reviews. (Longer North American leases may have rents tied to the rate of inflation or, more often, to tenant's turnover; this is rare in the UK.)

The pattern of rental in the typical prime UK investment property is therefore stepped upwards (in a period of inflation or growth) at 5 yearly intervals. Rents at each review point are renegotiated in line with the open market rental or estimated rental value (ERV). It is arguable that ERVs reflect the fixed nature of the review period and are higher than their annual equivalents would be, but there is no published empirical proof for this. Where longer review periods arise (7 year, 14 year and 21 year reviews still appear in continuing UK leases) the principle of 'uplift' may be applied to increase the rent beyond the equivalent ERV for a 5 year review pattern.

In summary, therefore, the return from property is generated as follows.

(1) Capital: the investment may produce a return of capital by resale which may exceed or be less than the original investment. In freehold investments, there is an effective limit (land value) to any loss; in leaseholds, a decline to nil value must eventually be suffered.

(2) Income: the investment provides a varying income depending upon rental values, themselves a product of the demand for use of the property and the supply of alternatives. Variance of the income is reduced by leases and long review periods; upward only reviews will produce, at worst, a level income.

1.3.6 Summary

To summarise this broad overview of five investment types, it is useful to identify similarities.

Ordinary shares and property are fundamentally different from bank deposits and fixed interest securities in two major respects. Firstly, ordinary shares and property are both what Sharpe (1985) calls real or equity investments, representing ownership of tangible assets. Bank deposits and fixed interest securities are not real investments, but are instead investments in money itself. This difference gives rise to a second: broadly speaking, equity or real investments perform well in periods of inflation (they are inflation-proof to some degree), while money investments perform badly (inflation-prone). The period of inflation witnessed in the UK from the 1950s to the present was the cause of a rise in property and share prices in relation to alternative non-equity investments.

Sitting uncomfortably between these pairings is the relatively new index-linked gilt which is not a real investment, but which will perform well in inflationary periods. Figure 1.5 illustrates this.

	Real investments	Monetary investments
Inflation proof	Equities Property	Index-linked gilts
Inflation prone		Bank deposits Fixed interest securities

Figure 1.5 A classification of investments

There are, of course, many other examples of investments which demonstrate or question those classifications. Leaseholds producing a fixed profit rent are inflation-prone real investments, as are fixed freehold ground rents, for example. So this limited list of five investment types is neither finite nor comprehensive. It does, however, serve to set property investment in a context of alternative investment opportunities.

1.4   COMPARATIVE INVESTMENT APPRAISAL

The context of alternative investment types within which property may be appraised is justified by the investment policies of the UK's major investors, the larger insurance companies and pension funds, which have in recent decades pursued a policy of portfolio diversification by retaining a mix of ordinary shares and fixed interest gilts but increasing holdings of property and, more recently, of index-linked gilts. The theoretical basis of such a diversification policy is considered later (see chapter two); the progress of institutional investors in the property market over the last decade, when for many funds property holdings were built up from nominal levels to around one-quarter of all assets, is described in chapter four and is well charted elsewhere. (See Plender, 1982; Darlow, 1983; Fraser, 1984a; McIntosh and Sykes, 1984.)

More critically, the property valuation profession has in recent years been the subject of scrutiny by outside specialists as a result of this growing involvement in the property market by institutional investors. An early example is a report published by stockbrokers W. Greenwell & Co. in 1976, commonly referred to as 'The Greenwell Report' (Greenwell & Co., 1976). This report contained a critique of property investment appraisals and was regarded as displaying remarkable temerity in recommending a change in appraisal techniques. It can hardly be said that Greenwells were misguided by a lack of understanding of the art: the very methods they promoted (equated yield/DCF appraisals) are now being practised more consistently by valuers. And the need for this questioning arose out of the secondary banking collapse fuelled by the property crash of 1973–4 for which, according to John Plender, valuers must accept some responsibility: 'blind faith in the wisdom of the valuer will leave the British banking system vulnerable to collapse if property investment bubbles over into speculation' (Plender, 1982).

Greenwell & Co. must take some credit for the appearance in 1980 of the interim report of a major research project into property appraisal methods (Trott, 1980), which repeated the main Greenwell appeal for DCF-based valuation techniques. At the same time, other outside forces with either a general interest or expertise in the practice of investment were (and are) making inroads into the valuer's old areas of influence.

Despite these inroads, can the valuer relax safe in the assumption that his main territory remains largely undisturbed? The answer lies in his capacity and propensity for adaptation. It is arguable that in some cases the stockbroker may be able to provide more convincing, analytical and well-presented advice than the parochial – and probably short – valuer's report will do. Of course, specialist advice (regarding lease, structure, planning, forecasts of rental prospects) will have to be incorporated, but the valuer, or even the surveyor, does not have a monopoly of these areas of professional expertise.

The valuer/surveyor's market edge remains one based on convenience – the customer can buy all his goods in one shop. But where larger transactions are concerned the ability to subcontract is ensured by fee levels. And in institutional purchases the use of equity capital circumvents any restrictive lender requirement for a valuation to be carried out by a chartered (or similar) surveyor.

The valuer's reputation is endangered particularly by a belief that his methods are incorrect, illogical and, by deduction, capable of leading to inaccurate appraisals. The Greenwell Report insinuated that valuations were often too high as a result of blind reliance on an over-simple methodology. The main aim of the valuer, therefore, must be to ensure accuracy.

However, as argued at 1.1 above, this is not enough. It is not even capable of being defended. Appraisals must also be rational; and this implies that they must be capable of comparative interpretation in order to deflect the claims of the investment professions upon the valuer's territory. While stockbrokers view property as an investment, most valuers and surveyors view property as bricks, planning permissions and legal interests. The more important clients are mobile between all types of investments: while numbers can be compared with numbers, bricks cannot be compared with share certificates.

The need is for the valuer now to provide comparative investment advice. M. J. Patrick recently made a plea for greater cross-media awareness:

> Senior decision-makers, with overall responsibility for all investment, including property, are not surveyors but have backgrounds as actuaries or accountants. Understandably they are not necessarily impressed with statements that property is 'different' and incapable of being reported in a manner similar to that used for fixed interest and equity funds . . . as investment becomes more competitive there are a growing number of advisers attempting to make inroads into areas which, traditionally, have been the preserve of professional surveyors. These advisers have already demonstrated considerable skill with other investment media. They bring with them new (to property) and more analytical approaches to property investment. Consequently if surveyors are to maintain their position they must, at the very least, attune themselves with alternative approaches . . . (Patrick, 1983).

Illustrative of this problem is the manner in which the UK property valuer appraises leaseholds. Comparison is the valuer's main tool, but rather than comparing a 10-year leasehold with (for example) 10-year dated bonds the valuer goes through a tortuous route (see chapters three and four) by which he attempts to make the leasehold appear to be broadly comparable to the freehold by perpetualising the terminable income. He does this in order to compare property investment with property investment rather than with alternative investment media. This is no longer acceptable (see chapter eight).

To restate the problem, valuers are increasingly required to provide analytical, defensible and accurate valuations that are capable of comparative interpretation. Traditional training within the surveying profession can hinder the development of valuers into investment specialists.

Yet valuers are being placed under specific pressure to come up with answers to problems which, we suspect, have already been addressed by outside professions. Two examples of this are the current unanswered questions in DCF-based investment valuations – what discount rate should be applied, and how should we forecast future income flows? In the solution of each of these a lateral approach, taking us into the stock of knowledge concerning the appraisal of *other* investments, will lead to a greater awareness of the place of property in the investment spectrum. Valuers and property analysts need to be able to develop such an awareness for three reasons:

(1) The return on other investments may be a measure against which a property investment should be appraised. For example, should the redemption yield on conventional gilts be generally accepted as an indication of the equated yield which should be used in DCF-based property appraisals?

(2) The return on other investments may be a guide to the future value of property. If conventional gilts yield 16% when prime shops yield 3½%, when no rental growth is currently exhibited (as in 1982), it is possible to conclude that prime shops will fall in price, as indeed they did. Advice to a vendor or purchaser should reflect that view.

(3) Subject to (1) above, the return on other investments may be a guide to the implied necessary future performance of property. For example, levels of implied rental and capital growth can be computed given information regarding redemption yields on bonds and initial yields on property. Such information will aid the investor's choice between alternative property investments and improve the quality of professional advice.

Richard Ratcliff (1965) summarises our views, and our reasons for producing this book.

In the upward push of the appraisal fraternity toward the cherished professional goal, an essential reform is the rationalisation and updating of conventional valuation theory and methodology. We need to understand the valuation process as a form of economic analysis or research leading to a prediction of the most probable selling price of the property under conditions of uncertainty. We must shake off the older view of appraisal as the measurement of an inherent quality of real estate. We must recognise that 'the' value of a property cannot be expressed in a single unchallengeable figure. The appraiser must frankly admit that his predictions are fraught with various degrees of dependability. Thus he is responsible for giving to his client the benefit of his opinion of the degree of certainty of his findings, expressed as a probability qualification to the value figure in his report. We must view real estate valuations as investment analysis, a counterpart to security analysis.

Chapter two progresses our aims by introducing investment analysis.

Chapter two

PRINCIPLES OF INVESTMENT ANALYSIS

2.1 QUALITIES OF INVESTMENTS

What is a good investment? A simple answer to this seemingly simple question is 'one which produces a high return'. Previously we have identified returns as deriving from three sources: income, capital return and psychic income. A good investment is one which produces high levels of these in comparison with the price paid.

Most investments are traded in an atmosphere of uncertainty. It is not possible to predict with accuracy what the level of return will be. Even fixed interest gilts held to redemption produce a return which is uncertain in real terms and dependent upon future inflation levels for purchasing power value.

Investors will attempt to reduce uncertainty to its minimum by market research and other means. Information which is freely available is impounded into prices, so investments promising a high return will (all other factors being equal) sell for more. Jacob and Pettit (1984) describe this 'efficient market hypothesis' as follows.

Market participants, acting in their own self-interest, use available information to attempt to secure more desirable (higher returns, ceteris paribus) portfolio positions. In doing so they collectively ensure that price movements in response to new information are instantaneous and unbiased and will 'fully reflect' all relevant information. Competition among participants to secure useful information will drive security prices from one equilibrium level to another so that the change in price in response to new information will be independent of the prior change in price. Price changes will be a random walk in response to the information.

Investors in the five categories summarised in chapter one will typically hold some information which is not uncertain. This will be:

(i) price of the investment;
(ii) current income produced. For bank deposits, this is the current interest rate; for fixed interest gilts, the coupon; for index linked gilts, the next interest payment (based on the retail price index already published); for ordinary shares, the last dividend payment; and for property, the current contract rent.

Absolute certainty over the current income level leads to the use of the *initial yield* as a common market measure by which investments can be related. This is given by $\frac{\text{net current income}}{\text{price}}$. The level of this initial yield will be determined by several factors which determine the quality of an investment. A high quality investment is expected to produce a low initial yield because the market would bid a high price in relation to the level of current income, which depends upon a series of considerations or features which are unrelated to the current income level, and which are considered below.

2.1.1 Income and capital growth

The current income level may not be a good indicator of future income levels. Consequently, the initial yield may not indicate the continuing income yield that will be produced by an investment over its holding period. Where that yield is expected to increase, the initial yield may be low, the result of a higher price being paid.

Fixed interest gilts produce a fixed income. The price should reflect that fact. There is no prospect of income growth or, conversely, of monetary income loss. The initial yield is a perfect indication of the continuing income yield ('running yield').

Index-linked gilts, on the other hand, produce an index-linked income. As long as inflation is expected to be positive, income growth may be anticipated and the initial yield should therefore be lower, *ceteris paribus*, than for fixed interest gilts.

Ordinary shares produce dividends which depend upon (a) profits and (b) management dividend and reinvestment strategy. The latter is often used to smooth away variations in the former, so that a broad relationship between inflation and dividends may be theorised via profit levels, and in an inflationary era the profits of an average company might be expected to increase (except in the curious circumstances of 'stagflation': see Fraser (1984a)).

For property, a similar relationship between *inflation* and rents may be discernible. The Investors Chronicle Hillier Parker Rent Index (May 1985) shows that over the period 1977 to 1985 inflation was accurately matched by rental values as measured by the index (see Table 2.1 overleaf).

Other causes of income growth may be considered additionally to inflation. There may be prospects for *real growth* in addition to inflation (see, for example, the period 1965 to 1973 in Table 2.1) which may be discernible above the cyclical nature of the market. Particular sectors of the market, by type or region, may demonstrate this particularly well (see shops, 1977–1985, in Table 2.1). One of the major problems of this type of analysis is the quality of data. There are no such things as definitive rental value indices and it was not until the mid 1960s that any indices of rental value movements were published. A recent study (Crosby, 1985) constructs shop rental value indices for Nottingham City Centre for 1910 to 1981. The results from 1910 to 1960 are set out in chapter three (Table 3.1, page 69) and show that between 1910 and 1960 a real growth rate above inflation of 1.25% pa was achieved. Theorising over-simplistically, a supply artificially restricted by planning controls may be set against increasing demand as behaviour patterns change and population increases to cause real rental growth. A similar effect may be translated into real dividend increases for ordinary shares; it is not present for fixed interest (conventional) gilts.

There may also be *monopoly profits* which accrue to property owners. Property interests are unique: although the impact of heterogeneity will vary according to circumstances, extra gains may be made by exploiting the resulting monopoly position. An extreme example of this is marriage value. The owner of a mid-length leasehold interest will almost certainly be unable to sell to an investor at a price which matches the gain which the freehold reversioner could make by its surrender. Monopoly profits may accrue as a result to both freeholder and leaseholder. Other 'special purchasers' may appear: funds which are especially keen to buy a south-east prime shop, for example, for portfolio balance.

Less clear-cut is the gain made upon re-zoning or betterment. This may be diluted by competition, but the siting of a new motorway or the re-allocation of land planned for commercial development may well produce capital gains in excess of inflation and a reasonable real growth. These can also be termed monopoly profits: they may be the product of the exploitation of monopolistic information or of monopolistic land ownership.

Finally, *gearing* or leverage, the use of borrowed funds to exaggerate capital and income growth, is particularly suited to property investment. Simple house purchase illustrates this strategy. Suppose a house purchaser has a choice of an all cash buy for £50 000 or a £30 000 interest-only 10% loan and £20 000 equity input. Suppose prices increase by 50% over 3 years. The following comparison emerges:

Table 2.1 Investors Chronicle Hillier Parker Rent Index (adjusted for inflation)

Index

	1965	1969	1972	1973	1974	1975	1976	1977 May	1977 Nov	1978 May	1978 Nov	1979 May
ICHP Rent Index	87	106	121	155	155	127	112	100	101	103	108	112
Shops	87	102	123	142	140	119	110	100	103	109	117	123
Offices	86	113	131	188	180	140	115	100	100	101	104	106
Industrial	88	98	101	114	127	115	107	100	101	101	104	110

Change (%) per annum on previous reading

	1965	1969	1972	1973	1974	1975	1976	1977 May	1977 Nov	1978 May	1978 Nov	1979 May
ICHP Rent Index	–	5.0	4.5	28.3	−0.4	−17.7	−12.3	−10.5	2.0	4.6	8.8	8.6
Shops	–	3.6	6.2	15.4	−0.8	−15.3	−7.5	−9.2	5.6	11.6	16.1	11.4
Offices	–	7.1	5.2	42.8	−4.1	−22.2	−17.6	−13.2	−0.7	3.1	4.8	4.4
Industrial	–	2.9	0.8	13.3	11.2	−9.4	−6.5	−7.0	2.7	−1.1	6.8	12.5

Note: 1965–1969 and 1969–1972 are expressed per annum.

Retrospective growth rate (%) per annum to May 1985

ICHP Rent Index	0.8	−0.3	−1.4	−3.5	−3.8	−2.3	−1.1	0.2	0.1	−0.3	−0.9
Shops	1.5	0.9	−0.2	−1.4	−1.5	0.0	0.9	2.2	2.0	1.3	0.3
Offices	0.6	−0.9	−2.3	−5.3	−5.4	−3.6	−1.9	−0.4	−0.3	−0.6	−1.0
Industrial	0.0	−0.7	−1.0	−2.1	−3.3	−2.6	−2.2	−1.6	−1.8	−1.9	−2.5

Note: The above table shows the compound annual growth rate from each Rent Index time point to the present. For example, industrial rental values declined at the rate of 2.2% per

	All cash	60% mortgage
House value in 3 years	£75 000	£75 000
Equity in 3 years	£75 000	£45 000
Less initial equity	£50 000	£20 000
Less interest payments made (compounded)	0	£ 9 930
Equity gain	£25 000	£15 070
Equity gain %	50%	75.35%

A 75% capital increase resulting from gearing may be compared with an ungeared 50% gain. This particular investor would be best advised to buy additional similar property elsewhere – if it can be found – and make 75% on the whole £50 000 currently available for investment by repeating the gearing level.

Such gains can be maximised by increasing the gearing level in times of

1979 Nov	1980 May	1980 Nov	1981 May	1981 Nov	1982 May	1982 Nov	1983 May	1983 Nov	1984 May	1984 Nov	1985 May	1985 Nov	1986 May
110	107	107	105	104	102	102	101	101	101	102	101		
123	117	116	112	112	110	111	111	111	113	117	119		
103	100	102	101	102	100	99	99	99	99	98	97		
109	108	106	101	97	96	95	93	92	91	91	88		
−3.4	−5.5	0.2	−5.2	−1.7	−3.5	−0.2	−1.0	−1.3	1.3	1.8	−1.3		
−1.3	−8.3	−2.7	−6.0	−0.4	−2.7	0.9	−0.2	0.5	4.6	6.5	3.2		
−5.3	−5.0	4.2	−2.0	0.7	−4.2	−0.3	−0.3	−1.5	0.6	−0.8	−2.6		
−3.0	−1.8	−2.6	−9.4	−7.6	−3.5	−1.5	−3.6	−3.4	−1.9	0.0	−5.5		
−1.7	−1.5	−1.1	−1.2	−0.8	−0.6	−0.1	−0.1	0.1	0.6	0.2	−1.3		
−0.6	−0.6	0.3	0.6	1.5	1.8	2.6	2.9	3.7	4.8	4.9	3.2		
−1.4	−1.0	−0.6	−1.2	−1.1	−1.3	−0.8	−0.9	−1.1	−1.0	−1.7	−2.6		
−3.7	−3.8	−3.9	−4.1	−3.4	−2.8	−2.7	−2.9	−2.7	−2.5	−2.8	−5.5		

annum between 1976 and May 1985. Over the same period shop rental values increased at the rate of 0.9% per annum.

high price increases, where interest rates are low, and where taxation rules are favourable. The risk of financial failure resulting from interest rate increases or falling prices is at the same time increased by such a policy; but the general inflationary trend since the second world war and the particular experience of 1960–1972, when many massive gains resulted from such policies (see Marriott, 1967 and Rose, 1985), provides an example of a sustained period which demonstrated the benefits of gearing. While equities may be geared (for example by the use of options), property is the perfect asset in this respect.

These four constituents of growth have produced many valuable property companies and underpin the popular nature of property investment. Income growth is directly translated into capital growth, and it might be surmised that (*ceteris paribus*) the geared purchase of property in an improving area close to a new development or traffic improvements in a period of inflation is an excellent investment, examples of which have been common over the last 25 years.

2.1.2 Operating expenses

Once the purchase of an investment has been completed, the investor must face the prospect of continued expense necessitated by ownership. For bank deposits, such operating expenses are nil, apart from the investor's own time spent in checking accounts. For securities, the management of a given investment (rather than a portfolio) is again reduced to keeping an eye on the financial pages. For property, on the other hand, operating expenses derive from several sources. Repair and maintenance costs, insurance premiums, rent review fees, management (rent collection, periodic inspection, services management) fees, shortfalls in service charges, rates (in some circumstances), re-letting fees, refurbishment costs, dilapidations claims, and various legal expenses arising out of disputes with the public, tenants or adjoining owners contribute to a potentially high annual expenditure for the property investment owner, and may increase required initial yields.

2.1.3 Liquidity, marketability, transfer costs

Liquidity (for our purposes) is the ease and certainty with which an asset can be converted to cash at, or close to, its market value. Bank deposits are almost perfectly liquid; gilts are usually convertible to cash within one day; equities may be transformed to cash within a week to a month. Property, on the other hand, is illiquid. A quick sale will not usually be possible unless a low price is accepted. Even then, the period between a decision to sell and receipt of cash can be as long as three months.

Contributing to property's illiquidity are a trio of factors. *Marketability* describes the reserve of potential buyers for an investment and the speed and ease with which they may be contacted. For large property investments – buildings worth more than £10m., say – the number of potential buyers may be small. For unusual investments (for example Land's End) the potential market may be difficult to target and advertising may be highly inefficient. On the other hand, the stock exchange ensures the marketability of most gilts and equities.

The *indivisibility* of property as an investment contributes to its lack of marketability and therefore to its illiquidity. The possibility of sale of part of an investment reduces the impact of this problem and enables flexible financial management. Property can be physically divided, divided into freehold and leaseholds, or split into time shares, but it remains in general a fundamentally indivisible investment, with a high minimum outlay. This explains the drive towards a unitised property market current in 1988. However, until a unitised market becomes established or syndication becomes acceptable and popular in the UK, the purchase and sale of small units of a property investment will not normally be possible. This is not true of the alternatives.

The *transfer costs* necessitated when a decision to sell is finally translated into cash are higher than those associated with the alternatives. Stamp duty, conveyancing fees and agents' fees on purchase are nearly matched by conveyancing fees and agents' fees on sale: these may total 3% and 2.5% respectively. A more likely transfer cost for equities is around ½% for a reasonable volume and is likely to be less for gilts.

Illiquidity and its associates may therefore be said to be highest for property in comparison to the chosen alternatives. It has been argued (Fraser, 1985b) that the infrequency of property trading as compared with trading frequency in the stock market (see chapter four, Table 4.3) reduces the importance of this factor: but infrequency of trading probably results from illiquidity. The fact remains that cash tied up in property is, pound for pound, less liquid than cash tied up elsewhere. This has two implications: firstly, it increases the chances of a company becoming financially embarrassed and put out of business by lenders (see page 34); secondly, it decreases the chances of attractive alternatives being acquired. For property companies, the illiquidity of property may be said to be much more of a problem than it is for the larger institutions. In any case, it should increase required initial yields.

2.1.4 Psychic income

For many smaller investors property has an appeal unmatched by the alternatives. For some, this may be a prestige value: for others, it may be the opportunity for exercising positive management and, while perhaps increasing return, offering self employment. Driving past farmland may hold more appeal for some (even fund managers) than reading the financial pages; building naming rights may be a more tangible example of the psychic income which may be derived from property ownership. Whatever its effect – noticeable in some cases, non-existent in others – psychic income is a positive input into the quality of property as an investment, which may reduce the required initial yield.

2.1.5 Tax efficiency

The tax efficiency of an investment refers to the degree to which a gross return is reduced to a net return for the individual investor. Given the different and complex tax positions of individuals, institutions and companies alike, it is impossible to generalise regarding the relative appeal of a real estate investment. However, it warrants thorough attention in each individual analysis.

2.1.6 Risk

Introduction

Of very great importance is the degree of risk attached to an investment. Some finance texts view risk as the major determinant of return; modern portfolio theory contributes to this importance by regarding the investment decision as a trade-off between expected returns and risk (see Brigham, 1985). Branch (1985) is more circumspect, suggesting that 'investors will generally trade off some expected return for a reduction in risk'. A simple conclusion may be drawn: risk increases the required initial yield.

But what is risk? Reilly (1985) suggests that it is 'uncertainty regarding the expected rate of return from an investment'. Is there anything intrinsically unattractive about uncertainty when the expected rate of return may be much higher, or much lower, than expected? The answer to this question is supported by empirical rather than theoretical evidence. The typical investor is demonstrably risk-averse.

Experiments carried out in university classes usually bear this out. Despite the unreality engendered by the lack of real money in such an environment the following game is a useful test of risk-aversion. The tutor offers for sale ten tickets, each of which give the right to a cheque. Five cheques for £50 and five cheques for £100 are to be distributed on a random basis with a 50/50 chance of each being handed over in return for a ticket in any one case. The class holds 15–20 students. Tickets are sold by means of sealed tender, so that only the ten highest bids are successful. Unsuccessful bidders lose no money.

The prices obtained for tickets always indicate risk-aversion. £75 would not be an unrealistic offer, balancing a chance of £25 profit with an equal chance of £25 loss. But students rarely bid up to £75. One such series of bids from 15 students was as follows:

£80			
£75			
£74			
£74		£50	
£70		£50	
£70	offers accepted	£50	offers refused
£65		£40	
£60		£40	
£50			
£50			

In a more competitive market place, the successful £50 bidders would be less fortunate. The £80 bidder showed some property market optimism and a confidence in his luck. The £75 bid was, as suggested above, a neutral offer but the other bids illustrate risk-aversion. They equated the 50% chance of a considerable gain with the 50% chance of a much smaller loss. The median bid of £60 equated a £40 gain with a £10 loss. (The two £40 bids show an excessive degree of suspicion over the sincerity of the tutor.)

Thus uncertainty regarding the expected rate of return from an investment is seen as unattractive and results in devaluation. 10 certain £75 returns would have produced £750; the tickets offered netted only £668 for the same eventual cost to the offeror. Risky investments are less valuable.

Sources of risks

The sources of property risk are manifold, and many are unique to this investment form. They may be distinguished as follows.

(i) *Tenant risk* is the chance that the tenant will affect returns by his actions. The most serious concern of the investor will be the chance of voids, that is the possibility of the tenant vacating the premises and paying no rent. Even where long leases are signed by tenants, the possibility of bankruptcy must be considered. Legal actions are expensive and ponderous where actions to recover rent are undertaken.

Tenants may fail to perform repairing and insuring obligations. They may cause physical damage to or stigmatize a property. They may alienate adjoining owners or other tenants.

These prospects lend a risk to property which is near-unique. Perhaps the closest parellel is the risk of investing in ordinary shares which derives from bad management policies; it is much reduced, if it can be paralleled at all, in government securities and bank deposits.

(ii) *Sector risk* is the chance that sectoral price movements affect the subject investment. Such a risk is certainly present in the ordinary share market, where the choice of sector may be vital. Electricals may underperform industrials and chemicals; within that sector, micro-electronics may underperform household goods.

A property's sector risk is more sharply focused than this. Given the 'lumpiness' of property investment, where large sums of money may be tied up in one investment, property is particularly prone to sector risks in two dimensions. A parallel sector risk distinguishes offices (for example) from shop, industrial, residential, agricultural, development or recreational investments. In the period 1977 to 1983 industrials, on the whole, performed in a volatile and ultimately unprofitable manner (see Table 2.1).

A second dimension of risk which is not paralleled elsewhere is the

Table 2.2 Shop rents and yields, 1977–1985

Shops – rent index	(May) 1977	1978	1979	1980	1981	1982	1983	1984	1985
All shops	100	11,	147	170	181	195	203	219	244
North	100	119	166	187	202	224	230	255	282
South-east	100	109	138	171	196	206	222	236	265
Midlands	100	115	137	161	176	202	210	221	250
Scotland	100	121	152	188	192	191	194	200	221
London	100	121	147	159	157	160	165	184	203
Shops – ave yields (%)									
All shops	6.1	5.3	4.8	4.8	4.7	4.7	5.0	4.8	4.8
North	5.9	5.1	4.5	4.5	4.4	4.4	4.6	4.5	4.5
South-east	5.6	4.8	4.3	4.3	4.1	4.1	4.4	4.1	4.1
Midlands	6.1	5.3	4.7	4.7	4.6	4.6	4.8	4.6	4.6
Scotland	5.9	5.4	5.3	4.9	4.8	4.8	5.3	4.8	4.7
London	6.8	5.9	5.4	5.4	5.4	5.4	5.7	5.7	5.7

Source:
Investors Chronicle Hillier Parker Rent Index (November 1985); Average Yields (November 1984, November 1985)

locational factor. Table 2.2 above shows regional variations in rental value and capitalisation rates between 1977 and 1985.

The annual rate of return on a shop property, performing in line with the regional rent movements and yield fluctuations, would be as follows:

	1978	1979	1980	1981	1982	1983	1984	1985
North	37.6	58.1	12.6	10.5	10.9	−1.8	13.3	10.6
London	39.4	32.7	8.2	−1.3	1.9	−2.3	11.5	10.3

(Assumes annual reviews)

North   Average return 1977–85 = 17.75%
London   Average return 1977–85 = 11.68%

Performance differences occur between sectors (shops, offices, industrials) and regions caused by changes in the rents and capitalisation rates. Although shop average yields have fallen since 1977, industrial yields have risen. (The ICHP average industrial yield was 8.5% in 1977 and 10.2% in May 1985.)

The average industrial yield shows a greater variation by region. The south east industrial average yield was 8.8% in 1977 and by 1985 had returned to the same figure. The industrial yield in the north was also 8.8%

in 1977 but had risen to 11.9% by 1985 (May) and rents had remained static since 1980, with corresponding real declines in value.

An industrial property in the north, bought in 1977 and having performed as the index, with the yield increase of 8.8% to 11.9%, would show an 8 year average annual return of just 1.47% between May 1977 and 1985. A property in the south east would have an annual average return of 10.4% over the same period.

Overlaid upon this is international risk. UK funds have been seen to spread their property investments in recent years through the UK, Europe and North America. Both the relative performance of property rental values and yields in these areas and exchange rate fluctuations contribute to a pronounced sector risk in individual property investment which cannot so easily be diversified away by exploiting the lower unit of investment which typifies other markets. (On the other side of the coin, depending upon the nature of the liabilities of the investor, international diversification can be an efficient reducer of risk in the portfolio context: see page 37).

(iii) *Structural risk* is the chance of high repair costs, high maintenance costs, or refurbishment becoming necessary, and eventually rebuilding becoming necessary, either through structural failure or economic or functional obsolescence. Such risks are not paralleled in other markets other than indirectly and even then in a highly diversified manner. (For example, there may be a structural risk attaching to the performance of ordinary shares in a heavy industry company with one old manufacturing plant, but this risk type would be much reduced in the case of a chain of retail shops, where many more units (if owned freehold) would diversify such risk and reduce its impact upon performance.)

Much work remains to be completed in the general area of property depreciation and obsolescence (see page 204). It is not currently easy to generalise about the life of building types. It is, however, possible to say that freehold interests in prime shop units are much less prone to structural risk (often the buildings are old yet solidly constructed, having transcended the usual cycle of redevelopment; they are simple, ground floor cubes; and the responsibility for shop fronts, fittings and so on is transferred to the tenant) than are modern industrial units (where the nature of occupation, the nature of construction and technological impact upon industry reduce economic life). It is also clear that land is less likely to depreciate in normal circumstances, so that property investments with a proportionately larger land value are less prone to obsolescence and hence to structural risk. Office buildings in the City of London (for example) are less prone to structural risk than similar buildings in Houston where land values are less protected by physical boundaries and planning restrictions, and are in any event lower due to the relative eminence of the City of London as a financial centre.

Other structural risks may be passed on to tenants in the form of full repairing and insuring leases, but the ultimate responsibility for obsolescence and fundamental defects rests with the property owner who consequently shoulders a risk unique to this form of investment.

(iv) *Legislation risk* is the chance of changes in case law and statute law which directly affect investment returns. Certain property investors have suffered in this respect in past decades by the introduction and extension of the Rent Acts, the Leasehold Reform Act, the Town and Country Planning Act and others (see Baum, 1983). As one man's meat is another man's poison, so the concept of 'shifting value' identified in the Uthwatt Report (1942) probably resulted in balancing gains for others. For example, the rental values of residential properties outside the Rent Acts increased as protected tenancy rents became artificially depressed. More generally, legislation risk can have an upside as well as a downside. The introduction of Sunday trading, for example, would doubtless increase the value of out of town shopping centres.

Property is therefore especially prone to legislation risk. Equities are not exempt from this: health and safety regulations can have a massive impact upon drug companies, for example. Nonetheless, the experience of some residential landlords upon extension of the Rent Acts and the introduction of the Leasehold Reform Act 1967, while probably of limited impact, sharply focused property investment as a high legislation risk sector.

(v) *Taxation risk* is related to the above category, and describes the chance of imposition of new taxes upon the investment type or of alterations in current taxes. Property can be uniquely prone to taxation risk. Prior to massive institutional investment, it was possible to generalise that the person in the street was much less likely (aside from home ownership) to be a property investor than a stock market investor; that is still true in terms of direct investment. Property is easily identified as a taxation target and is not electorally disastrous, as long as home ownership is avoided. This fact in itself explains the tax incentives given to single house ownership (capital gains tax exemption, tax relief on mortgage interest, the now-abolished partial tax relief on insurance premiums for pre-14 March 1984 policies used in endowment mortgages) in a context of relative disincentive for private property investment. (In the USA, tax allowances and particularly beneficial depreciation schedules coupled with syndication of ownership interests and a free rental market in all sectors made it much easier to invest in property outside the family home prior to the 1986 tax reforms; and only in 1985 was tax relief on multiple property ownership abolished in Australia.) Taxes upon UK property investments apparently affect only the corporate sector and the wealthy. (Many institutional funds are tax-exempt.)

Local authority rates are constantly under the public eye and are unlikely to vary greatly; however, while they tax occupation rather than ownership, it is clear (Debenham, Tewson and Chinnocks, 1984) that rate increases cause rent (and return) reductions. The introduction of rate free (for 10 years) Enterprise Zones, for example, increased property values within the zones (albeit at the expense of immediately surrounding areas: see, for example, MacGregor *et al*, 1985).

More importantly, new taxes such as Development Land Tax, introduced in 1976, can have an enormous impact upon return. The introduction of Capital Gains Tax in 1965 was of great redistributive effect; the indexation of Capital Gains Tax in 1982 has reduced this impact.

Various income tax reliefs for particular categories of property investment – woodlands, for example, or industrial buildings – are constantly in danger of adjustment or abolition. Taxation risk for property is a major factor which is less likely to attack the alternative markets.

(vi) *Planning risk* is the risk that central or local government planning policies (in the broadest sense, including transport policy, regional policy, power policy and so on) impinge negatively or positively upon property investment values. At the regional level, policies of redistribution (such as the siting of government departments in depressed areas) will have broad effects; at the local level, proposals for such traffic improvements as the M25 and the Channel Tunnel have an immediate impact upon values. At the individual level, particular planning decisions have an enormous impact upon value, both in relation to adjoining properties and, more dramatically, in relation to the subject. The picture of a previously subsistence level smallholder with 11 acres of what is now a housing estate on the edge of Leicester, sitting in the Habitat-furnished kitchen in the farmhouse on his 200-acre farm, with the maximum amount in each of 3 building societies and a bemused smile on his face, remains with one of the authors as an illustration of the 'upside risk' of property investment. The downside corollary is a speculative purchase of land with development potential which eventually settles upon someone else's land, and it is of course downside risk that equates with most investors' perception of risk as an investment quality.

The effect of planning is so enormous that further elucidation is probably unnecessary. Let it suffice to say that the effects upon other sectors of the investment market are less pronounced.

(vii) *Legal risk* is the chance that the title to an investment is unsatisfactory or that it is discovered that a right exists over the subject land which affects its value. It is the risk that a rent review notice is missed; or, conversely, that a request for an excessive rent is not challenged in time by a tenant. These possibilities are generally unique to property. Each will be someone's loss balanced by someone's gain; to all, they represent risks. ·

Figure 2.1 illustrates the impact of these various risks upon property investment return.

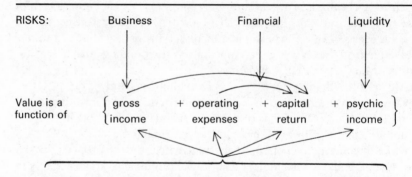

RISKS: Tenant   Sector   Structure   Legislation   Taxation   Planning   Legal

Gross income and *operating expenses* directly cause changes in *capital return*, which may also be caused by other independent factors (eg Capital Gains Tax).

Business risk is uncertainty in gross income flows. *Financial risk* is induced by financing methods and is directly reflected in interest rates, increasing the debt service element in (operating) expenses. *Liquidity risk* may reduce the capital return as a result of lack of marketability at a full price.

Tenant risk acts upon the gross income much as business risk does. *Sector risk* has a similar effect but also acts directly on yields and thus capital values. *Structural risk* has an impact on the cost of operating the investment and may also reduce resale value and hence capital return. *Legislation risk* may affect both rents and yields independently (eg Rent Acts). *Taxation risk* may act upon income or expenses allowed against income (Income or Corporation Tax) and capital return (Capital Gains Tax). *Planning risk* may change income flow, capital return and even psychic income through restricting the owner's use of the property asset. *Legal risk* may result in inadequate rent or an alteration in yield through defective title.

Figure 2.1 Property investment risks

In contrast with the above risk classifications, designed for application to property and within which there are direct and indirect applications to alternative markets, finance theory applies three broad categories of risk to investment. Reilly (1985) summarises these as follows:

Business risk   is the uncertainty of income flows caused by the nature of the firm's business;

Financial risk   is the uncertainty introduced by the method of financing an investment;

Liquidity risk   is the uncertainty introduced by the secondary market for an investment. How long will it take to convert the investment into cash, and what price will be received?

Applying these classifications to property is approached by imagining each property investment as an individual business. Business risk is then a derived risk which is reduced enormously by fixed rents in leases or between rent reviews and by upward only rent reviews. Liquidity risk has already been covered. Financial risk affects property which is acquired by using some borrowed funds, and is the corollary of a geared purchase. While all investments are sensitive to some extent to interest rate fluctuations, it can be seen that property which is highly geared (as it often is) carries with it a high financial risk.

In summary, property is subject to many risks, several of which are unique to this sector. General risk classifications which are applied to the alternatives show property to be prone to all general categories but relatively protected from business risk by leasing practice. These general classifications are of very limited value in explaining property risks, and the fuller examination which preceded this classification may be of considerably more value. This depends, however, on the definition of risk.

Money or real risk?

Risk may be analysed in terms of money income (what is the possibility of variations in the actual income and capital returns from the expected?) or in terms of real income (what is the possibility of variations in the real value of actual and capital returns from the expected?). The choice is a significant one and depends greatly upon the *liabilities* of the investor. A predictive comparison of property with (for example) fixed interest gilts is simpler on the former basis, while a comparison with index-linked gilts is simpler when predicated on the latter basis.

The money risk of fixed interest gilts if held to redemption is almost nil, founded on the prospect of government default. There is some money risk if a sale before redemption is possible. Real risk is, on the other hand, quite high due to the fixed money income produced and the possibility of variations in the real value of money.

The money risk of equities is higher, as dividends and share prices vary. Real risk should intuitively be less than for fixed interest gilts due to a broad correlation between inflation and dividends and between dividends and share prices, although empirical evidence may be found to dispute this.

The money risk of index-linked gilts is considerable, even if held to redemption, due to uncertainties regarding future inflation levels; while the real risk is very low, created only by lagging of the inflation linking (see chapter one). If a sale before redemption is a possibility, additional real risk is experienced as a result of future inflation expectations, themselves subject real risk is very low, created only by lagging of the inflation linking (see chapter one). If a sale before redemption is a possibility, additional real risk is experienced as a result of future inflation expectations, themselves subject to change, being reflected in price and altering the inflation linked nature of the return (see example 2.1).

EXAMPLE 2.1

Assume a suitable target rate for a purchase of index-linked gilts is 13%. In 1985 a 5-year index-linked gilt, coupon 3%, has been issued with interest paid annually in arrear at a price of £100. Inflation between 1985 and 1988, when the gilt was resold, ran at 5% pa. Inflation between the resale date and redemption was expected to run at 10% p.a.

The income is given as (£100 × c) where c = coupon, increasing at a rate of $(1 + g)$ where g = compound inflation rate from issue to year of income.

In years 1986, 1987 and 1988, the annual income is as follows:

$$
\begin{array}{lll}
1986: & £100 \times (0.03) \times (1.05) & = £3.15 \\
1987: & £100 \times (0.03) \times (1.05)^2 & = £3.31 \\
1988: & £100 \times (0.03) \times (1.05)^3 & = £3.47
\end{array}
$$

In years 1989 and 1990 it is expected to be as follows:

$$
\begin{array}{lll}
1989: & £100 \times (0.03) \times (1.05)^3 \times (1.10) & = £3.82 \\
1990: & £100 \times (0.03) \times (1.05)^3 \times (1.10)^2 & = £4.20
\end{array}
$$

The resale price is given by £100 $(1 + d_1)(1 + d_2)(1 + d_3)(1 + d_4)(1 + d_5)$.

This is £100 $(1 + 0.05)(1 + 0.05)(1 + 0.05)(1 + 0.10)(1 + 0.10)$ = £140.07.

In 1988, an investor with a target rate of 13% would pay a price given by

$$
\frac{£3.82}{1.13} + \frac{£4.20}{(1.13)^2} + \frac{£140.07}{(1.13)^2}
$$
$$
= £3.38 + £3.29 + £109.70 = \underline{£116.37}
$$

For the 1985 purchaser, his return is the internal rate of return (i) of the following income flow.

$$
- £100 + \frac{£3.15}{1 + i} + \frac{£3.31}{(1 + i)^2} + \frac{£3.47}{(1 + i)^3} + \frac{£116.37}{(1 + i)^3}
$$

The internal rate of return (i) = 8.33% p.a.; this is a real return not of 3% p.a. but of 3.17% p.a. Were, alternatively, inflation expected at 2% p.a. after 1988, the IRR would become 3.40% p.a.; this is a real return not of 3% p.a. but of −4.4% p.a. The real risk of index-linked gilts therefore depends upon the timing of a sale prior to redemption and upon future expectations of inflation.

Bank deposits display almost negligible money risk but have considerable real risk produced largely by the propensity of the fixed capital return to be reduced in real value by inflation, and the imperfect and only very indirect linkage between interest rates and inflation.

The money risk of a property investment is, as we have already shown, potentially very high. It is probably higher than its real risk, which is reduced by a broad correlation between inflation and rental values and between rental values and capital values, so that property represents a medium-risk (in real terms) investment type, roughly on a par with equities (although property review patterns possibly argue in favour of the latter), riskier than index-linked gilts but less risky than fixed interest gilts (see figure 2.2).

Real risk might be a preferable basis for investment comparison. But we are sure that, at present, property investment appraisals should be carried out in a manner which lends itself to investment comparison; and that comparison is most practicable by using money values in cash flow predictions. Consequently we err on the side of a money risk hierarchy for the rest of this book. In these terms, fixed interest bonds held to redemption are least risky; bank deposits are next; index-linked gilts are next, and property, with the levelling of return produced by leasing practice, is exceeded only by equities in terms of money risk.

This, however, ignores our final debate over risk definitions.

RISK:	REAL	MONETARY
LOW		
│	Index-linked gilts	Fixed interest gilts
│	Equities	Bank deposits
│	Property	Index-linked gilts
│	Bank deposits	Property
V	Fixed interest gilts	Equities
HIGH		

Figure 2.2 A possible real and monetary risk hierarchy

Individual or portfolio risk?

Fraser (1985b) has produced evidence based on the JLW Property Index (Jones Lang Wootton, quarterly) for his proposition that, whether measured in money or real terms, and whether measured in terms of downside risk or overall risk, property has, between 1977 and 1985, been the least risky investment category of the three major institutional investment vehicles (fixed interest gilts, equities and property). At the individual property level, this empirical evidence is impossible to reconcile with *a priori* reasoning. One would expect to be correct in a presumption that, in money terms at least, property is riskier than fixed interest gilts held to redemption.

There are two reasons for this apparent contradiction. Firstly, Fraser's analysis examines period by period returns rather than yields to redemption.

Secondly, Fraser's analysis relates to portfolios of property and gilts rather than the individual constituent assets. The JLW Property Index is constructed by forming a hypothetical portfolio of 138 properties (as at Summer 1985) mixed in type (offices, shops, industrials and others) and by location. Many of the risks which attach to individual property investment have been diversified away. For example, shifting value – if it exists – would naturally compensate falling value in one location by rising value in another, thus smoothing out variations.

Table 2.3   ICHP Rent Index (extract from Table 2.1)

	1982 May	1982 Nov	1983 May	1983 Nov	1984 May	1984 Nov	1985 May
ICHP Rent Index	102	102	101	101	101	102	101
Shops	110	111	111	111	113	117	119
Offices	100	99	99	99	99	98	97
Industrial	96	95	93	92	91	91	88

Similarly, as Table 2.3 shows, the extremely stable real value profile of the ICHP Rent Index from May 1982 to May 1985 masks considerable variations in the three broad sectors of offices, shops and industrials. Even within those categories there are many more inter regional, inter city and inter property variations hidden away. Consequently, the use of indices containing a large number of properties, which may be outside the scope of a typical investor, will present a misleading riskless view of property as an asset. The reliance of such indices upon valuations compounds this problem.

Markowitz developed a basic portfolio model (Markowitz, 1959) which showed how risk may be reduced within a portfolio by combining assets whose returns demonstrated less than perfect positive correlation.

(What follows is a simplistic and non-technical introduction to modern portfolio theory and the Capital Asset Pricing Model, predicated in terms of a single period expectations model. A simple numerical example at page 249 illustrates the principle. Readers who require a full discussion of MPT should refer to a standard finance text: see, for example, Brigham, 1985; Reilly, 1985; or Sharpe, 1985.

Given that the typical investor is risk-averse, the combination of two or more investments whose returns fluctuate over time and in different conditions *but in opposite directions* can reduce risk without at the same time reducing return. Thus, if it can be shown that as industrial properties decline in value shops increase in value and *vice versa*, a two-asset property portfolio is superior to that of either individual asset. The investor de-values a risky asset; two risky assets in combination would be worth more than the sum of the two individual values.

Measuring risk by use of standard deviations (see chapter eight) and return by internal rate of return or net present value, it is possible to plot on a graph the risk/return combination of two equally priced and perfectly negatively correlated investments. Let us imagine that these are the shop and industrial investments referred to above.

Imagine that the shop (X) has an expected IRR of 14% and a standard deviation of IRRs of 24%; and that the industrial property (Y) has an expected IRR of 18% and a standard deviation of IRRs of 52%. Whether an investor would choose X or Y would depend upon his risk/return

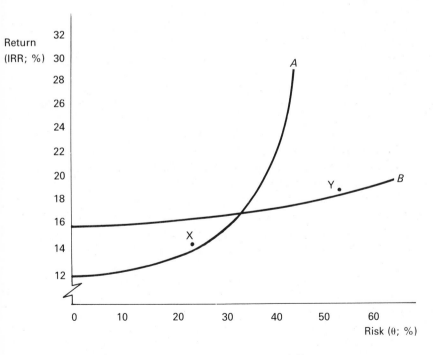

Figure 2.3 The risk–return trade-off

indifference: a risk-averse investor (A) would choose X; a risk-seeking investor (B) would choose Y.

Let us further imagine that investments X and Y are infinitely divisible, and that the purchaser's available funds can be expended in any combination of X and Y from 100% X to 100% Y (this may be possible through unitisation of property investments). Given their perfect negative correlation, a 50:50 combination will have nil risk; the return will be the average of the two IRRs, that is 16%.

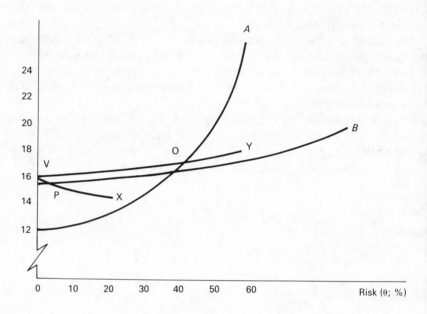

Figure 2.4 Risk and return in a two-asset portfolio

Figure 2.4 shows all possible combinations, joined in a continuous line. Note that investor A would choose 100% X or any combination of X and Y up to a maximum amount of the risky asset Y given by the point O. Investor B would choose 100% Y or any combination of Y and X up to a maximum amount of the low-return asset X given by point P.

Note that both A and B can narrow down their choice further. For either, less than 50% of investment Y produces a two-investment portfolio which has a higher risk – for a lower return! This choice should be a portfolio combination between points V and O. There is an efficient set of combinations shown by that part of the curve connecting points V and Y, known as the efficient frontier (see Figure 2.5). All other combinations can be disregarded.

We must now relax the simple assumption of a two-property portfolio.

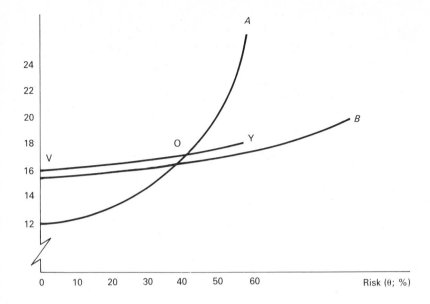

Figure 2.5 The efficient frontier

Given a much larger choice of property, equity and other risky investments, any two or more of which may be combined, a whole set of efficient frontiers may be constructed (see Figure 2.6 overleaf).

Note that all risk-return combinations of *IJ* are bettered by alternatives. Note also that certain parts of all other curves are bettered at some point. A new efficient frontier of portfolios may be constructed roughly along a line reconnecting points *A* and *H* (line AH).

Note that 100% of the least risky asset *A* and 100% of the highest return asset *H* are alternative positions on the efficient frontier. In between may be any number of combinations of two or more property (and equity) assets. The investor's choice will depend upon his risk return indifference.

Any point along line *AH* is a risk/return trade off. But some investments may be found which are risk free. For some investors, it may be preferable to invest wholly in risk free investments. What happens to the efficient frontier if risk free assets are combined with an efficient portfolio of risky investments? It can be shown that the standard deviation of a portfolio that combines a risk free asset and a portfolio of risky assets is the linear proportion of the standard deviation of the risky asset portfolio. In other words, given a standard deviation of 0 for a risk free investment, a 50:50 combination of that risk free investment with the risky portfolio will produce a risk of 50% of the risky portfolio. A new linear efficient frontier may be constructed (see Figure 2.7). Assume the risk free return is 12.5%.

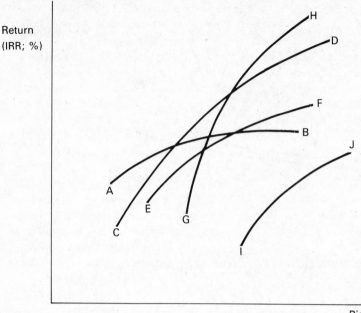

Figure 2.6 Multi-asset portfolio efficient frontiers

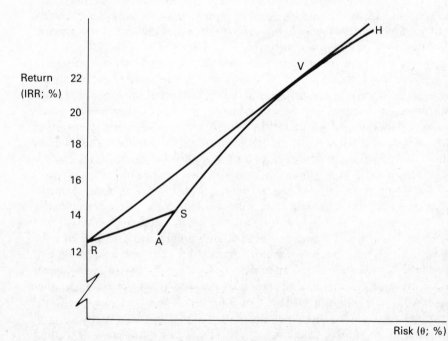

Figure 2.7 The efficient frontier with a risk free asset

It is clear from Figure 2.7 that one set of combinations (RV) dominates all other possibilities (including, for example, RS). Depending on the investor's risk return indifference, a point along this line should be selected. This (slightly modified) is known as the capital market line.

By definition, all portfolios on the capital market line are efficiently diversified. It is not possible to reduce risk for an increased or equal return even by adding further negatively correlated investments. The risk of this portfolio is the risk of the whole market (systematic): there is no residual or non-market risk, and it is now the volatility of the market which produces risk for the portfolio.

Adding further investments will not affect the unsystematic risk of the portfolio, which has been diversified away. It may, however, have an effect upon its systematic risk. How volatile is a new investment in relation to the market portfolio? If it exaggerates the upturns and downturns in the portfolio, it is a risky asset and should only be purchased if the rate of return it promises is sufficiently high: that is, one that suggests that positive abnormal returns will be made.

Beta (β) is the measure of volatility of an investment in relation to the market portfolio, that is, a portfolio comprising every known asset weighted in terms of market value. A β of 1.0 implies that as the market increases in value by 10%, the expected value of the new investment increases by 10%. A β of 2.0 implies that as the market increases in value by 10% the expected value of the new investment increases by 20%. A β of 0.5 implies that as the market increases in value by 10% the expected value of the new investment increases by 5%.

We have already discussed the possibility of investing in a (monetary) risk free asset – say fixed interest government bonds held to maturity. The rate of return on such an investment can be called the risk free rate (RFR).

The market portfolio is not risk free. It is free of unsystematic risk; therefore, all it contains is systematic risk. The return on the whole market will vary in value over time in relation to the return on the risk free investment. The expected return on the market portfolio [E(Rm)] should therefore be higher than the risk free rate. It comprises the risk free rate plus an expected risk premium [E(Rp)].

$$E(Rm) \quad = RFR \quad + E(Rp)$$
$$\text{or} \quad E(Rm) \quad = RFR \quad + \beta[E(Rm) - RFR]$$

The return on a risky investment can be similarly derived. It should comprise the risk free rate plus a risk premium which reflects the systematic risk of the investment relative to the market. Where an investment is twice as risky as the market, the expectation is that it should earn twice the risk premium. The measure of this relative riskiness is β. Thus the return on a risky investment a (Ra) is given by the following:

$$Ra = RFR + \beta(Rp)$$

Empirical studies in the UK have shown that Rp has in recent years been close to 9%. Given a risk free rate (the return on short-term Treasury Bills or the redemption yield on short dated government bonds, in either case with maturity matching the single period which forms the basis of the model) of around 10% at the time of writing, the expected return on the market can be estimated.

$$Rm = 0.10 + 0.09$$
$$= 19\%$$

The required return on risky investments can also be calculated. Let us assume (without necessarily recommending the use of CAPM in the property market: see chapter eight, particularly pages 246–9) that an historic examination of the performance of property investments in relation to the whole market has produced estimates of betas for offices, shops and industrials. (Brown (1985) has attempted exactly this type of analysis.) Let us assume that the results are as follows:

Shops: $\beta = 0.4$
Offices: $\beta = 0.3$
Industrials: $\beta = 0.5$

(Note that all three categories are less risky than the market, a result which would support Fraser's examination based on the JLW Property Index described on page 37.)
The expected or required returns are as follows:

Shops: $Rs = RFR + \beta(Rp)$
                $= 0.10 + 0.4\ (0.09)$
                $= \underline{13.6\%}$

Offices: $Ro = RFR + \beta(Rp)$
                $= 0.10 + 0.3\ (0.09)$
                $= \underline{12.7\%}$

Industrials: $Ri = RFR + \beta(Rp)$
                $= 0.10 + 0.5\ (0.09)$
                $= \underline{14.5\%}$

The implications of such an analysis for property investment appraisal are enormous. However, the theoretical basis of the capital asset pricing model is not accepted without question; its application to property is not necessarily settled; and tests for betas in the UK property market are rare and uncorroborated.

Despite these reservations, much can be learned about the behaviour of the property market from this theory. Seven sources of individual property investment risk were identified earlier in this chapter, and at a portfolio level it is clear that many are in the nature of unsystematic risks which can be diversified away by balanced portfolio construction.

Tenant risk – largely the risks of voids leading to nil rents – can be normalised by the purchase of a large number of properties. As the number of investments held increases, the chance of a total void (say 10%) approaches the certainty of a partial 10% void across the portfolio. As long as the expected cash flow reflects this prospect risk is now negligible.

Sector risk can be diversified away, to some extent, by its very nature. While it may not be possible to construct a property portfolio which mirrors the performance of national indices (see Brown, 1985), balancing by type, by region and by city will result in considerable risk reduction.

Planning risk can be diversified away. We have already referred to shifting value: one planning refusal may be balanced by a permission elsewhere; a drift in values towards the south east caused by the M25 and Channel Tunnel proposals can be normalised by holding property in both north and south.

Legal risk is similar and can be largely removed by diversification. As one bad title is suffered it may be that another legal right which is valuable but was not paid for is discovered.

Not wholly unsystematic, however, are the following.

Taxation risk can affect all property in the same (negative or positive) manner. The introduction of a new tax on property ownership is an example of how all property may be prone to a taxation risk which is itself *systematic*.

Legislation risk is similar. Imagine the effect on values of a new Law of Property Act which abolishes freehold ownership or nationalises land. The risk is again *systematic*.

Structural risk is, in some respects, diversifiable. A spread of building types, construction materials and so on will convert the possibility of excessive loss into the certainty of a normal burden of repair and rebuilding. However, the impact of fashion upon building design may not be altogether unsystematic. While a balanced portfolio might reduce the risks of technological change and its impact upon industrial design, more basic changes in architectural practice may affect all properties in the same manner. For example, natural light may be found to be less efficient for all properties than a new type of artificial lighting. All buildings would then become obsolete to a greater or lesser extent. New lift designs might have a similar, though less dramatic effect. And microtechnology might eventually change the pattern of property employment so drastically that all sectors of the market are prone to the same risk.

In conclusion, property as an investment is (like all investments) prone to both unsystematic and systematic risks. While the former may be diversified away, the latter cannot. The effect of balanced portfolio construction is thus to reduce but not abolish property investment risk. Is it possible to generalise about this? Is the high individual risk of property irrelevant: or is the lower portfolio risk the correct measure?

Much depends upon the behaviour of the typical investor in the particular sub-market under consideration. Does the investor practise a policy of diversification within the property market? Does he have sufficient funds to do this properly? The answers to these questions can only be provided by reference to the particular. If the prime institutional investment market is the sub-market under consideration, then the answer to the first question is probably positive, but to what extent, and in how rational a manner, it may be difficult to judge.

The answer to the second question is that it is extremely unlikely. Given the current minimum level of investment necessary to purchase prime investment property, few if any funds can diversify internationally, regionally, by city and by property type in order to diversify away tenant risk, sector risk, planning risk, legal risk and some structural risk. Even the largest insurance companies may not be in this position. The analyst's strategy must therefore be to identify the most likely purchaser, the relevant conception of risk, and its effect upon the likely selling price or return to that purchaser.

The vast majority of transactions in the UK property market involve purchasers and vendors who are not able to avoid unsystematic risk. For this reason we do not propose to proceed with portfolio analysis as the basis for the major part of this text. We will, however, use the theory again (in chapter eight) in an illustrative example.

2.2 INITIAL YIELD ANALYSIS AND CONSTRUCTION

Early in this chapter we explained the use of the initial yield as the popular measure of the quality of an investment. Because the initial income level of an investment is usually known or can be predicted with some certainty it can be compared with price to produce a readily understood yield measure.

$$\text{initial yield} = \frac{\text{current income}}{\text{price}}$$

It should now be recognised that a series of features which affect the quality of the investment affect the initial yield level through the operation of market demand and the price determination process. As market conceptions of any or all of income and capital growth, liquidity, operating expenses, psychic income and risk change for the better, the effect upon price will be positive. Given no change in current income, which is determined largely irrespective of these considerations, the effect must be upon initial yield.

The initial yield is therefore a highly complex measure of the quality of an investment. In theorising what the level of initial yield should be for an investment, a process of yield construction may be undertaken.

Irving Fisher's classic work on interest (Fisher, 1930) established the basis for yield construction. Yields can be broken down into rewards for three factors: time preference, or impatience (i); expected inflation (d); and risk (r). A rate can be constructed from these inputs so that the interest rate $I = (1 + i) (1 + d) (1 + r) - 1$. Simplifying this, a risk free rate (RFR) can be constructed from i and d, and the rate on risk free investments such as short-term Treasury Bills combines rewards for these two factors, so that

$$RFR = (1 + i) (1 + d) - 1 \text{ and}$$
$$I = (I + RFR) (1 + r) - 1$$

(Note that an approximation is given by $I = RFR + r$. This is the format adopted in the illustration of yield construction below.)

This is the basis for a process of yield construction, but some further development is necessary.

The first step in a process of yield construction for a property investment is to find a risk free (or neutral) rate obtainable elsewhere in the investment market. What return is available from investments which are free of income and capital growth in money terms, absolutely liquid, free of operating expenses, devoid of psychic income and money risk free?

Of the alternatives presented in chapter one, the closest proxy for the risk free rate is the redemption yield on fixed interest gilts (but see pages 8–11 for qualifications to this). The cash flow is certain, removing growth and risk; the investment is liquid; it has little prestige or hobby spin-offs; it is cheap to manage. In chapter one we showed how the effective IRR (redemption yield) of Exchequer 12½% 1990 could be calculated as 10.64%. This will serve as our risk-free rate.

The initial yield on our property investment (let us assume a prime shop) can be constructed by a normative process as follows. The risk free rate is adjusted in a series of stages to account for the factors which affect shop properties. (All figures used have no logical or empirical foundation: they are for illustration only.)

A risk adjustment (a risk premium, R) may first be applied. Given that the gilt is risk free, and (whether viewed in an individual or portfolio sense) that the shop investment is risky, assume $R = 1.5\%$. Operating expenses may require another 0.5%. Illiquidity may urge an extra 2.5%. So far the required initial yield is up to 15.14%. The effect of psychic income is negative but very small: for convenience, say 0.14%. Rental and capital growth prospects also have a negative effect on initial yield, but the effect should be much larger: say 7%. The result is a required initial yield of 8%.

	neutral	risk	oper-ating expenses	illi-quidity	psychic income	growth	initial yield
(1)	10.64%	+ 1.5%	+ 0.5%	+ 2.5%	− 0.14%	− 7.0%	= 8%

A positive process of yield analysis, using market information to observe what actually happens in practice, would show that in 1985 4% would be a much more likely initial yield for a prime shop. It may be tempting to draw one of several conclusions.

(i) If the adjustments used reflect the preferences of an individual investor, he should not purchase the investment at the market price.

(ii) The market price and initial yield suggest that successful bidders for the property are less pessimistic about risk, operating expenses and/or illiquidity, or are more optimistic about psychic income and/or growth, or a combination of both factors. For example, if a portfolio risk measure is used and a small (1%) risk premium is viewed as necessary, and illiquidity is not a problem due to intended infrequency of trading, the construction (normative) process can be equated with the analytical (positive) process as follows:

	neutral	risk	oper-ating expenses	illi-quidity	psychic income	growth	initial yield
(2)	10.64%	+ 1%	+ 0.5%	+ 0%	− 0.14%	− 8.0%	= 4%

Alternatively, assuming much greater optimism regarding growth, the process might become:

	neutral yield	risk	oper-ating expenses	illi-quidity	psychic income	growth	initial yield
(3)	10.64%	+ 1.5%	+ 0.5%	+ 2.5%	− 0.14%	− 11%	= 4%

In recent years the low level of initial yields for shop investments has been questioned, and most analyses have centred on the excessive rental growth expectation that appears to push initial yields so low. It may be more useful to adopt a portfolio analysis in this highly competitive, institutional investor-dominated yet tiny sector of the market which establishes series (2) as the more appropriate and realistic construction process (see Fraser, 1984a and 1985b).

Whatever the lessons to be learned from such a process, two clear conclusions can be drawn.

(1) In the *valuation* process (estimation of the most likely selling price) the estimation of adjustments in the normative process of yield construction is extremely difficult, is guided by almost no empirical evidence and has an enormous effect upon result. It is concluded that such a valuation method is impossible to adopt. In practice, it has been neglected in favour of the positive process of yield analysis. Part two of this book shows how yield analysis has been used, and how the technique performs in the current property investment market.

(2) In the *analysis* process (estimation of worth to an individual investor) the yield construction process is more promising. The opportunity exists to agree adjustments with the individual. But again the quantum of adjustment is difficult to judge and the result is highly sensitive to changes.

It is concluded that the process of appraisal by initial yield construction (theory) is dangerous and impossible to practise. Appraisal by initial yield analysis (empricism) is, however, possible: in fact, it is the market standard. That is not to say that it provides a satisfactory methodology. The implications of initial yield (implicit) appraisals are considered in part two.

Part Two

MODELS

Chapter Three

CONVENTIONAL APPRAISAL TECHNIQUES: PRE REVERSE YIELD GAP

3.1 INTRODUCTION

The basis of a logical and defensible technique for investment property appraisal must evolve from the attitudes and perceptions of those who carry out the valuation and analysis of property investments and those investors who purchase, hold, and sell the property. The influences on them range from the concepts and techniques taught to them in the formative years of their careers to the market conditions which apply at the time of each transaction and their perceptions of future changes in those conditions. During the 1970s and 1980s a large number of articles and comment have discussed and criticised the techniques used by valuers to appraise property investments. Many articles and comment suggest that the conventional techniques being criticised have remained static in the past. For example: 'For many decades the conventional methods of investment valuation were accepted as logical, practical, and seemingly immutable' (Trott 1980, p. 1).

Trott also suggests that it was not until the property crash of 1973 that serious criticism evolved. To investigate the historical context of appraisal techniques is a necessary preliminary to a discussion of whether any major changes have taken place in property and other investment markets and whether any such changes have rendered conventional models obsolete.

3.2 DEVELOPMENT OF MODELS 1884–1933

The simplicity of appraisal techniques prior to the twentieth century is illustrated by Norris (1884). The appraisal technique for rack rented freeholds, reversionary freeholds and leaseholds is reduced to a single rate calculation where the freehold in perpetuity is the maximum value and the values of the reversionary interest and the leasehold interest must summate to a total which equals the whole, 'such that the sum of the two is always equal to the total value of the freehold in perpetuity' (Norris, 1884, 6). It is useful to illustrate this in passing. Rack rented or fully let freeholds are a common form of traded property investment, and the initial yield appraisal of such investments is quite straightforward (see example 3.1). The reversionary freehold results from lettings at rents which are, for whatever reason, below the current rack rental; the initial yield appraisal is slightly more complicated (see example 3.2). For every reversionary freehold there must be a valuable leasehold, whose value is derived from the resultant difference between rent paid and rack rent. The valuation is again straightforward (see example 3.3). Note that the sum of the valuations in 3.2 and 3.3 equates with the valuation in 3.1.

EXAMPLE 3.1

A fully let freehold; net rent passing and net estimated rental value (ERV) £21 000 p.a.; appropriate initial yield 6.25%.

ERV (Y)	£21 000 p.a.	
YP perp. at 6.25%	16	
Valuation		£336 000

EXAMPLE 3.2

As example 3.1 but net rent passing is £10 000 and there are 2 years to the next rent review.

Current rent	£10 000 p.a.	
YP 2 years at 6.25%	1.8270	
		£18 270
Reversion to ERV	£21 000 p.a.	
YP perp. at 6.25%	16	
PV 2 years at 6.25%	0.8858	
		£297 633
Valuation		£315 903

EXAMPLE 3.3

The leasehold interest corresponding to example 3.2.

Rent received	£21 000 p.a.
Rent paid	£10 000 p.a.
Profit rent	£11 000 p.a.
YP 2 years at 6.25%	1.8270
Valuation	£20 097

(This idea was the basis of the rational model (Sykes, 1981) 97 years later.)

In 1908 the third edition of Curtis on the Valuation of Land and Houses was revised and enlarged (Davies, 1908). Examples of valuation of rack rented and reversionary freeholds and leaseholds are given as follows:

EXAMPLE 3.4

Rack rented freehold – property let at rack rent of £100 p.a.

ERV	£100 p.a.
YP perp. at 4%	25
Valuation	£2 500

This accords with example 3.1 above.

EXAMPLE 3.5

Reversionary freehold – property let on ground lease with 37 years unexpired, ground rent £12 p.a., rack rent £75 p.a.

Ground rent	£12 p.a.	
YP 37 years at 3%	22.1672	
		£266
Reversion to ERV	£75 p.a.	
YP perp. at 5%	20	
PV 37 years at 5%	.1644	
		£247
Valuation		£513

Note that a lower rate is used in the capitalisation of the term incomes. This differs from example 3.2.

EXAMPLE 3.6

Leasehold rack rent £120 p.a., ground rent payable £20 p.a. on lease with 71 years unexpired.

ERV		£120 p.a.
Ground rent	£	20 p.a.
Profit rent		£100 p.a.
YP 71 years at 6%	16.4005	
Valuation		£1 640

Note that this accords with example 3.3, but that a higher yield is now used.

EXAMPLE 3.7

Leasehold: net income £150 p.a. with 35 years unexpired.

Profit rent		£150 p.a.
YP 35 years at 7%		
and 4%	11.9650	
Valuation		£1 795

A different approach is now used: a dual rate capitalisation process is used for a shorter leasehold.

The practice of using a lower rate on the term of a reversionary freehold was consistent in every example within the text although no comment was made for justification. The valuation of leaseholds by both single and dual rate concepts was justified on the basis that practice conflicted with theory (Davies, 1908, 41), the theory put forward in the text being the recoupment of capital through an insurance company policy. The author commented that single rate was used in practice, often with an increase in yield over and above the equivalent freehold of (generally) 1% or 2%.

The sixth edition of Curtis was published in 1924 (Smith, 1924). In the preface the editor comments, 'Little remains of the matter originally written by Mr Curtis, but many of the examples prepared by Mr Davies are retained.'

The subsequent edition of Curtis (Smith, 1933) is similar to the previous edition in that all the examples used to illustrate technique are used in the 1924 edition. Within both these editions the valuation of a rack rented freehold followed the established course of estimating a net income flow and capitalising in perpetuity at an appropriate yield.

EXAMPLE 3.8

'A well placed freehold shop is let on lease at £68 per annum, which is a secure rent, the lessee paying rates and insurance and doing all repairs, but not paying land tax, which is £2 per annum. What is the value of the freehold interest?' (Smith, 1933, 81).

	Rent	£68 p.a.	
Less:	Landlord's outgoings		
	Land tax	£ 2 p.a.	
	Net income	£66 p.a.	
	YP perp. at 5½%	18.1818	
	Valuation		£1 200

The valuation of reversionary freehold property can be illustrated by one example from the same text.

EXAMPLE 3.9

'A freehold house is let on lease, which will expire in 20 years' time, at a ground rent of £10 per annum. The net annual value is £100 per annum. Value the ground rent at 4 per cent and the reversion at 5 per cent' (Smith, 1933, 86).

Ground rent	£10 p.a.		
YP 20 years at 4%	13.5903		
		£136	
Reversion to a house worth, per annum in possession,	£100 p.a.		
YP perp. at 5%	20		
PV 20 years at 5%	0.3769		
		£754	
Valuation			£890

The approach has not altered. A vertically sliced term is valued at a lower yield than the reversion.

The valuation of leasehold property is again undertaken by both single rate and dual rate tables in the seventh edition of Curtis.

EXAMPLE 3.10

'What is the value of a leasehold house, yielding £100 a year net, held on lease for an unexpired term of 28 years, the purchaser requiring 6 per cent on his investment, assuming a sinking fund at the same rate?' (Smith, 1933, 120).

Profit rent   £100 p.a.
YP 28 years at 6%   13.4062

Valuation   £1 341

The next example in the text immediately introduced the dual rate concept.

EXAMPLE 3.11

'What is the value of a leasehold house, the net income after paying ground rent and other deductions being £150 a year, unexpired term 35 years, interest 7 per cent, reinvestment 4 per cent?' (Smith, 1933, 120).

Profit rent   £150 p.a.
YP 35 years at 7%
        and 4%   11.9650

Valuation   £1 795

The concept of a tax adjusted, dual rate capitalisation is introduced as a specific problem in short leaseholds (Smith, 1933, 123–6) but it is not pursued in the application of method to any examples later in the text which are all undertaken on a single or dual rate basis.

3.3 DEVELOPMENT OF MODELS 1943–1962

In 1943 Curtis was replaced by the first edition of *Modern Methods of Valuation* (Lawrence and May, 1943).

The typical valuation of freehold reversionary property and leasehold property is illustrated by one example where a compensation claim is worked out for freehold and leasehold interests in a shop with living accommodation.

EXAMPLE 3.12

'A corner shop and dwelling house in a good shopping centre in the town. The freehold is let on a 99 years' lease expiring in 36 years' time at a ground rent of £10 per annum.

The head lessee let the shop 16 years ago on a 21 years' repairing lease at a rent of £100 per annum. The premises are now worth a rent of £180 per annum on a repairing lease' (Lawrence and May, 1943, 304–5).

Valuation

(i) Freeholder:

Ground rent	£10 p.a.	
YP 36 years at 4%	18.9083	
		£189
Reversion to ERV	£180 p.a.	
YP perp. at 5½%	18.1818	
PV 36 years at 5½%	.1455	
		£476
Valuation		£665

(ii) Head Lessee:

Rent received	£100 p.a.	
Ground rent	£ 10 p.a.	
Profit rent	£ 90 p.a.	
YP 5 years at 6%		
and 3%	4.0265	
		£362
Reversion to ERV	£180 p.a.	
Ground rent	£ 10 p.a.	
Profit rent	£170 p.a.	
YP 31 years at 7%		
and 3%	11.1112	
PV £1 in 5 years		
at 7%	0.7130	
		£1 345
Valuation		£1 707

(iii) Sub lessee:

ERV	£180 p.a.	
Rent paid	£100 p.a.	
Profit rent	£ 80 p.a.	
YP 5 years at 8%		
and 3%	3.7264	
Valuation		£298

It appears that by 1943 the incidence of taxation was still being ignored in the valuation of leasehold investments, but this is not the case (as will be illustrated later in this chapter; see page 64).

By 1962, *Modern Methods of Valuation* had moved onto a fifth edition (Lawrence, Rees and Britton, 1962). The valuation of freeholds retained the past approach for both rack rented and reversionary property.

EXAMPLE 3.13A

'Value the right to receive an income of £1 000 per annum for the next 3 years with a reversion to full rental value of £1 500 per annum' (Lawrence, Rees and Britton, 1962, 62–4).

Current rent	£1 000 p.a.		
YP 3 years at 5%	2.7232		
		£2 723	
Reversion to ERV	£1 500 p.a.		
YP perp. at 6%	16.6667		
PV 3 years at 6%	0.8396		
		£20 990	
Valuation			£23 714

Although this technique was adopted for almost all examples in the text, the layer method was introduced as an alternative approach.

EXAMPLE 3.13B, AS 3.13A

Current rent	£1 000 p.a.		
YP perp. at 5%	20		
		£20 000	
Top slice income	£500 p.a.		
YP perp. at 9%	11.1111		
PV 3 years at 9%	0.7722		
		£ 4 290	
Valuation			£24 290

The valuation of leaseholds was introduced as before but now with both dual rate unadjusted for tax and dual rate adjusted for tax capitalisation techniques. The text has a very similar example to the one illustrated before from the first edition of *Modern Methods of Valuation* (see page 58).

EXAMPLE 3.14

'Premises in a provincial town, occupied by a draper, consist of a shop and upper part. They are held from the freeholder on a 99 years building lease from 1903 at a ground rent of £25 per annum. The lessee let to the draper for 21 years from 1950 at £300 per annum. The present rental value is £700 per annum. Valuation date 1961' (Lawrence, Rees and Britton, 1962, 367).

Freeholder:

Ground rent	£25 p.a.		
YP 41 years at 6%	15.1380		
		£378	
Reversion to ERV	£700 p.a.		
YP perp. at 7½%	13.333		
PV 41 years at 7½%	0.0516		
		£481	
Valuation			£860

Head lessee:

Rent received	£300 p.a.		
Ground rent	£ 25 p.a.		
Profit rent	£275 p.a.		
YP 10 years at 7½%			
and 2½%	6.0880		
		£1 674	
Reversion to ERV	£700 p.a.		
Ground rent	£ 25 p.a.		
Profit rent	£675 p.a.		
YP 31 years at 8½%			
and 2½%	9.3686		
PV 10 years at 8½%	0.4423		
		£2 797	
Valuation			£4 470

Sub lessee:

Profit rent	£400 p.a.		
YP 10 years at 9½%			
and 2½% adj.			
tax at 7/9d	4.1541		
Valuation		£1 662	

(Note that a different approach has been adopted for the head lessee's and sub lessee's interests.)

The examples illustrated show a continuity of approach to the valuation of fully let freehold investments and reversionary freeholds, where term yields are at lower levels than reversionary yields. The approach to leaseholds shows less consistency with a shift towards the use of dual rate tables with adjustments for tax on the sinking fund element.

The valuation of reversionary freeholds within reported Court and Lands Tribunal decisions of the period does not show quite the same consistency as the text books, with the use of lower yields on the term only emerging after the second world war. The valuation of leasehold interests does mirror the changing application of techniques with a continual movement from single rate tables to dual rate tables and then a further movement to the use of tax adjustments.

3.4 THE MODELS

3.4.1 Fully let freeholds

Valuations as shown in example 3.1 were standard in both textbooks and in practice.

3.4.2 Reversionary freeholds

Textbooks consistently demonstrated a term and reversion technique based on a lower yield on term than that used to capitalise the reversionary income. The 1908 edition of Curtis (Davies, 1908) makes no comment on the reasons for this approach. It could be assumed that the reasons were so obvious in the minds of the authors that they did not feel that the reasons needed airing. An alternative theory may be that the attitude of instruction rather than debate was prevalent in the textbooks of the time, and there was no need to provide reasons for anything that was normal practice.

The sixth and seventh editions of Curtis (Smith, 1924, 1933) also make no comment on the continued use of lower yields on the term. However, in other general comments, both editions relate the rate of return to questions of security of income and the connection could be assumed.

Pre second world war practice does not confirm the use of lower yields on term. In both court proceedings and old valuation files inspected by the writers reversionary freehold valuations are undertaken on a single, or equivalent, yield basis. Considering this dichotomy between teaching and practice, it is surprising that some discussion of the point is not present in the text books.

The post war texts continue the approach of the pre war texts in using lower yields on the term. The valuation of reversionary freeholds illustrated in cases shows a change from an equivalent yield approach to a lower yield on term. It would appear that, after the war, practice changed its approach to that used in teaching.

The first edition of *Modern Methods of Valuation* set out the case for a lower term yield for the first time.

> The £100 income, being less than the property is really worth, is very well secured and may reasonably be capitalised at a lower rate per cent than would be appropriate in dealing with the full annual value of the premises (Lawrence and May, 1943, 9).

A second reason for lower term yields appearing in reversionary valuation post war is changing market conditions. Our rental evidence of shops in Nottingham (Table 3.1, page 69) shows a greater level of rental growth for the first 10 years following the war than for any period prior to the war. Between 1910 and 1939, the average annual rental growth rate was 2.08% p.a. From 1945 to 1950 the annul rate was 12.2% p.a. A shop let on a 21 year lease in 1935 and valued in 1950 would, according to the index, have a rental value well over double the rent paid under the lease. Apart from the 1920s when rental growth forged ahead at a rate of 6.1% p.a., rental decreases were as likely as rental increases. Apart from reversionary valuations of ground rents, the security of rents paid was not significantly better than the full rental value in terms of ratio of rent paid to rental value. After the second world war the position changed.

In this instance practice showed a willingness to amend its techniques when a theoretical argument was shown to be relevant by the extent of differences between rents being paid and rental value.

3.4.3 Leaseholds

Throughout the period under study, the practice of leasehold valuation has shown changes. Norris (1884) used a single rate approach based on the same yield as the equivalent freehold. By 1908, the textbook comment shows a fundamental difference in theory and practice, where practice was stated to rely upon a single rate basis while theory suggests that a dual rate basis was appropriate (Davies, 1908, p. 41). This dilemma continues into the later editions of Curtis. 'Sinking funds, however, cannot be compounded at the same rates as those upon which leasehold property is purchased, and in this case theory and practice do not agree' (Smith, 1933, 101).

The dilemma is solved by Smith with reference to one of the basic ideas of valuation theory. As the method of analysis of sales is often a single rate technique, the valuer must always use identical techniques to analyse and value, so a valuation on single rate techniques is appropriate (Smith, 1933, 102). One of the major defences of a change in techniques is the basis of comparison; comparisons are the best evidence of yields, and it does not matter how units of comparison are analysed as long as the same method is used to value. It appeared that this factor overrided all concepts of value, and the lack of a logical basis was accepted. This argument mirrors exactly the arguments against the innovation of contemporary techniques of investment valuation and the same dilemma is evidenced in the 1943 edition of *Modern Methods of Valuation* (Lawrence and May, 1943, 50). The same conclusions are arrived at: namely that the analysis of comparables will outweigh any conceptual problems.

The 1933 edition of Curtis introduced a further problem with the valuation of leaseholds; that is, the effect of income tax on the amount being deposited in the sinking fund each year. Having suggested that in short leasehold valuations income tax was a very relevant factor in recoupment of capital, the author again states 'although strangely enough it is often found in practice that purchasers seem to take no account of it' (Smith, 1933, 123).

The author then proceeds to suggest that it *is* taken into account, by using a higher yield in the capitalisation. The 1943 edition of *Modern Methods* again repeats the dilemma and comes to the same conclusion, that a reliance on analysis of transactions will eradicate any major errors (Lawrence and May, 1943, 58).

The 1962 edition of *Modern Methods* (Lawrence, Rees and Britton, 1962, 65) discusses the same points but is assisted by a reference to the production of tables to take into account the tax problem. It has already been illustrated that the text book coverage had moved from a single rate basis prior to the first world war to a dual rate basis between the wars, and by 1960 was using tax adjusted tables for short leaseholds and recommending a tax adjustment as theoretically correct. During the 1960s the final movement to most leasehold valuation by tax adjusted tables was made.

Examples of valuation practice mirror the change. Cases investigated show the same movement from single rate, at the turn of the century, to dual rate tax adjusted valuations by the 1960s. Our investigation of valuations of commercial premises carried out in the Nottingham area show (as typical) single rate valuations in the 1930s, dual rate unadjusted valuations in the 1950s (long leasehold) and dual rate tax adjusted valuations in 1960s. By 1970, most leasehold valuations were carried out on a tax adjusted basis.

The foregoing analysis indicates two major conclusions, both significant to our discussion of the role of contemporary investment valuation techniques. Firstly, the suggestion that techniques and applications have remained static during this century is shown to be incorrect. Applications in practice have been changed when practitioners are convinced that change is desirable. The catalyst for change would appear to be academic, that is, text book comment on the underlying theories, helped by the production of tables or the means to implement changes in technique or application without undue hardship. Secondly, valuers rely on instruction and the acceptance of rules of valuation ('as you devalue, so must you value'). Rules of valuation were often taught by instruction rather than by debate of concepts. Later chapters will attempt to show that the reliance on valuation rules regardless of concepts and logic has led the profession to defend techniques and applications which have lost a logical base.

The use of valuation rules is especially prevalent in the choice of yields for investment property valuation and this aspect of technique and application is examined in the next section.

3.5 YIELD CHOICE

The theoretical background to the derivation of capitalisation rates did not appear to change between 1900 and the early 1960s. In 1962 Lawrence, Rees and Britton commented

> In Chapter 1, it was shown that, in order to use the investment method of valuation, the valuer must determine the rate of interest appropriate to the particular interest in the property being valued. He will normally do this by an analysis of previous market transactions. The valuer is not, however, merely an analyst. He must have a clear idea not only of what the market is doing but also why the market is doing it and, if he is to advise adequately on the quality of the investment, what the market is likely to do in the future' (Lawrence, Rees and Britton, 1962, 11).

This quotation encapsulates the theoretical approach of the valuer to determining yields. Yield construction is apparently rejected in favour of yield analysis (see chapter two), as the best evidence of the yield to be used is the yield on comparable property transactions. But it is clear that the writer considered that comparable evidence should be viewed and analysed in the context of a logical approach as to why investors invest in property and a knowledge of alternatives.

In 1933, the seventh edition of *Curtis* commented:

> The comparative advantages of the investment and its disadvantages in relation to competing securities will be weighed and a conclusion come to. The valuer will form his opinion from the records of the property market, his past experience in buying or selling, the existing market conditions, and his expert knowledge of the circumstances and conditions of the actual property to be valued, and of property generally of that class (Smith, 1933, 5).

Again, it is clear that the author feels that a sound technique should be based on an analysis of property market data but clarified by an understanding of the place property has within a wider investment spectrum. The 1924 edition of *Curtis* comment is almost identical and also relates the return required to 'its disadvantages in relation to competing securities' (Smith, 1924, 5).

The third edition of *Curtis* comments that the rate of interest should be compared to the yield on Consols (undated government stock) (Davies, 1908, 47) and this is confirmed by Norris.

> As to Real Estate, it is clear that the largest beneficial interest which can vest in its possessor is that of a Freehold in Perpetuity, or Fee Simple, in present possession; and the value of this beneficial interest has been ordinarily assumed, in the case of land, to be thirty years' purchase upon the net annual rental – for the reason that, when bought into the market, it must enter into competition with other investments which are in their nature secure or guaranteed, and therefore permanent; and of these the chief, almost the only one, is consols: and as consols can be purchased in general to pay about 3½ per cent interest upon the purchase money, allowing for expenses - ie., at thirty years' purchase - their value is found by experience to regulate that of freehold Landed Estates, to some extent, so that the purchaser may be enabled to sell out of the funds to reinvest in land, without material loss (Norris, 1884).

In the 1943 edition of *Modern Methods of Valuation*, Lawrence and May state:

> The rate of interest required by prospective purchasers of the various classes of landed property will therefore be governed by the general level of interest rates prevailing at the moment . . . particularly with the ideal security . . . Government Stock (Lawrence and May, 1943, 8).

Thus the theoretical approach to selection of capitalisation rates is well defined: but the following examination of the practical application of investment valuation techniques suggests that the above theme of comparative investment appraisal has been lost.

The above statements are usually found in the opening chapters of texts yet subsequent detailed applications of method concentrate almost exclusively on the analysis of comparable property investments to determine yields. The problem has been identified by Philip White.

> If one compares the books and courses which students of valuation use today, and particularly the contemporary examination papers, with those in use 15 or 20 years ago, it is clear that . . . the education and training of valuers is largely unchanged. Concepts of value are not seen to be important, methods of valuation are reduced to 'cook book' routines, and arithmetical anomalies are accommodated as practical approximations (White, 1977).

The basic texts referred to so far do introduce concepts of value but the comments of Philip White are confirmed on further examination. For example, Smith (1933) refers to '. . . the rules which must be followed, more or less strictly, if a successful valuation is to result.'

Having established that the economic considerations of investment appraisal require a breadth of knowledge regarding a wide range of conceptual and mathematical ideas, the text book immediately informs the student that a knowledge of 'rules' will enable him to survive his professional career. 'Workshop Manual' routines are therefore established and the textbooks degenerate into a collection of approved solutions for a wide range of possible circumstances that may arise in valuation practice. Smith exemplifies the problem with his recommendations for leasehold valuation. 'In calculating the value of leasehold properties the rules of practice may be applied and stated as under . . .' (Smith, 1933, 118). The text then outlines seven steps including '4. Determine the rate per cent of interest which a prospective buyer would usually expect the property to yield. This will be decided according to the market experience of similar properties. . .'

The student or practitioner is taught to ignore the concepts and wider implications of yield construction or choice and to reduce it to a comparison basis with similar properties. There is little argument within the texts that the best evidence of what the yields are in any particular location is what similar properties have sold for recently. 'In any particular case, evidence of actual transactions is usually the best basis for capitalising rental values' (Lawrence, Rees and Britton, 1962, 219).

The textbook approach to yield choice is clear. Following the preamble concerning the conceptual and logical basis of yield choice and the establishment of comparative investment appraisal, no attempt is made to quantify property yields in this wider context. Instead a succession of solutions are produced which rely exclusively on the comparison of property investments with other property investments and the wider context is submerged. The comments of White concerning 'cook book routines' are confirmed as the student valuer is taught the rules of market analysis and valuation.

For the first 60 years of this century, the use of the investment method of valuation for freehold and leasehold interests has seen minor amendments in application. These amendments have started from a theoretical discussion in textbooks leading relatively slowly to changes in practice. The contention that no changes have taken place is incorrect but the extent and effect of these changes is small. One of the major barriers to change is the existence of rules in the valuation process, a kind of practical safety net into which all valuers will fall if things go awry. The impression is given in the early texts that observance of these rules will enable a valuer to complete a successful career, while ignorance of these rules will lead to downfall. The changes which did take place were based on sound conceptual arguments at the time, put forward innumerable times prior to a slow acceptance. Therefore valuers will change their attitudes and techniques if a long sustained argument is put forward from a logical platform. But what changes in market conditions and expectations in the period to 1960 urged changes in technique?

3.6 EXPECTATIONS OF INVESTORS, 1910–1960

The expectations of investors in different types of investment medium can be analysed on the basis of market indicators and knowledge of the past. We use a number of indicators to help this analysis. These are the rate of inflation or the reducing purchasing power of the pound; the yields acceptable in capital markets; and indices on Nottingham shop rents. Table 3.1 sets out the information used for the following analysis.

The yield on conventional gilts between 1910 and 1960 ranged between a yearly average of 2.6% and 5.4%; 5.4% was the yield in 1960 and between 1910 and 1950 the range was from 2.6% to 5.3%. The average yield was 3.75% with a standard deviation of 0.72% between 1910 and 1950, and an average of 3.9% with a standard deviation of 0.75% between 1910 and 1960.

Inflation ran at an average of 3.05% p.a. between 1910 and 1960. Up to 1950 the average was 2.79% p.a. On a year to year basis the income from gilts showed a 1% real return up to 1950. Between 1950 and 1960 the inflation rate was over 4% p.a. and the yield on gilts steadily rose from 3.5% in 1950 to 5.4% in 1960 to maintain a real return. A rise in gilt yields in times of inflation may have been expected but the volatility of the inflation rate is in marked contrast to the stability of gilt yields. The average five yearly prices index growth is set against the average gilt yield in the same period in Figure 3.1.

The figure illustrates two points. The first is that investors in gilts did not seem to mind that in some years the value of their income was reduced to a negative real return. The second point is the variability of inflation. The second point may help to explain the first. Investors probably thought that prices were equally likely to go down as they were to go up. Although long term analysis shows an upward trend (1910 to 1960 : 3.05% p.a.), investors could point to a number of disturbances in the period such as the two world wars and the depression of the early 1930s. They could also point to the fact that the negative inflation rate occurred in the most stable time and (given stability) they would expect the same thing to happen. From 1945/1946 onwards they may well have been expecting the same conditions of 1920 to 1929. The evidence of rising gilt yields in the 1950s, predating the 1961 reverse yield gap, suggests that investors' perceptions changed then

Table 3.1 Nottingham city centre retail property: table of rents, inflation and initial yields, 1910–1960

Years	Prime rent Index (1)		Average rent Index (2)		RPI (3)	Prime initial yields (4)	Gilts (5)
	1910 = 100	1946 = 100	1910 = 100	1946 = 100	1913 = 100		
1910	100.0	43.3	100.0	38.2	94	5.0	3.1
1911	96.9		96.0		95	5.0	3.2
1912	95.4		92.9		98	5.0	3.3
1913	95.4		91.6		100	4.5	3.4
1914	95.4		91.6		101	6.5	3.3
1915	95.4		91.6		121	–	3.8
1916	95.4		91.6		143	–	4.3
1917	96.9		94.6		173	–	4.6
1918	99.2		99.3		199	6.75	4.4
1919	101.5		104.4		211	5.0	4.6
1920	104.6		109.8		244	5.0	5.3
1921	106.9		114.8		222	4.5	5.2
1922	109.2		120.5		179	5.5	4.4
1923	111.5		125.6		171	6.0	4.3
1924	118.5		132.3		172	6.25	4.4
1925	123.1		138.7		173	6.0	4.4
1926	127.7		148.8		169	5.5	4.6
1927	133.8		157.6		164	5.0	4.6
1928	140.0		168.4		163	4.0	4.5
1929	147.7		180.1		161	5.0	4.6
1930	153.8		198.7		155	6.0	4.5
1931	135.4		159.9		145	9.0	4.4
1932	135.4		158.9		141	8.0	3.7
1933	135.4		158.2		137	6.5	3.4
1934	135.4		160.3		138	6.5	3.1
1935	135.4		161.9		140	6.0	2.9
1936	135.4		166.7		144	6.0	2.9
1937	143.8		177.8		152	5.5	3.3
1938	152.3		187.2		153	5.0	3.4
1939	146.2		181.5		158	5.0	3.7
1940	140.0		172.1		179	7.5	3.4
1941	140.0		170.0		197	–	3.1
1942	140.0		170.0		210	–	3.0
1943	140.0		170.0		217	–	3.1
1944	140.0		170.4		222	7.0	3.1
1945	161.5		192.8		226	6.0	2.9
1946	230.8	100	262.0	100	236	5.0	2.6

Table 3.1 (Cont.):

Years	Prime rent Index (1)		Average rent Index (2)		RPI (3)	Prime initial yields (4)	Gilts (5)
	1910 = 100	1946 = 100	1910 = 100	1946 = 100	1913 = 100		
1946	230.8	100	262.0	100	236	5.0	2.6
1947		105.6		108.9	249	4.5	2.8
1948		110.2		116.0	268	4.5	3.2
1949		111.9		124.1	275	4.5	3.3
1950		114.1		131.4	283	4.5	3.5
1951		116.7		138.0	311	4.5	3.8
1952		123.3		146.3	338	5.0	4.2
1953		139.8		160.9	349	5.5	4.1
1954		158.6		170.0	355	5.25	3.8
1955		179.8		198.3	371	5.0	4.2
1956		200.0		224.5	389	5.5	4.7
1957		212.0		253.7	404	5.5	5.0
1958		222.6		276.5	416	5.5	5.0
1959		233.4		293.3	418	6.0	4.8
1960		242.7		308.3	422	6.0	6.4

Sources:

(1) + (2) + (4) Compiled by Crosby from data obtained from number of sources. Main source: Harlow Shelton & Co., Chartered Surveyors, Nottingham.

(3)   National Income Expenditure and Output of the UK 1865–1965 (for reference, see Crosby, 1985).

(5)   Abstract of British Historical Statistics and 2nd Abstract of British Historical Statistics (2½% Consols, undated stock, gross redemption yields) (for reference, see Crosby, 1985).

and the majority of the market had responded to these perceptions by 1960–1961.

The property market had different indicators, but perhaps the same reasons for not reacting positively to economic indicators until after 1960. The reaction of rents, as indicated by shop rental values between 1910 and 1960 in the Nottingham city centre, also shows a series of cycles with an overall trend upwards. In the war periods of 1914–1918 and 1939–1945 shop rentals declined and also declined sharply in the depression of the 1930s. Between these disturbances shop rentals grew. In the period 1918 to 1930 rental values doubled while the cost of living was reduced by approximately 25%. The average rent index 5 yearly changes between 1910 and 1950 are shown in Figure 3.2.

The effect of the very high increases in rent during 1945–1950 may have

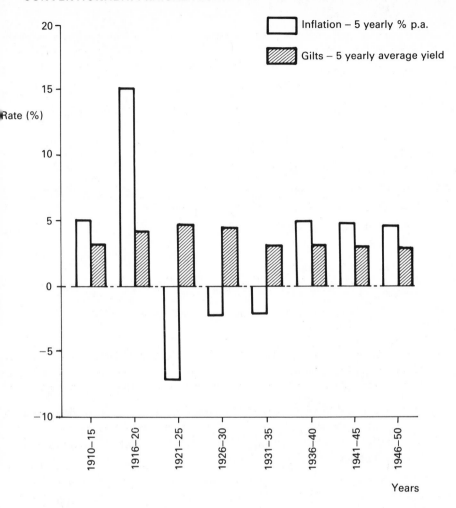

Figure 3.1   Comparison of yields on gilts with RPI, 1910–1950
Source: Table 3.1.

heightened alarm in that a repetition of 1920–1930 may have been part of investors' perceptions. Even though the average growth rate between 1910 and 1950 was 3.13% p.a., the investor's past experience did not give confidence that this would continue. The period 1910–1930 is a similar image to 1930–1950, and this supports the view of a possible expectation of rental falls within the decade 1950–1960. After all, the level of knowledge of both valuer and investor was limited. No rental evidence in the form of indices was published and only past experience of periods of growth and decline could be utilised. The upward trend may not have been as well perceived as the fluctuations.

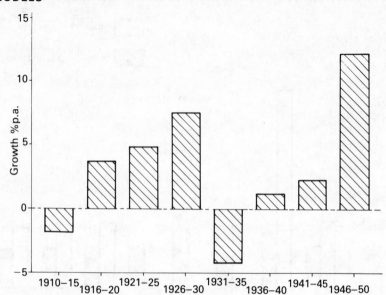

Figure 3.2 Nottingham rent index change, 1910–1950
Source: Table 3.1.

Comments within valuation reports by surveyors show the reluctance to accept a continuing upward trend in inflation and rental values. In 1944 the expectation of some inflation after the war was present. For example:

> We feel it is difficult to forecast the possible trend in rents when the war is over but if a certain degree of inflation is likely to be present – as seems possible – it would be prudent to ask a higher rent for each succeeding period of seven years.

The expectation of future inflation after the war may have been a result of the continuance of inflation after the first world war in 1918 up to 1920 prior to the reduction in 1921.

A valuation report of 1959 contained the following: '. . . but this depends on the future trend of rental values. Since the war this has been upward, but it is difficult to see this trend continuing. . . .' Even after 14 years of price rises and rental increases, the reluctance to accept that this might continue is still apparent. The increase in rents from 1945 to 1950 was 12.2% p.a.; from 1950 to 1955, 8.6% p.a.; and, from 1955 to 1960, 9.2% p.a., a 15 year average of 10% p.a.

Nottingham city centre prime rental values (Long Row) rose from £3.00 Zone A in 1946 to £7.50 in 1961. Albert Street was estimated at £2.00 Zone A in 1946 and £6.00 in 1961. Clumber Street increased from £1.50 Zone A to £4.25 over the same period. In 37 different locations across the Nottingham city centre only two rent points (both on Lower Parliament

Street) did not show at least a doubling of rental value. The suburban centres of Nottingham grew by an average of 7.8% p.a. between 1946 and 1961, with the average Zone A of £0.36 rising by over three times to £1.11 (Crosby, 1985).

The rental evidence shows a period of constant and relatively stable growth in shop rents around 10% p.a. between 1945–60 while prices increased at an average of 4.25% p.a.

An examination of gilt yields between 1945 and 1960 shows the yield from gilt edged stock (2½% Consols) going through a period of transition.

Between 1946 and 1960 the yield on gilts rose from 2.6% to 5.4%. At the same time the initial yield on prime shops was the same in 1947 as it was in 1960. The yield gap reduced from 2.7% in 1947 to 0.1% in 1960.

The changing relationship between gilt and shop yields indicated the start of the reverse yield gap between fixed income and growth investments. The

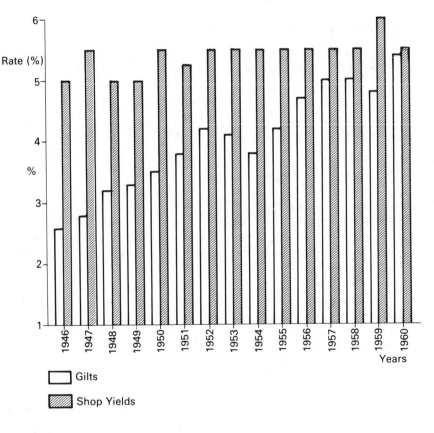

Figure 3.3 Prime shop initial yields and gilts, 1946–1960
Source: Table 3.1.

yield on UK ordinary shares was 4½% in 1947 and 5% in 1960 (Senior, 1975). As the average yield on gilts was 3.75% between 1910 and 1950, and the yield on gilts in 1950 was 3.5%, it seems probable that inflation was not seen as a problem in the investment market at that point. The yield on gilts only exceeded one standard deviation from the 1910–1950 mean in 1956 (4.7%) so it further seems probable that the market as a whole reacted to inflation, and its effect on real incomes, in the second half of the 1950s. The leaders of the herd can be assumed to have reacted before that.

Property investors and valuers did not have to react in the same way as property could be a growth investment and had showed the ability to react to a decline in the value of money. The yield evidence does not necessarily suggest that the changing perceptions of the investment market were ignored by property investors and valuers up to 1960. Even though the investment market had seen that growth potential was equally important as security (by 1959–1960 riskier UK share yields were initially about the same as risk free gilts), yields on property did not rise to maintain a risk differential. There are two possible reasons for this:

(i) valuers and investors were equally aware of economic changes and perceived that growth investments did not warrant a yield higher than gilts on account of security.

(ii) valuers and investors had missed both points. They were unaware of the concept of value, had ceased to look beyond property for value comparison and still did not perceive property as a growth investment.

Evidence shows that the latter more closely represents the reality. Rent review patterns, for example, are an instructive source.

Property need not be a growth investment. The valuer and investor can structure leases in such a way that the income from property is fixed under a lease for many years. Lease lengths can be for any number of years as determined by owners and tenants. Some published comment exists regarding the length of leases and the advent and extent of rent reviews within leases.

Senior (1975) suggested that leases on prime shops were 'long leases without review prior to 1960'. No indication of how long they were, or to what they were reduced to, is made. In the technical appendix to the Investors Chronicle/Hillier Parker Rent Index (Investors Chronicle/Hillier Parker, 1979) the normal review pattern for shops is quoted as:

1965–1969	14 years
1972–1973	7 years
1974 onwards	5 years

Bowie (1972) suggests that average review patterns were, from the mid 1950s to the early 1960s, 21 years; from the early 1960s to 1967, 14 years; from 1967 to 1972, 7 years.

Neuberger and Nicholl (1976) suggested that analysis of valuation office data in 1973 for industrial property showed only 18% of transactions had reviews under 10 years while 65% had reviews of 25 years or less. The same report suggests that Property Services Agency data for office property in 1973 show a majority of asking rents based on 20 year leases with five year reviews.

Walls (1977) suggested that probable review terms or lease lengths were:

Date lease entered into	Probable review period
1945	35
1955	25
1960	14
1967	7
1970	5

An impression of reducing review periods can thus be gained from the evidence. However, the amount and quality of data and the variability of the opinions leave no definite conclusions.

To clarify the situation, we carried out an analysis of lease lengths and review patterns on shop properties. Lease details were extracted from prime shops regardless of UK location. The data was banded for time periods of around five years (Figure 3.4).

The evidence suggests very little change in perception. Landlords were willing to grant tenants long leases and appeared to have very little faith in continuing rental growth. The security of income offered by good covenant tenants was perceived to outweigh any opportunities of participating in rental growth. This conclusion ignores any resistance to change from tenants. However, our previous comment regarding landlords' fear of a collapse of growth, coupled with a lack of perception of change, is more probable, as evidenced by a number of landlords still granting leases such as one in Eastwood, Nottinghamshire, where the tenant was given a 21 year lease from 1956 with an option to renew for a further 21 years at the same rent.

Further evidence of perceptions can be taken from the yield table formed by Senior (1975) regarding the level of yields on ground rents. Ground rents let on very long leases, often 99 years, were the property market's nearest equivalent to an undated gilt edged stock. The income was secure as often the property rental value exceeded the ground rent many times over and the reversion was so far off as to be of very little value. The comparison of gilt yields and ground rents as determined by Senior is illustrated in Table 3.2.

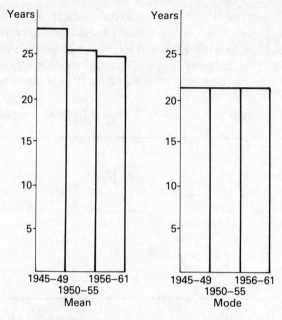

Figure 3.4 Prime shop property, UK, 1945–1961: lease/rent review periods
Source: Crosby (1984, 1985).

Table 3.2   Gilt and ground rent yields (%)

Year	Gilts	Ground rents (60 years unexpired)	Differential
1947	2¾	4/5	1¼/2¼
1948	3¼	4/5	¾/1¾
1949	3½	4/5	½/1½
1950	4½	4/5	−½/½
1951	4	4/5	0/1
1952	4¼	–	–
1953	4	–	–
1954	3¾	4/5	¼/1¼
1955	4¼	4/5	−¼/¾
1956	4¾	4/5	−¾/¼
1957	5	4/5	−1/0
1958	5	4/5	−1/0
1959	5	4/5	−1/0
1960	5¼	4/5	−1¼/¼

Source: Senior (1975).

The yields on ground rents with more than 60 years unexpired remained constant at 4.5% while the yield on gilts rose. Assuming a yield of 4.5%, the yield gap started at +1.75% in 1947 and was reversed by 1960 at −0.75%, a relative shift of 2% over 13 years. If gilts were representative of the safest risk free form of investment then investors in 1960 could have received a higher return with lower risk and would have been ill-advised to buy ground rents.

The evidence of yields from the investment market suggests that the realisation that inflation was following a long term upward trend was formed in the 1950s and by 1956 gilt yields approached 5% or 1% above the average for the period 1910–50. By 1960 the initial yield on UK equities was lower than that on UK gilts, which suggests that by then the majority of investors were prepared to pay less for certain income than they were for growth potential. The evidence also suggests that property investors were slow to react and the evidence of yields on ground rents and rent review patterns confirms that property investors had not perceived any major changes in the economy within which they operated.

Given this lack of perception, the behaviour of investors over the period can now be reconciled with the valuation model adopted to determine whether the model was based on a defensible logic.

3.7   THE RATIONALE OF THE APPRAISAL MODELS

3.7.1   Fully let freehold

The valuation of a rack rented freehold shop property in (say) 1950 would have been undertaken on the basis of a capitalisation of the rent at the appropriate yield. For example, the prime shop yield in Nottingham was estimated to be 4.5% at that time (see Table 3.1). Assuming a rent of £4 000 p.a., the calculation based on direct comparable analysis would be as shown in example 3.15.

EXAMPLE 3.15A

ERV	£ 4 000 p.a.
YP perp. at 4.5%	22.2222
Valuation	£88 889

The landlord would expect the rent to be fixed for 21 years at least, possibly 35 or 42 years, if the tenant represented a very good covenant. The valuation has a logical basis if viewed in the light of the following propositions.

(i) Property is more risky and less liquid than fixed interest government securities (2½% Consols) (see chapter two), which yielded around 3½% to redemption at that time.

(ii) There is no assumption of an upward trend in rents. The likelihood of a fall in rents is just as possible as an increase and therefore the object of fixing a rent for as long as possible is seen as a positive advantage to minimise the risk of a fall in income. The upward movement of rents is not necessary as the initial yield is already 1% above the yield on fixed interest stock.

These assumptions are consistent with the previous analysis of investors' perceptions prior to the movement towards the reverse yield gap which took place later in the decade. The valuation is a conveniently presented discounted cash flow valuation.

EXAMPLE 3.15B

Assume that the rent is fixed for 21 years; that the market would expect another 21 year lease to be granted at the end of the current lease; and that rental values are not expected to show a long term upward or downward trend. Remember that gilts yield 3½%. A discounted cash flow valuation with a 1% risk premium would be as follows:

Years	Rent £	YP 21 yrs at 4½%	PV at 4½%	£
1– 21	4 000	13.4047	1.0000	53 619
22– 42	4 000	13.4047	0.3968	21 275
43– 63	4 000	13.4047	0.1574	8 442
64– 84	4 000	13.4047	0.0625	3 350
85–105	4 000	13.4047	0.0248	1 329
106–126	4 000	13.4047	0.0098	527
127–147	4 000	13.4047	0.0039	209
148–168	4 000	13.4047	0.0015	83
169–189	4 000	13.4047	0.0006	33
190–210	4 000	13.4047	0.0002	13
				88 880

As the additions to value are becoming small, a summation of this series is approximately correct. The total value of cash flows is £88 880 (compare £88 889, page 79). If the cash flow series above is proceeded with, the valuations will equate, because the above series can be shown to equate with the conventional valuation format.

Let: Rent = R
         YP 21 years at 4½% = YP
    PV at 4½% for 21 years = PV

The above series reads:

$$R(YP) + R(YP)(PV) + R(YP)(PV)^2 + R(YP)(PV)^3 \ldots$$

This is a geometric progression increasing at a common ratio of PV, where

$$YP = \frac{1 - \dfrac{1}{(1+i)^n}}{i}$$

$$PV = \frac{1}{(1+i)^n}$$

and where

$$i = \text{interest rate}$$
$$n = \text{period}$$

The series to infinity can be summated to

$$\frac{R}{i}$$

which in this case gives $\dfrac{£4\,000}{0.045} = £88\,889$

Note that R/i is the conventional valuation format for a fully let freehold.

3.7.2 Reversionary freehold

The normal technique for a 1950 valuation of a term income with a reversion to a new lease in the future would be as shown in example 3.16.

EXAMPLE 3.16

Property is let on a 21 year lease, with 6 years unexpired in 1950. The rent under the lease is in the region of 50% of the rental value in 1950 (Nottingham average rent index 1910 = 100: 1935 = 161.9: 1950 = 344.3). Assuming the same rental value of £4 000 p.a. in 1950, the rent under the lease is taken at £2 000 p.a.

The approach would be to capitalise the reversion at a yield higher than the term. Our previous discussion leads to a conclusion that the term yield is a 1% reduction rather than the reversion yield being a 1% addition. Adopting this approach the term yield would be at 3.5% with the reversion at 4.5%.

Current rent	£2 000 p.a.
YP 6 years at 3.5%	5.3286
	£10 657

$1/4.5\%$
$1/(1+0.045)^6$

	Reversion to ERV	£4 000 p.a.
	YP perp. at 4.5%	22.2222
	PV 6 years at 4.5%	0.7679

£68 257

Valuation   £78 914

(i) The term yield is now level with the yield on gilt edged stock. The term rent is seen as secure, the tenant occupying property worth twice as much as his rent payment. The income is fixed under a contract and the risk of default or fluctuation is minimal. Whether the term is as risk free as gilts is open to question but a yield of 3.5% is arguably the correct yield for the very best property, which would additionally presume a letting to an impeccable tenant.

(ii) The rent on reversion is estimated to be the rental value at the time of the valuation. Having regard to the perceptions of investors this would have represented the valuer's best estimate of what he actually thought the position would be. There is no implication of growth within the capitalisation rate and the valuer had no reason to suspect a definite increase any more than the review taking place in a trough, such as happened after 1930. The reversion would have taken place in 1956, 11 years after the war ended, and a sustained period of rental growth had only been evidenced for a longer period than 11 years once since 1910 (1918–1930). The more recent history of depression, recovery, war, recovery, was a shorter term cycle (three years down, six years up, six years depressed, six years up, to 1950).

(iii) The rent on reversion would have been assumed to be fixed on a long lease of either 21, 35 or 42 years in order to stabilise any possibility of fluctuating returns.

(iv) The yield for the capitalisation of the reversion would have been selected on the basis of comparison with similar or fully let property investments and represented a level of return that would be sufficient if it was the internal rate of return from the investment. Again, this is a discounted cash flow valuation. The margin above gilts represented the extra risks attached to property and had no inherent growth implied within it. The investor's willingness to accept a lease with no rent reviews is a testimony to that fact.

Given these assumptions and perceptions, the approach represents a logical, defensible, technique to both the capitalisation and prediction of income flow. The valuation assumes a fixed rent to reversion, a reversion to a rental level consistent with the valuer's estimate of current rental level, and a sustaining of this level into the distant future. This income profile is consistent with expectations (see Figure 3.5).

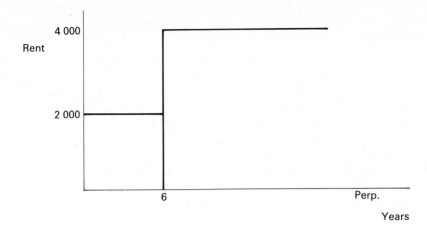

Figure 3.5 Income profile

3.7.3 Leasehold

The approach to leasehold investment valuation is based on the same expectations regarding maintenance of rental values and the fixing of rents on long review patterns.

The approach has been less consistent since the turn of the century than the approach to freehold investment valuation, but by 1950 the use of dual rate tables was accepted. The use of tax adjustments was well documented, and would become the normal approach after 1960.

EXAMPLE 3.17

The valuation of the leasehold interest in the previous property; rental value £4 000 p.a., rent paid £2 000 p.a.; unexpired term six years.

ERV	£4 000 p.a.	
Rent paid	£2 000 p.a.	
Profit rent	£2 000 p.a.	
YP 6 years at 5.5% and 2½% adj. tax at 40%	3.1654	
Valuation		£6 331

(i) The profit rent remains at the same level as existing and expires in six years' time.

With perceptions of fluctuating rental values rather than continually rising values the leaseholder could be expected to sublet the property for the whole of the remaining term with no reviews. The net income would therefore remain constant.

(ii) The interest expires in six years' time and upon expiry the lessee has no further interest in the property, and therefore no value. He has an investment which terminates, and all the return is in the form of income. The investor must recoup his capital out of income while a freeholder has his interest in perpetuity and the expectations are that this will mean that he can maintain the value of an asset. In order to compare the investment in a leasehold interest with a freehold the investment must be made perpetual. The dual rate approach was evolved to make this comparison, with a tax adjustment justified by the fact that for the taxpaying investor the sinking fund would be derived from a taxed profit rent.

(iii) Having made the investment comparable with a freehold and in the absence of rental growth expectations the only question remaining is whether a leasehold is more risky than a freehold. The perceptions were that it was, so a higher return was used. In practice the valuer would look for other leasehold comparisons in accordance with his training (to look for similar comparisons) but, in the event of absence of such comparisons, a margin was adopted over and above the freehold yield for similar property on the basis that the technique had made the spendable income of the leasehold comparable with the income from the freehold. In textbook examples 1% higher was a normal margin.

(iv) The sinking fund rates adopted were justified because sinking funds were available at yield levels in the order of 2/3% net of tax.

(v) The sinking fund element of net income was not treated differently from the rest of the income for income tax purposes so a tax adjustment was also logical.

This technique therefore again represents a logical, defensible approach.

The major conclusion from the foregoing analysis is that, in the context of the future expectations of investors and valuers, conventional techniques had a logical and defensible basis in 1950 and by analogy at other times prior to a change in investors' perceptions which occurred in the later 1950s. Whether these valuation models continued to be defensible after the change in perception will be considered in chapter four.

CONVENTIONAL APPRAISAL TECHNIQUES: POST REVERSE YIELD GAP

4.1 THE APPEARANCE OF THE REVERSE YIELD GAP

In 1980 the interim report of the Royal Institution of Chartered Surveyors research project into property valuation methods (Trott, 1980) was published, concluding that the collapse of the property market in 1973 was the catalyst for serious criticism of methods. This was the same report that suggested technique had not changed in the past.

The environment within which the valuer was operating was already beginning to change in the late 1950s, as evidenced by fixed interest initial yield movements. This change was not lost on the authors of *Modern Methods of Valuation* in 1962. 'With regard to the . . . assumption that money 'maintains' its real value, this does not happen in times of inflation' (Lawrence, Rees and Britton, 1962, 13).

The rise in fixed income yields up to 1960 has already been noted along with the continuous increase in the retail prices index since the second world war. The movements from 1960 onwards show a continuation of these trends.

The average level of inflation from 1960 to 1970 was 4.03% p.a. (see figure 4.1).

The yield on gilts had already started to rise in the last half of the 1950s and continued to do so during the 1960s. By 1970 the yield on consols stood at 9% (see figure 4.2). The average yield over the period was 6.77% which was above the average inflation rate of 4% p.a. A major realignment had taken place and the level of interest rates was again higher than the inflation rate. By the end of the 1960s the rising level of inflation (6.27%)

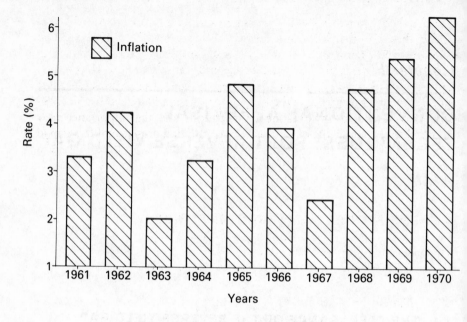

Figure 4.1 Annual growth of retail prices, 1961–1970
Source: C.S.O. (1983).

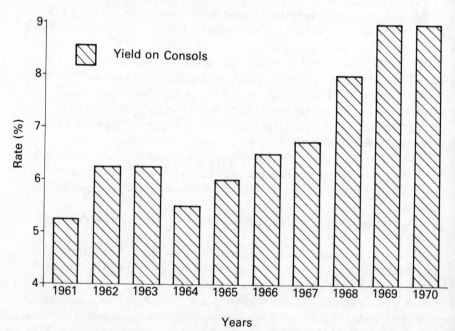

Figure 4.2 Average yield on Consols, 1961–1970
Source: Senior (1975).

was matched by a rise in yields to maintain a differential of between 2% and 3%. In the 1950s this differential had not been present. The average yield on gilts was 3.9% between 1950 and 1955 while inflation was at 5.6% p.a. From 1956 onwards the yield on gilts responded upwards and this response can be seen to continue in the 1960s (see chapter three at page 74). The emergence of the reverse yield gap between gilts and UK equities in 1960 confirms the change in investment perceptions and the importance now attached to the real value of returns. The continuing presence of this gap in the 1960s (by 1970 the reverse yield gap was 4%) shows the long-term acceptance of the attractions of purchasing growth investments in times of inflation.

4.2 THE PROPERTY MARKET RESPONSE

The property market response is summarised in three indicators: the yield on property investments, rental levels and lease terms.

4.2.1 Yields

The majority of sources show an upward drift in the latter part of the decade (see Table 4.1 below). According to Senior, the most dramatic move in property yields came in ground rents with more than 60 years unexpired. These yields were reported as 4–5% in 1960 but by 1970 were at 12% (see Table 4.2 overleaf).

Table 4.1 Prime and average shop yields, 1960–1970

Year	MLP/EIU average	Senior prime	Senior secondary	Nottm prime
1960		5.5	7.0	6.0
1961		5.5	7.0	5.5
1962		5.5	7.0	5.5
1963	6.5	5.5	7.0	5.5
1964	6.25	5.5	7.0	5.5
1965	6.75	6.0	7/8.0	5.0
1966	6.50	6.0	7.0	5.5
1967	6.37	6.5	7.5	6.0
1968	7.25	7.0	7.5	6.5
1969	7.30	7.0	7/8.0	5.0
1970	7.70	7.5	8.0	5.5

Sources: Senior (1975); Crosby (1985); Enever (1977).

Table   4.2 Ground   rents,
1960–1969

Year	Yield (%)	Gilts	Gap
1960	4/5.0	5.25	.75
1961	4/5.0	6.25	1.75
1962	5.0	6.25	1.25
1963	5.0	6.0	1.00
1964	6.0	5.5	−0.50
1965	8.0	6.0	−3.00
1966	10.0	6.5	−3.50
1967	12.0	6.75	−5.25
1968	12.0	8.00	−4.00
1969	12.0	9.00	−3.00

Source: Senior (1975).

4.2.2 Rents

Shop rental values also show an increase in the decade. The Nottingham average index rose by 8.9% p.a. and the prime index rose by 7.8% p.a. The Michael Laurie analysis of commercial property values shows an average increase of 13.0% p.a. between 1962 and 1970.

The sixth edition of *Modern Methods of Valuation* (Lawrence, Rees and Britton, 1971) suggests that the high level of retail trading in this decade had increased the demand for shops and caused real value appreciation in rental and capital values. A correlation between shop rents and retail sales has been suggested (Hillier Parker, annually: see page 203 for a further discussion). In the years 1962–1970 retail sales volume rose by 14.4%, an average of 1.7% p.a. (C.S.O. 1983). Shop rents rose by 8.9% p.a. in absolute terms and by 4.7% p.a. in real terms. Prices rose on average by 4.03% p.a. The evidence of the rental value and yield statistics is that, in this period of sustained real growth in rents, yields were forced up.

The yield on ground rents may offer the reason for this anomaly. Investors in property did not seem to realise the devaluing effects of inflation until after 1960. The gap between gilt and ground rent yields stood at 1.75% in 1961. A change is apparent in 1964–1965, which reversed the relationship of the previous 8 years in which ground rent yields had been lower than gilts. It has already been established that while gilt markets showed signs of changing perceptions in 1956, there is no sign of a change in property market perceptions until 1963–1964.

4.2.3   The review period

The movement in shop yields during the latter half of the 1960s may have been as a result of this change in perception. As ground rents were looked on with increasing suspicion, investors were now looking for participation in growth potential and, although shop rents were increasing at very high real growth rates, the ability to participate in growth had been seen to be very poor up to 1960, witnessed by typical rent revision terms.

The normal review or lease term up to 1960 was 21 years. An analysis of the review patterns of prime shop property in the 1960s shows the beginnings of an estate management change as regular reviews were introduced into prime shop leases in this period. In the period 1945–1961 only 4.9% of leases analysed had rent reviews within the lease term and the normal lease term was 21 years. In the period 1962–1970 rent reviews were included in 62% of leases. Between 1962 and 1965, 21 years remained as the normal review/lease term but the average fell from 25 years to 20 years. Between 1966 and 1970, the normal review term was 7 or 14 years and the average term was 13 years. Again, dramatic change came in the late, rather than the early, 1960s.

An analysis of lease particulars in the East Midlands region for prime shop property in 1962–1963 shows that the average lease/review term was 17 years with a mode of 21 years. By 1967–1968 the normal review pattern had fallen to 7 years with an average of 12 years. In contrast the normal lease term for secondary property was 7 years at both times (Crosby, 1985). This analysis supports the conclusion that growth potential, and the ability to participate in it, was a major factor in the upward shift in yields in the mid to late 1960s. The investor had realised that growth was a very important consideration but few apart from the most recent of leases enabled participation in that growth.

The analysis appears to suggest that the property market's response to changes in the economic criteria of investors lagged behind the investment market's response by up to 10 years. By the early 1970s the response had been made. The average review pattern for prime shop yields in the period 1971–1975 was 7 years and the mode 5 years. Prime shop lease terms in the East Midlands in 1972–1973 were on either 5 or 7 year reviews with an average of 6 years. Prime shop yields fell from a peak of 7.5% in 1970 to around a low of 4.5% in 1972 and early 1973. Investors' and valuers' expectations and perceptions had changed during the decade and a number of other changes would lead to the valuation techniques debate of the 1970s and 1980s.

4.3 INSTITUTIONAL INVESTMENT

4.3.1 Growth of institutional involvement

The growth of the financial institutions and their involvement in commercial property investment has been well documented elsewhere (see for example Darlow, 1983 and McIntosh and Sykes, 1984). In 1964 insurance companies held assets of nearly £4 billion in fixed interest gilts and preference and debenture shares and only £1.9 billion in equities. £851 million was in land, property and ground rents, including buildings owned and occupied by them for their business, mortgages, leaseback finance, fixed interest finance of property companies and direct ownership of fixed income properties. Although statistics on property investment holdings of the institutions are difficult to interpret, it is beyond dispute that since the early 1960s insurance companies and pension funds have put a considerable portion of their new funds into property.

During the 1970s the long term funds of the insurance companies increased their total property holdings from under £2 000 million to over

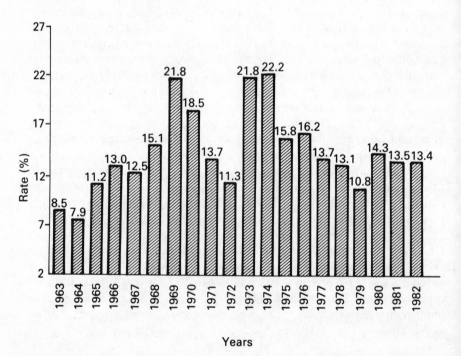

Figure 4.3 Property as a percentage of total acquisitions (insurance companies and pension funds), 1963–1982
Source: Darlow (1983)

£17 500 million by the end of 1982 (Debenham, Tewson and Chinnocks, 1983). For example, Legal and General Assurance Co. held 22.2% of their composite fund in property fund units in 1981. The implication for property valuers of this involvement is the view taken by most funds that property is not a 'special' form of investment and that it must take its place alongside the other major investment media. A major fund has confirmed this: 'We believe the days are past when commercial property was regarded as something exceptional in . . . investment.' (Legal and General, 1982).

This view has meant an increase in the analysis of the performance of property and an increasing interest in appraisal techniques from advisors of the institutions, investment analysts, stockbrokers and actuaries.

4.3.2 Performance analysis

In 1980, Richard Ellis stated that it was 'only in recent years that any real degree of effort had been made to research and analyse the institutional property market'. Since then considerable resources have been deployed in property investment research.

Progress in this field has been facilitated by computerisation as well as investment in research staff. The results of performance analysis have enabled comparisons to be made with other investment media in line with institutional fund managers' views that property must be seen in the same light as gilts and equities.

Long term performance analysis has created fuel for the debate regarding technique. The timing of purchases has revealed itself as a critical factor in performance (Richard Ellis, 1983) and research has also disturbed other views regarding the long term nature of property investment and the property types and locations which are expected to do best in the future. Knowledge of the past is helping to formulate policies for the future by aiding the isolation of relationships, and is therefore encouraging a form of analysis which requires prediction of the future. These ramifications fall on techniques which cannot adequately cope with the changing needs. There is a resultant pressure upon property specialists to produce rigorous analyses which is being fuelled by criticism from the institutions' financial advisors.

4.3.3 The role of financial professionals

Financial professionals developed a stronger interest in the property market when institutional investors expanded their property holdings in the 1970s. The last decade has, as a result, witnessed increasing criticism of valuation techniques.

In 1976 stockbrokers Greenwell and Co. criticised both valuers' reliance on direct comparison when so little of the stock of property investments was traded each year (see Table 4.3) and also criticised traditional techniques for

Table   4.3 Insurance   company
turnover ratios

Year	Property	Gilts	Equities
1978	2.8	81.6	9.8
1979	2.6	90.4	10.7
1980	1.5	79.2	14.3
1981	1.6	80.1	15.1
1982	2.2	86.3	17.5

Source: Debenham, Tewson and Chinnocks
(1983).

masking the assumptions behind a valuation (Greenwell and Co., 1976). The same company noted the lack of an index of average yields in the property market in 1984 (now remedied) and criticised prime yield indices as 'discredited indicators of value' questioning, by implication, conventional initial yield valuation techniques. And the Economist Intelligence Unit suggested in 1981 that 'those who claim that there is room for improvement in valuation techniques have established their case' (Daniels, 1981).

Greer (1979) has neatly summarised the pressures which encourage perpetuation of outdated techniques in property investment appraisal.

Both professional and academic literature reflects a deep vein of dissatisfaction with traditional approaches to the problem of risk in real estate investment analysis. A veritable flood of articles have appeared in recent years seeking to introduce techniques which have long been commonplace in other fields. Unfortunately, little of this path-breaking work has found its way into practice or into introductory textbooks or courses.

Each generation of real estate analysts educates its own successor. Training and professional certification are largely controlled by trade groups, which in turn are governed by successful practitioners who were educated by their professional predecessors. As a consequence of this 'intellectual inbreeding', real estate analysts employ methods and techniques which represent the state of the art in other fields a generation ago. Old, less-effective tools of analysis tend to be perpetuated in spite of the ready availability of something better.

This explains, but does not excuse, the prevalence of outmoded technology in real estate analysis. Intellectual cross-fertilisation from corporate finance and the decision sciences in general can enable real estate analysts to cast off the stigma of obsolescence and compete more effectively with professionals from such other fields as public accounting and management consulting who are experiencing increasing success in invading the traditional turf of appraisers and feasibility analysts.

4.4 EXPECTATIONS OF INVESTORS, 1960 ONWARDS

The pre-1960 perceptions of investors had justified initial yield valuation techniques based on the following assumptions.

  (i) It is assumed there is no growth in future rental over present rental values.
 (ii) It is assumed that rents are fixed on long leases without review.
(iii) The capitalisation rate (on a level, equivalent yield basis) is the internal rate of return expected from the investment.
(iv) An approximate 2% yield differential between prime shops and gilts reflected the disadvantages of property investment.

Since the inception of the reverse yield gap and the acceptance of rent reviews, a number of these assumptions have been disturbed.

  (i) The assumption of growth in the future is the essence of the reverse yield gap. The quantification of this implication is examined in chapter five.
 (ii) The practice of fixing rents on long leases without review changed and analysis shows that by 1980 the normal review pattern was 5 years.
(iii) The capitalisation rate depends on the preconceived level of growth in the future. The rate does not represent an expected internal rate of return over the life of the investment.
(iv) The internal rate of return expected is not known and is the subject of later discussion. However most commentators refer to a 2% margin above the internal rate of return on gilts to cover the disadvantages of property investment (see chapter two).

The impact of these changes is exemplified by the valuation of a reversionary freehold, as illustrated on page 79 (example 3.16). It would show a different expected future income profile (see figure 4.4) in 1970 than in 1950.

  (i) Taking the yield on gilts to be approximately 10% the yield required from the property is now higher.
 (ii) The rent on reversion is expected to be higher than the current rental value now.
(iii) Rent reviews are expected in the new lease so regular upward revisions at five yearly intervals should be incorporated.

Current techniques employ a reversion to the current rental value and then capitalise in perpetuity. If the implication of the reverse yield gap is

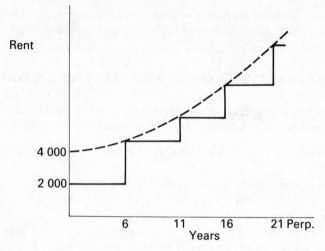

Figure 4.4 Expected future income profile – post reverse yield gap

accepted then the level of income expected is not explicit in these valuations and the capitalisation rate is the product of the purchaser's expectation; within the capitalisation rate growth is implied.

It would appear strange that techniques have not changed since the 1960s given the changes in investors' perceptions. Although the logical base of the conventional model appears to have collapsed it is still in almost universal use in the UK for the market valuation role. The case for conventional or more contemporary techniques in this role is examined in chapter seven.

4.5 VALUATION OR ANALYSIS?

In chapter one, a clear distinction was made between the estimation of likely selling price and the worth of an investment to an individual, bearing in mind the individual's own requirements. This distinction may not be so clear cut and we believe there is some middle ground.

Morley (Darlow, 1983, 216) defines market value by reference to the definition contained in the Royal Institution of Chartered Surveyors' guidance notes on Asset Valuation (see chapter one, page 3). He defines 'appraisal' as

considering the value or worth of the interest to specific purchasers taking into account:
(i) individual circumstances
(ii) his investment portfolio
(iii) different assumptions regarding the future.

This can be distinguished from the RICS definition of market value (exchange price).

But, as Heselgrave (1983) asks, 'should not price always equal worth in a free market of knowledgeable buyers and sellers?' He suggests the answer lies in the nature of the property market, a lack of centralised market place, secrecy of information and its reliance on transactions for comparison purposes. This introduces some middle ground.

Market value is influenced by the way in which valuers approach valuation. They have no perfect knowledge of information, and do not have available perfect comparisons. No two comparisons can be the same in terms of location and are unlikely to be the same in terms of lease structure, design, size, and all other physical factors. An element of subjectivity will be transferred into an apparently objective valuation. Heselgrave illustrates price by traditional techniques and worth by a discounted cash flow approach similar in concept to the change in technique caused by a change in perception outlined previously in this chapter. His assessment of worth does not include individual investor's requirements, so 'worth' has been generalised away from the concept of one owner to the whole market for that investment. This implies that the criticism is that, on account of techniques, there can be two valuations, related to market price and investment worth. It is implied that market inefficiency is the rule.

Wyatt (1983) confirms this possibility. 'The valuer's function is to interpret the market and its pricing mechanism – including the illogicalities. The analyst's function is to study the illogicalities and to spot under-valued investments.' Yet the distinction between a valuer and an analyst seems artificial and smacks of the intellectual inbreeding criticised by Greer. There is no reason why a valuation surveyor should not be educated or practise in the fields of market analysis and comparative investment appraisal.

The conclusion is clear. The use of poor price fixing techniques leads to a distinction between value and worth, worth being based on a more rigorous technique. Wyatt suggests that 'In time, the pricing mechanism may adjust to a more rational basis' (Wyatt, 1983).

Heselgrave suggests that the main reason for price not equalling worth is the irrational behaviour of the market. 'Although property investments are bought and sold in a sophisticated market, it is not one which always acts rationally, and it is therefore possible for the astute investor to identify a bargain which has been overlooked by others' (Heselgrave, 1983).

Heselgrave also suggests price is determined by direct comparison and worth by future income flow. He also suggests that 'for a particular investor' it may be worth more than the price. The implication of the article is that this is true not of a particular purchaser, but of many purchasers.

The advisors of sophisticated investors using methods of quantitative analysis which Greer suggests are in advance of valuers' techniques find the comparative approach hard to understand on two counts.

(i) With so little evidence of transactions and no such thing as an identical comparison, how can valuers rely on this as a complete approach, especially when there is no logical base to the way in which the unit of comparison, yield, is applied (Greenwell and Co., 1976)? (Insurance companies turned over only 2.2% of their property holdings in 1982 (see Table 4.3).)

(ii) There is no central information source; the market is characterised by secrecy and a lack of generally available information.

The different role of the stockbroker/analyst may lead him to this conclusion. The central market place for stocks and shares and a large number of transactions enable a daily market price to be established by comparison and the assessment of market value is not problematic.

The stockbroker/analyst's main efforts are therefore directed towards analysis and this focus of their professional expertise leads inevitably to concern at the concentration of professional wisdom towards market valuations based on comparison in the property sector, particularly as these very methods appear to make meaningful analysis impossible. The clear need is for valuers to adopt a market valuation model which lends itself to explicit analysis.

Such a model should not be totally reliant on available comparable evidence, and should function when no comparables are available.

The model should be more explicit than the conventional model which hides important issues such as growth potential and risk factors within a single capitalisation rate.

This approach would need to be market based but would be more specific regarding perceptions of investors. Lawrence and May when discussing the valuation of leasehold interests in 1943 found themselves with the same dilemma of suggesting one method of approach when the market used another. The text proposed the use of dual rate tables instead of single rate, as it believed using a single rate 'may mislead a client as to the effective rate at which he will receive interest on his capital.' The use of dual rate tables 'is more in accordance with the facts of a terminable income.' The authors reminded their readers that 'it is essential that the same basis should be used both in the valuation and in the analysis of recent sales.'

The same arguments hold for the current debate. Devaluation and valuation on the same basis is an excuse for retaining the status quo. No doubt in 1943 valuers continued to use an old technique simply because everybody else did; the circle of analysis – valuation – analysis took years to break. A similar slow process of change is taking place in the valuation profession today.

4.6   A CRITIQUE OF THE CONVENTIONAL VALUATION MODEL

We have so far only begun to identify the problems which result from continued use of conventional valuation techniques. We have showed the following.

  (i) While conventional techniques had a logical and defensible basis prior to 1960, the appearance of the reverse yield gap between gilts and equities, the increase in property rental values and the introduction of rent reviews in leases fundamentally changed the applicability of these techniques to what became and are now viewed as equity or growth investments. What was previously a convenient discounted cash flow basis in which the yield or capitalisation rate used represented the expected internal rate of return of the investment (see page 78) now became a wholly implicit model in which complex growth expectations were hidden alongside equally complex risk judgements.

 (ii) As initial yields became lower than those attainable in the gilt market, cross-investment comparison became impossible on this basis. The increasing role of institutional investors and financial professionals in the property market and a growing role for performance analysis pointed more and more to deficiencies in existing property investment appraisals.

(iii) The conventional appraisal model is in any case unhelpful for analysis by the implicit nature of the yield employed. An explicit appraisal model would enable more accurate and more informative cross-investment comparisons to be made.

 (iv) A gulf appeared to grow between market valuations on an illogical basis and assessments of worth (analyses) on a rational basis, pinpointing areas in which conventional market valuations were thought to undervalue or overvalue investments.

The remainder of this chapter is devoted to a critical appraisal of the conventional models now used in practice. The major criticisms against these models are illustrated by their application to fully let freeholds, reversionary freeholds and leaseholds. These criticisms are further examined in chapter seven after the contemporary alternatives have been investigated and comparisons of approach on the basis of logic and objectivity can then be made.

4.6.1   The fully let freehold

Of all three categories of property investment, the fully let freehold is least prone to inaccurate valuation by conventional techniques. Comparable information is generally more readily available, as there are two inputs into the valuation only: estimated rental value, which will equate with the passing rent and capitalisation rate. If it can be shown that abundant evidence of sales of similar property shows a consistent relationship between ERV and price, then it may be suspected that an accurate valuation may be produced by employing that same relationship.

However, growth remains implicit and risk adjustments can be made in only the most rudimentary manner (see chapter eight). Meaningful analysis based on this format is thus impossible and the peculiarities of individual investments (review pattern, quality of covenant, refurbishment and obsolescence, operating expenses and so on) can only be dealt with by the heavyhanded and subjective method of yield adjustment.

4.6.2   The reversionary freehold

For purposes of comparison, a single example will be used.

EXAMPLE 4.1

This concerns a small good quality freehold office investment, let at a net rent of £15 000 p.a. with the final six years of a fixed-rent 21-year lease to run. The net rental value of the building is estimated at £30 000. An identical building next door, recently let on five-yearly reviews at its full rental value, has just been sold for £500 000.

Analysis:

$$\text{Capitalisation rate } (k) = \frac{£30\ 000}{£500\ 000} = 6\%$$

Three conventional techniques of valuing reversionary freeholds are currently recognised. These are the term and reversion, equivalent yield and layer (or hardcore) approaches.

(i) Term and reversion

Term rent	£15 000 p.a.	
YP 6 years at 5%	5.0757	
		£76 135
Reversion rent	£30 000 p.a.	
YP perp. at 6%	16.6667	
PV 6 years at 6%	0.7050	
		£352 480
Valuation		£428 616

Analysis:

$$\text{Initial yield} \quad = \frac{£15\ 000}{£428\ 616} = 3.50\%$$

$$\text{Yield on reversion} \quad = \frac{£30\ 000}{£428\ 616} = 7.00\%$$

$$\text{Equivalent yield} \quad = 5.97\%$$

I Notes

(1) The capitalisation rate (k) is derived from evidence of sales of comparable property. This is almost always fully let property, as in this case. Hence k relates to the risk profile of the full rental value and the prospect of growth by means of five-yearly rent reviews.

(2) The capitalisation rate used in the term valuation is derived from k but is adjusted to reflect the supposed increased security (reduced risk) of the term income. The usual adjustment is $(k - 1\%)$ or $(k - 2\%)$ with little attempt made to reflect the circumstances of each case in this deduction. The reduced risk is the result of the profit rent (in this case £15 000) enjoyed by the leaseholder, who is unlikely to risk losing this income by defaulting on his rent payments and perhaps forfeiting his lease.

(3) The reversionary income is today's estimate of full rental value. No attempt is made to predict changes in full rental value. The use of a 'growth-implicit' yield of 6% (k) in the deferment is therefore justified although its exact implications are open to question (see Crosby, 1983). Sykes and McIntosh (1982) state a variation where $(k - 1)\%$ and $(k + 1)\%$ are used in the respective valuations of term and reversion. The use of $(k + 1)\%$ is open to question.

II Criticisms

(1) Is the term income always of increased security? A definitional problem arises here. Is full rental value the best possible rent which can be squeezed out of a lessee, or is it the best rent which is reasonably attainable? Most valuations are carried out on the basis of the latter definition, as it excludes the problem of the special purchaser or lessee and thereby reduces the margin for error and criticism. If the property is of prime quality, it is probable that an increase in rent to full rental value will make little difference to the lessee's inclination to continue in occupation, especially when the lessee is a large company (prime covenant) to which rent might be a small percentage of profit.

(2) Why adopt a rule-of-thumb deduction? If the principle of a capitalisation

rate deduction is acceptable, should it not be adjusted according to the level of rent payable in relation to full value?

(3) Bowcock (1983a) has identified an error resulting from the use of two interest rates in a single period. k and $(k - 1)\%$ are used in the capitalisation of the term income and in the deferment of the reversion income, which can result in blatantly erroneous valuations, forcing Bowcock's conclusion that

> 'the use of more than one remunerative rate of interest in a conventional investment valuation is unsatisfactory, and should be discouraged'.

(4) The use of k is only appropriate where the income to be capitalised has an element of growth potential (in this case the prospect of income growth by means of five-yearly reviews). Whenever growth potential is not a feature of the income – even when the reversion is but one or two years away – it is incorrect to imply rental growth by using k, which must result in over-valuation of the term.

(ii) Equivalent yield

Term rent	£15 000 p.a.	
YP 6 years at 6%	4.9173	
		£73 760
Reversion rent	£30 000 p.a.	
YP perp. at 6%	16.6667	
PV 6 years at 6%	0.7050	
		£352 480
Valuation		£426 240

Analysis:

$$\text{Initial yield} = \frac{£15\ 000}{£426\ 240} = 3.52\%$$

$$\text{Yield on reversion} = \frac{£30\ 000}{£426\ 240} = 7.04\%$$

$$\text{Equivalent yield} = 6\%$$

I Notes

(1) The equivalent yield (r) is sometimes called the equated yield without growth (see Jones, 1983) and can be termed the overall or average return on current rent estimates. In the equivalent yield valuation the

same capitalisation rate is applied throughout, so that k must be equal to r, which is not the case in term and reversion or layer (see below) approaches. The reduction in the capitalisation rate in the term valuation is rejected, thereby avoiding the mathematical problem referred to by Bowcock (1983a).

(2) As a method of analysis, this has its proponents. Jones suggests that 'the use of equivalent yields in property investment analysis has yet to be fully exploited' and the RICS research report (Trott, 1980) recommends 'that the use of equivalent yield analysis be encouraged'. As a method of valuation, the RICS report concludes that it is

a simple method of utilizing the evidence of comparable transactions more accurately and flexibly. In view of this it is perhaps surprising that it does not appear to be widely used, or even understood, in the profession at large.

However, Sykes suggests that it is the preferred method of the institutions and their valuers (Sykes, 1983a).

II *Criticisms*

Perhaps any mass drive towards such understanding would be misdirected. The equivalent yield as a tool of analysis may be useful as an equated yield or internal rate of return on current rental estimates, but as a single capitalisation rate applied to reversionary investments it falls foul of the major criticism of the term and reversion approach. The term income is fixed; it is therefore incorrect to use k, which implies growth, to capitalise it.

(iii) **Layer (hardcore) approach**

    (a) Simplified approach

Layer rent	£15 000 p.a.		
YP perp. at 5%	20		
		£300 000	
Marginal rent	£15 000 p.a.		
YP in perp. at 7%	14.2857		
PV 6 years at 7%	0.6663		
		£142 788	
Valuation			£442 788

      Analysis:

$$\text{Initial yield} = \frac{£15\,000}{£442\,788} = 3.39\%$$

$$\text{Yield on reversion} \quad = \frac{£30\ 000}{£442\ 788} = 6.78\%$$

$$\text{Equivalent yield} \quad = 5.81\%$$

(b)   Modified approach

Preliminary calculations are carried out as follows in order to determine a more appropriate yield for the marginal income. The value of the reversion is assumed to be split into two parts, marginal and layer. Following the assumed market practice evident in term and reversion valuations, k is applied to the whole full rental value while $k - 1$ would be applied to the more secure layer.

Valuation of whole:		
Full rental value	£30 000 p.a.	
YP in perp. at 6%	16.6667	
		£500 000
Valuation of layer:		
Layer rent	£15 000 p.a.	
YP perp. at 5%	20	
		£300 000

As part of the valuation of the reversion, therefore, the marginal income is worth £500 000−£300 000 = £200 000. The appropriate yield to produce this result is:

$$\frac{\text{Marginal rent}}{\text{Capital value}} = \frac{£15\ 000}{£200\ 000} = 7.5\%$$

Valuation:		
Layer rent	£15 000 p.a.	
YP perp. at 5%	20	
		£300 000
Marginal rent	£15 000 p.a.	
YP perp. at 7.5%	13.3333	
PV 6 years		
at 7.5%	0.6480	
		£129 592
Valuation		£429 592

Analysis:

$$\text{Initial yield} = \frac{£15\ 000}{£429\ 592} = 3.49\%$$

$$\text{Yield on reversion} \quad = \frac{£30\,000}{£429\,592} = 6.98\%$$

$$\text{Equivalent yield} \quad = 5.95\%$$

I *Notes*

(1) In the simplified approach the full rental value is seen as being notionally split into two parts: a layer income, which coincides with the term rent, and a marginal income, which constitutes the excess of full rental value over current rent. The layer income is regarded as less risky, and the marginal income as more risky, than the full rental value. Hence $(k - 1)\%$ and $(k + 1)\%$ respectively are used in the capitalisation.

(2) The modified approach is an attempt at greater sophistication. Applying market evidence of sales of fully let comparables, it is possible to calculate k as usual. Given the notional split of the full rental value into layer and marginal incomes; given that the layer income is more secure, and is deserving of capitalisation by a rule-of-thumb $(k - 1)\%$ adjustment; and given the capital value of the fully let property, it is possible to compute a capitalisation rate which can be said to reflect the extra risk of the marginal income.

(3) The advantages and applications of this approach are well documented in the RICS report.

(4) Sykes (1983a) states a popular current variation where an equivalent yield is applied to both layer and marginal incomes. If the equivalent yield is derived in the same way, the valuation becomes identical to that shown at (b) above, the format being immaterial.

II *Criticisms*

(1) It is difficult to accept the arbitrary split of the reversionary income into two parts. The risk of non-receipt attaches to the whole, and not to part, of the income. In cases where the current rent is low in relation to full rental value, the nature of the split becomes meaningless, as the marginal income might constitute a larger proportion of the full rental value.

(2) The apparently sophisticated modification relies upon acceptance of the rule-of-thumb 1% deduction in term capitalisation when using the term and reversion techniques, thereby implying the incorporation of criticisms of such a method. In any event, the modification is not market-derived, it is cumbersome, and it appears to be designed to ease calculations of tax-free capital appreciation (the split reversion approach) without generally assisting in the valuation of the typical reversionary investment. As a result, it is obsolete.

(3) Again, and even more so, the criticism of the other conventional

approaches and their capitalisation of fixed income at a rate based on k holds. This time, a notionally fixed layer income, certainly fixed over perpetuity (although this is now in the realm through the looking glass) is capitalised at $(k - 1)\%$, implying growth which is not to be achieved. An element of cancelling errors is provided by the geared nature of the marginal income which should justify even lower capitalisation rates.

(4) Bowcock (1983a) demonstrates the even more pronounced error of dual rates as it affects hardcore valuations. In the example he chooses, the valuation is

very unstable, the result depending entirely on the subjective opinion of the valuer . . . it is difficult to see how any objective analysis of property transactions could determine the correct marginal difference to be made between the hardcore and marginal rates to a convincing degree of precision.

Conclusions

All three conventional techniques are prone to errors of logic and errors of arithmetic. The layer method has the added disadvantage of being cumbersome and of being based on questionable and arbitrary judgements. The single damning criticism of all three techniques is the common, illogical practice of capitalising fixed term incomes at rates which imply rental growth in the term income.

Defenders of the conventional approaches argue that the investment, looked at as a whole, does have growth potential during the period of the term as the value of the reversion is likely to be increasing. But why should this not be dealt with in the valuation of the reversion itself? Similarly, proponents who accept the over-valuation implied by this treatment of the term point to an under-valuation of the reversion as justification. 'Two wrongs do not make a right': each part of the valuation should be defensible on its merits, so that the reversionary freehold valuation can be regarded as two accurate parts which add up to an accurate whole and not as a mysterious formula which happens to appear to work.

4.6.3   Leaseholds

Leasehold valuations by conventional techniques are even more prone to attack.

EXAMPLE 4.2

A leasehold interest has 20 years to run, subject to a fixed head rent of £10 000 p.a. The current rental value is £20 000 p.a., subject to five-yearly reviews. Market evidence suggests a freehold capitalisation rate (k) of 6 per cent for this type of property.

Much-criticised, the tax-adjusted dual rate valuation appears to remain in limited use. The tax exemption of the pension fund has prompted unadjusted dual rate valuations. Single rate valuations have also been suggested (see, for example, Enever, 1981). These three approaches will be taken as the available conventional techniques.

The three share a common feature leading to a problem requiring immediate consideration. The remunerative or capitalisation rate (k) is traditionally settled by reference to the initial yields obtained by purchasers of freehold investments in similar property with a small upward adjustment to account for the so-called extra risk of leasehold investment. This may be said to be the result of several inter-related factors: the top-slice nature of a leasehold, making the profit rent considerably more sensitive to changes in full rental value than the net freehold income is; the dual contractual burden suffered by the leaseholder; the risk of a dilapidations expense inherited from previous leaseholders; and others.

The adjustment to k is often accepted as plus 1 or 2% over the freehold remunerative rate, which would lead in this case to a remunerative rate of 7 or 8%.

The logic of such adjustment is not questioned here. Investors are generally said to be risk-averse (see chapter 2): so greater volatility in the net income, even if equal chances were applied to increases and decreases, would be seen as a factor justifying a higher yield.

However, the quantum of the adjustment is in the hands of the valuer. In the usual case, where market evidence is slight or imperfect, a considerable burden settles itself upon the valuer's intuition. This problem will be borne in mind for later reference: but for the purposes of the examples a remunerative rate of 6 per cent is used to isolate other errors and to reduce variations in an area where the valuer's inspiration is in danger of influencing his logic.

(a) Dual rate, tax-adjusted

Rent received	£20 000 p.a.	
Less rent paid	£10 000 p.a.	
Profit rent	£10 000 p.a.	
YP 20 years at 6% + 3% tax 40p	8.1950	
Valuation		£81 950

Analysis:
  Yield = 6% × £81 950 = £ 4917

Sinking fund (gross)	= £10 000 − £4 917
	= £ 5 083
Sinking fund (net)	= £ 5 083 (0.6)
	= £ 3 049.80
× A £1 p.a., 20 years at 3%	26.8704
Capital recouped	£81 950

I *Notes*

(1) As noted above, the 6% capitalisation or remunerative rate would normally be derived from sales of comparable freehold properties and adjusted upwards to account for extra risk.

(2) The accumulative rate of 3% is supposed to represent the net-of-tax return available on a guaranteed sinking fund policy taken out with an assurance company, being absolutely safe.

The sinking fund is designed to replace the initial capital outlay on what is a wasting asset. The historical organisation of the profession demanded that a property-wide means of comparison evolved: while leaseholds might best be compared with redeemable stock, reality required that they be comparable with property investments, that is freeholds. The wasting nature of the asset had, then, to be countered by the replacement of capital over the period of the lease so that an interest similar to a freehold can be shown to exist, provided the right steps are taken, and the right price is paid.

(3) The tax adjustment of 40% counters the fact that any tax-paying purchaser of the investment would lose a portion of his profit rent in tax. While the effect on the remunerative rate or yield is not regarded as important (all, or most, investment opportunities are quoted on a gross-of-tax basis) its effect on the sinking fund payment is vital. Without adjustment, the sinking fund would become inadequate as a result of income tax reducing the whole profit rent. As it has to accurately recoup capital, a 'grossing up' factor is applied to cancel out the effect of tax (see, for example, Baum and Mackmin, 1981): this grossing-up factor (in this case $1/1 − 0.4$) is the tax adjustment.

(4) A 'true net' valuation (using a net profit rent, a net remunerative rate and no tax adjustment) would produce an identical result.

II *Criticisms*

(1) Why use such a low accumulative rate? Bank deposits or building society accounts earn considerably more and yet are regarded as safe. It is true that they do not provide a guaranteed accumulation: but there is

probably an equal risk of increases and decreases in the rates offered. Even risk-averse investors would be unlikely to discount the yield they would accept on guaranteed accumulations by as much as is necessary to produce 3%. Borrowers would certainly not set up 3% sinking funds when the cost of the capital they have employed to purchase the interest may be four times as great.

(2) Why adjust for tax at 40%? Valuations are usually estimates of market value. Hence, the purchaser's tax rate is unlikely to be known, and a guess, or average, has to be made. Forty per cent may be a realistic average where the small-scale investor is interested: but this ignores the common case where a tax exempt fund is likely to buy, or where a company paying corporation tax is likely to purchase, either for occupation or investment. The considerable interest of gross funds in this market may be explained by the use of tax-adjusted valuations leading to low asking prices, and resulting in high equated yields for the purchasers.

(3) As noted in the RICS report, the combination of three variables in the tax-adjusted, dual rate valuation (renumerative rate, accumulation rate, tax rate) makes a full analysis of transactions hazardous. Different values for the three variables may combine to produce the same years' purchase figure.

(4) Other criticisms may be made: as, to a certain extent, these are common to all conventional techniques, they will be dealt with later.

These criticisms may be countered by an approach which is often used to reflect the interest of the gross funds and slightly more realistic accumulative rates.

(b) Dual rate, unadjusted for tax

Rent received	£20 000 p.a.	
Less rent paid	£10 000 p.a.	
Profit rent	£10 000 p.a.	
YP 20 years at 6% + 4%	10.6858	
Valuation		£106 858

Analysis:

Yield = 6% × £106 858   = £ 6 411.48

Sinking fund   = £10 000 − £6 411.48

    = £ 3 588.52

×A £1 p.a., 20 years
    at 4%   29.7781

    £106 859*

* Rounding error

I *Notes*

(1) A slightly higher net accumulative rate is used here to allow what might be seen as more realistic valuations to be made. It is significant that the 1978 (10th) of *Parry's Valuation Tables* includes dual rate tables with 4 per cent accumulative rates for the first time. It is interesting to note, however, that, if this technique is designed for the gross fund, the gross rate of sinking fund accumulation – 4 per cent – is actually lower than the equivalent rate in the previous example (3% net at 40% tax is equal to 5 per cent gross).

(2) A tax adjustment is superfluous in this case as the income of a gross fund is not reduced by tax. If this, however, represented a market valuation, any bidding taxpayer would have to accept a very low yield in order to compete while allowing for recoupment of capital.

II *Criticisms*

(1) It is easily proven that a single rate years' purchase figure allows for recoupment of capital at the remunerative rate (see, for example, Baum and Mackmin, 1981). The justification for a dual rate approach is the argument that, *if a sinking fund were actually taken out in practice*, there would be no reason for the accumulative rate offered by an assurance company coinciding with the remunerative rate attainable upon purchasing the investment, thus necessitating a dual rate approach.

But are sinking funds actually taken out in practice? There are sound reasons for concluding that few investors would arrange for recoupment of capital in this way:

(a) *Occupiers* can usually be regarded as long term (more than the profit rent period) tenants. The initial capital outlay, probably an overdraft, or regarded as an investment of cash 'in the business', is recouped out of profits, which (hopefully) outlive the profit rent. A perpetual income may in many cases be the result, in which case a sinking fund is inappropriate.

(b) *Investors* are likely to be holders of a number of property interests. In such a case, recoupment of capital from a wasting asset like a leasehold is unlikely to be by means of a sinking fund: it can be by investing profit rents in similar investments. It is possible to show (see Baum, 1982) that an increasing income and portfolio is likely to grow from a small portfolio of leaseholds by continuous reinvestment. Note the behaviour of building societies, effectively mass purchasers of limited term property incomes by way of mortgage loans. Repayments are turned over immediately to become fresh loans: and all repayment calculations are carried out on a single rate basis. The requirement to invest in a similar investment can also be questioned: the investor will be happy to invest in any investment with the correct risk/return characteristics.

(c) *Borrowers* in either category will have a cost of capital well in excess of the 3% or 4% accumulative rate. Consequently, no purchaser would set up a sinking fund to recoup capital at a low accumulative rate when, as an alternative, he could reduce a debt costing much more.

(2) It has been well illustrated (Fraser, 1977) that, while the concept of the sinking fund in leasehold valuations is designed as an attempt to reconcile the differences between the freehold and the wasting leasehold asset, the recoupment of capital in times of inflation becomes inadequate. Freeholds are (if depreciation is set aside) likely to increase in capital and rental value over time. If the sinking fund replaces the initial capital cost of the leasehold, then the leasehold fails to keep pace with the freehold, and the rationale of the dual rate concept is not put into practice.

Various methods of adjusting the sinking fund to cope with inflation have been suggested by writers including Fraser, Greaves and Rose. Their approaches are fully documented in the RICS report, which concludes that 'index-linked annual sinking funds . . . are not practical and (should) be discouraged'. It appears that such methods approximate to the introduction of valuation programs for calculators when the market is adopting computers. In times of inflation, the sinking fund is obsolete, and methods designed to streamline the dual rate valuation are doomed to extinction.

(3) The fundamental mathematical error which is inherent in all dual rate valuations of varying profit rents is also well-documented (see Baum and Mackmin, 1981; Trott, 1980; Harker, 1983 and Bowcock, 1983a). The double sinking fund, annual equivalent and sinking fund approaches, and Pannell's method (for comparisons, see Baum and Mackmin, 1981, chapter 5) deal with the problem with varying degrees of success; nonetheless, the RICS report dismisses them as 'not practical', for similar reasons.

The RICS report is less critical about single rate leasehold valuations which 'should be encouraged . . . if implicit assumptions are made about future rental growth'.

(c) **Single rate**

Rent received	£20 000 p.a.
Less rent paid	£10 000 p.a.
Profit rent	£10 000 p.a.
YP 20 years at 6%	11.4699
Valuation	£114 699

Analysis:

Yield = 6% × £114 699   = £ 6 882

Sinking fund   = £10 000 − £6 882

                                         = £ 3 118

× A £1 p.a., 20 years
    at 6%   36.7856
                                         ——————————

                                         £114 698*

* Rounding error

I *Notes*

(1) As demonstrated by the analysis, the single rate valuation allows for the recoupment of capital at the remunerative rate. Whether such a rate could be earned in practice is not necessarily important for the reasons stated at (b) II (1) above (see also Colam, 1983).

(2) However, recoupment of capital would have to be out of taxed income, as profit rents are subject to income tax and reinvestment in any medium would only be possible with the after-tax income. Hence a net of tax valuation is necessary. The example used is a net of tax valuation for a gross fund: if the potential purchaser is a taxpayer competing with taxpayers, then a tax adjustment will be needed. In such a case the net profit rent should be capitalised by a years' purchase factor at a net-of-tax yield, otherwise a dual rate valuation will be the result.

(3) All foregoing criticisms appear to be met. The accumulative rate is no longer critically low; the problem of average tax adjustment can be avoided by investigating the market; there is no artificial assumption that a sinking fund is actually taken out, as reinvestment is at the remunerative rate, thereby obviating the problems of recoupment in times of inflation; and there is no mathematical error when valuing varying profit rents at a single rate of interest (but see Bowcock, 1983a).

However, a fundamental criticism – which attaches to *all* conventional leasehold valuations – remains.

II *Criticisms*

(1) The remunerative or capitalisation rate (k) is derived directly from evidence of sales of similar freehold properties, assuming a shortage of good evidence of comparable leasehold sales. In the examples, no risk adjustment is employed. Whether the remunerative rate *is* increased or not, the assumption must be made that the level of rent growth enjoyed by the owner of the freehold interest as implied by k must be exactly the same in the case of the comparable leasehold. Any adjustment of k is to account for risk, and not growth, differential.

There is nothing inherently wrong with the use of initial yields or capitalisation rates to imply rental growth. But for two reasons the capitalisation rate k (or $k + 1$, or $k + 2$) is likely to be incorrectly applied in the case of leaseholds because:

(a) leaseholds produce complex rental growth. Rental growth depends upon the relationship of head lease and sub-lease. Where the term or review dates do not coincide, the profit rental pattern can be complex and unrelated to the growth potential in a freehold, and;
(b) the sensitivity of the top slice leasehold income can be expressed in another way by leverage or gearing. Small changes in full rental value will produce geared, exaggerated changes in profit rent in the same way that equity increases at a faster rate than the capital value of a partially loan-financed asset (see, for example, Darlow, 1983; and Greer, 1979).

The table below expresses such a phenomenon, based on a leasehold interest of 30 years leased at a fixed head rent of £200 000, current rental value £400 000, three-yearly rent reviews being typical. Rental growth of 7% p.a. is assumed. Gp is annual profit rental growth on the base of the previous profit rental; Gi is the annual profit rental growth on the base of the initial £200 000 profit rent.

Year	Profit rent (£)	Gp	Gi
1– 3	200 000		
4– 6	290 017	0.131874	0.131874
7– 9	400 292	0.113400	0.122599
10–12	535 384	0.101783	0.115617
13–15	700 877	0.093937	0.110157
16–18	903 613	0.088379	0.105767
19–21	1 151 973	0.084309	0.102161
22–24	1 456 225	0.081256	0.099150
25–27	1 828 947	0.078920	0.096601
28–30	2 285 547	0.077117	0.094419

This complex gearing effect is certainly not accurately reflected by the use of a k-based rate derived from freehold analysis and implying a constant 7% p.a. increase in income. As the term goes on, the fixed head rent takes up an increasingly less significant part of the rental value, so that the profit rent growth (both Gp and Gi) tends towards 7%; but in the early years, more dramatic growth is enjoyed, and the use of k is inappropriate (see Figure 4.5).

Another major criticism of the use of growth implicit capitalisation

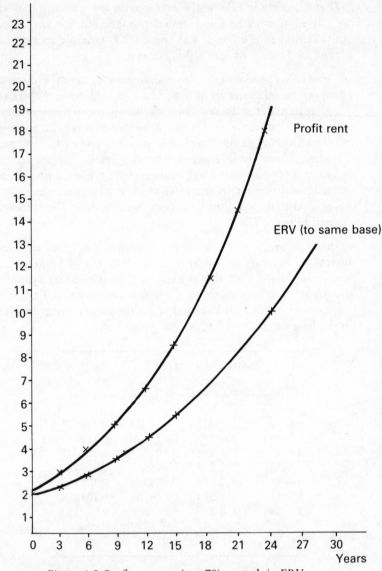

Figure 4.5 Profit rent gearing: 7% growth in ERV

rates is the difference in implied growth rates within identical yields on a perpetual income as against a terminable income (Crosby, 1985). This problem is examined in detail in chapter seven.

(2) Note that a mathematic error can exist in the valuation of varying profit rents even if a single rate approach is adopted where different yields are applied over the life of the investment (see Bowcock, 1983a; and Crosby, 1985).

(d) Conclusions

While the conventional dual rate valuation has had its apologists in recent years (see, for example, Millington, 1983), the weight of comment has been negative (Trott, 1980; and recently, for example, McIntosh, 1983a and Bowcock, 1983b). Such negative comment has largely been devoted to the well-documented problems of the sinking fund assumption, or allowance, while the single damning defect in all conventional approaches – the implicit growth assumption planted by the use of the all-risks, remunerative yield – is less widely recognised. The RICS report, for example, concludes 'that the theoretical weaknesses of the conventional dual rate method be emphasised to all practitioners' while demonstrating ambivalence over implicit single rate approaches ('if implicit assumptions are made . . . then the use of single rate valuations (should) be encouraged'). The conclusion of the authors is that, except in limited circumstances where the profit rental pattern may be fixed, the single rate valuation is little improvement over the dual rate approach, which, as Bowcock concludes, 'should be scrapped'.

A defensible, modern approach to the valuation of leaseholds should be capable of addressing the problems related not only to the sinking fund but also to gearing and other fluctuations in the profit rental pattern, implying the inevitability of a DCF-based methodology. Several such systems have been put forward in recent years, but have not been subjected to critical, comparative review. Even a text (Darlow, 1983) claiming to give 'an authoritive, state-of-the-art, review of advanced methods of investment valuations and analytical techniques' misses in this respect, and the need for a full consideration is urgent. Such a consideration follows.

Chapter Five

CONTEMPORARY TECHNIQUES: AN INTRODUCTION

5.1 INTRODUCTION

During the 1970s numerous alternative techniques and formulae were proposed as models for the capitalisation of income from property investments. The Royal Institution of Chartered Surveyors sponsored a research programme into property valuation methods which led to the publication of an interim report in 1980 (Trott, 1980). This report studied these numerous techniques and concluded that 'equated yield analysis and valuation' is the 'best way of comparing the returns on property with those of gilt edged stock.'

The report also concluded:

> . . . equated yield analysis is a practical and simple method of making explicit assumptions as to the likely pattern of future value changes and . . . its use in the determination of value to particular purchasers (should) be encouraged. However the subjective assumptions made in the method (e.g. as to the opportunity cost of capital and the growth rate) mean that valuations will not necessarily reflect the judgement of the market.

The implication is that techniques that rely on a subjective assumption regarding the future cannot be used for valuation but may be appropriate for analysis. In discussing discounted cash flow (DCF) techniques (of which equated yield analysis is a variant) Trott introduces the arguments for and against the use of these methods in market valuation.

In arriving at an estimate of market value, what matters is the observed behaviour of the market, and if the market does not use DCF methods then it is hard to see how these can be used to derive market value. But the advocates of DCF make the point that most investors are unlikely to purchase property in isolation from a consideration of the other investment opportunities available to them and that they will have regard to their own expectations of future rental growth . . . when deciding whether or not to buy a property investment at the ruling market price. . . . If the use of DCF methods affects investors' behaviour then the pattern of demand and supply will alter with a consequent effect upon the value in the open market.

This argument for the use of DCF in market valuation is then rejected and recommendations are made for equated yield analysis to be confined to analysis and not adopted for valuation. The comments of Heselgrave and Wyatt regarding the use of explicit cash flow techniques confirm that these methods have already taken on the role of a general check on market value as determined by existing techniques based on all risks yields (see chapter four). Whether explicit or DCF based models can, despite these reservations, be applied to valuation will be considered in detail in chapter seven.

This chapter examines the DCF-based and real value models which have been suggested as alternatives to conventional appraisal models, setting out in detail the underlying assumptions and their subsequent construction. A common factor in contemporary models is that they consider the explicit prospective future income flow generated by the investment. In one form or another, the models accept the implication of the reverse yield gap and require an assessment of value changes in the future. One means of attempting this is to identify a simple average rate of anticipated rental growth implied by that yield gap. Therefore, prior to an examination of explicit models, the underlying assumptions and mathematics of assessing market-based implied rental growth rates are investigated.

5.2 IMPLIED RENTAL GROWTH ANALYSIS

5.2.1 Introduction

The DCF approach is explicit regarding three major inputs. These are:
  (i) future growth in rental values;
 (ii) future changes in contractual income flow, and the timing of these changes; and
(iii) the yield required from the investment (the target rate).

Critics of the method complain about the subjective nature of these inputs. But the timing of future value changes is not a serious problem for assessment. The charge of subjectivity can only be made of growth rate and yield choice and it can be demonstrated that a simple analytical model can reduce the problem of choice to one factor (yield choice) by objectively assessing market concepts of future rental growth.

5.2.2 Analytical basis

In conventional valuations, the analysis of transactions to produce the capitalisation rate is a very simple affair.

EXAMPLE 5.1

A freehold shop property has just been let on a 25 year lease with 5 year rent reviews at £20 000 p.a. and subsequently sold for £400 000.

The analysis comprises the quantification of a direct relationship between the rental and capital values which takes the form of a multiplier.

$$\text{Analysis for YP: } \frac{\text{capital value}}{\text{rental value}} = \frac{£400\ 000}{£20\ 000}$$

$$\text{YP in perpetuity} = 20$$

This multiplier can be directly used to value another rack rented freehold. Unfortunately, as most properties are let on periodic review patterns most properties to be valued will be between reviews, so that the multiplier cannot be directly applied. The valuer is encouraged in such cases to convert the multiplier into a unit of comparison, a yield. This is simply done by finding the reciprocal of the multiplier.

$$k \text{ (capitalisation rate)} = \frac{1}{\text{YP}} = \frac{1}{20} = .05 = 5\%$$

To obtain k directly:

$$k = \frac{£20\ 000}{£400\ 000} = .05 = 5\%$$

Having obtained the unit of comparison (k), the valuer applies it to similar property income flows. But the subject income flow may be fixed under a lease without review, or may be subject to 3-yearly, 5-yearly or other review patterns. There may be other variations in the quality of the expected income flows. The rate can then be amended where the valuer feels special circumstances are relevant, but the amendments are at best intuitive and at worst guesswork.

If it is accepted that the unit of comparison is to be a yield, logic would suggest that yields from property must have some relationship with yields obtainable in other investment markets (see chapter one). Historical analysis and much published comment indicates that a fixed income prime property target rate should be higher than the redemption yield on conventional gilts (the relevant margin will be examined in chapter seven). For the purposes of constructing contemporary valuation models a 2% differential will be adopted. At the time of writing conventional gilts yield around 11% so a natural conclusion is for target rates (equated yields) of property to be 13%.

Another conclusion can now be drawn. The prime yield on shops is, at the time of writing, approximately 4%; prime and near-prime shop properties sell at capitalisation rates of between approximately 3½% and 6%. If a realistic yield would be nearer 13%, the purchaser must be expecting growth in rental and capital value in the future to make up the shortfall. As capitalisation rates have remained between about 4% and 6% for prime shops for the most part of this century, the major component of long term growth has been rental growth, and capital values have only grown on account of rents increasing. There are now few valuers who do not realise that low yields imply rental growth.

If it is known that a particular equated yield is required, or certainly projected for the purposes of valuation, and under what review pattern the property is let, or expected to let, then the future growth rate in rental value needed by the purchaser to make the investment worthwhile can be quantified. The implied rate of growth in rental value will be the constant annual growth rate in rental value required to produce the target rate or equated yield given an initial capitalisation rate and rental growth being realisable at periodic intervals (review dates).

5.2.3   Calculation of implied rental growth rate

There are numerous formulae used for calculating the implied rental growth rate. Three are considered below.

Capital value	$= £1$
Equated yield	$= e$ (decimal)
Rental growth p.a.	$= g$ (decimal)
Review period	$= t$ (years)
Capitalisation rate	$= k$ (decimal)

(1)   The basis of the calculation is to set up an equation where the equated yield is made up of the capitalisation rate plus the annual sinking fund to replace the capital gain at the equated yield over the review period. If the original capital sum is £1 the capital gain is equal to:

$$(1 + g)^t - 1$$

The annual sinking fund formula incorporating e and the review term t is:

$$\frac{e}{(1 + e)^t - 1}$$

The formula is therefore:

$$e = k + \left[\left\{\frac{e}{(1+e)^t - 1} \, ((1+g)^t - 1)\right\}\right]$$

Rearranging,

$$k = e - \left[\left\{\frac{e}{(1+e)^t - 1} \, ((1+g)^t - 1)\right\}\right]$$

Let p = rental growth over the review period, t and SF = annual sinking fund to replace £1 over the review period t at e.

$$\text{Then } k = e - (SF \times p)$$

g may then be derived from p, as $(1 + p) = (1 + g)^t$.

EXAMPLE 5.2

Capitalisation rate (k): 5% (from market evidence)
Review period (t): 5 years
Equated yield (e): 13%

$$k = e - (SF \times p)$$

$$0.05 = 0.13 - \left[\left\{\frac{e}{(1+e)^t - 1}\right\} \times p\right]$$

$$0.05 = 0.13 - 0.1543p$$
$$p = 0.08/0.1543$$
$$= 0.15847 \ (51.85\% \text{ over 5 years})$$
$$(1 + p) = (1 + g)^t$$
$$1.51847 = (1 + g)^5$$
$$1.51847^{0.2} = (1 + g)$$
$$g = 0.0871 \ (8.71\% \text{ p.a.})$$

(2) From the same basis, rearranging by subtracting k from both sides and dividing both sides by the annual sinking fund factor leaves

$$(e - k) \left/ \frac{e}{(1+e)^t - 1} \right. = (1+g)^t - 1$$

$$(e - k) \left[\frac{(1+e)^t - 1}{e}\right] = (1+g)^t - 1$$

$$g = \sqrt[t]{(e - k)\left[\frac{(1+e)^t - 1}{e}\right] + 1} - 1$$

Using example 5.2 again:

$$g = 5\sqrt{(0.13 - 0.05)\left[\frac{(1.13)^5 - 1}{0.13}\right] + 1} - 1$$

$$= 5\sqrt{0.08\,(6.48) + 1} - 1$$

$$= 0.0871$$
$$= 8.71\% \text{ p.a.}$$

(3)   A third formula is based on a DCF net present value approach to the problem. The required rate of return or target rate is the equated yield. The outlay is the capital value $(1/k)$; the inflows represent the value of the term income until the first review; the property is then assumed to be sold at the first review. The rental value on review is capitalised at the same capitalisation rate as represented by the current purchase and the capital value obtained is then entered as an inflow at the first review. The equation for an income of £1 is:

$$\frac{1}{k} = \left[\frac{1 - \frac{1}{(1 + e)^t}}{e}\right] + \left((1 + g)^t\right) \times \left[\frac{1}{k}\right] \times \left[\frac{1}{(1 + e)^t}\right]$$

$$(1 + g)^t = \frac{\left[\frac{1}{k}\right] - \left[\dfrac{1 - \frac{1}{(1 + e)^t}}{e}\right]}{\left[\frac{1}{k}\right] \times \left[\frac{1}{(1 + e)^t}\right]}$$

The formula can be rewritten in conventional valuation format to enable a valuer to solve implied growth rate calculations with the aid of familiar formulae or a set of valuation tables.

$$1/k = \text{YP perp. at } k; \quad \frac{1}{(1 + e)^t} = \text{PV £1 in } t \text{ years at } e;$$

$$\frac{1 - \frac{1}{(1 + e)^t}}{e} = \text{YP } t \text{ years at } e. \text{ Therefore:}$$

$$(1 + g)^t = \frac{\text{YP perp. at } k - \text{YP } t \text{ years at } e}{\text{YP perp. at } k \times \text{PV } t \text{ years at } e}$$

Using example 5.2 again,

$$(1 + g)^5 = \frac{\text{YP perp. at } 5\% - \text{YP } 5 \text{ years at } 13\%}{\text{YP perp. at } 5\% \times \text{PV } 5 \text{ years at } 13\%} = \frac{20 - 3.5172}{20 \times .54276}$$

$$= \frac{16.4828}{10.855} = 1.5185 : \quad g = 5 \sqrt{1.5185} - 1$$

$$g = 8.71\% \text{ p.a.}$$

The solutions reconcile and indicate that the rent must increase by 1.5185 times the previous rent at each review in the future if the required return from the property is to be achieved, excluding other considerations. It would be surprising if rents increased at a constant rate in the future, so this solution represents a long term average target. The solution can be improved (for example, it does not include an allowance for reducing rental growth prospects resulting from depreciation: see chapter eight); nonetheless, this simple model enables us to develop an explicit discounted cash flow appraisal model.

5.3 DISCOUNTED CASH FLOW APPRAISAL MODELS

5.3.1 Introduction

In simple terms, the major criticism of conventional appraisal models as applied to the post reverse yield gap property market is the implicit nature of the capitalisation rate employed and its failure to perform as a target rate or expected internal rate of return as it had performed prior to the appearance of the reverse yield gap. A DCF appraisal model which is explicit regarding the anticipated cash flow can now be developed employing a discount rate which represents the investor's target rate.

DCF appraisals in this format, but recommended for analysis rather than market valuation, were first suggested by Marshall who termed his model 'equated yield analysis' (Marshall, 1976) to draw attention to the internal rate of return/redemption yield nature of the discount rate employed (increasingly termed 'equated yield' in the property market, to distinguish from the all risks yield or growth implicit capitalisation rate used in conventional appraisals).

A variety of formats for the appraisal are possible, but the increasing use of computer based spreadsheets (for example Lotus 1–2–3) encourages a tabular format (see page 78 and chapter eight).

An immediate problem must, however, be faced. The perpetual nature of a freehold property investment implies an infinitely long cash flow projection. While the discounting process will reduce the value of future tranches of income, eventually to a nominal amount, by which point the projection may cease, the process may remain inconveniently lengthy. This may be a minor problem in computation, but remains a considerable problem in presentation. What is needed, therefore, is a method of shortening the process.

Several alternatives will be considered. These include a shortened cash flow model: a DCF by formula approach; the 'rational model'; and a real value hybrid.

5.3.2 An explicit cash flow model

A means of shortening the cash flow projection naturally presents itself when the behaviour of most investors in the market is considered. While property may in most cases continue to be considered as a long term investment, investment holding periods will not typically be perpetual. It may be quite possible to envisage a resale at some future point; often, a natural point of sale presents itself. The behaviour of the investment market confirms that a natural resale point will be coincidental with a reversion or rent review; the assumption of resale at such a point will permit the termination of cash flow projections, replacing future cash flows by the resale price. It will be shown later in this chapter that the choice of resale timing is not of importance in the appraisal; before we demonstrate this point, however, we need to consider how to estimate resale price. This is dealt with further in chapter eight.

Marshall's equated yield analysis format included termination of the cash flow after 30 years for a fully let freehold. Up to that point rental growth expectations cause the rental flow to be increased at each expected review date in the future. The yield used to discount the cash flows is the target rate; all growth potential is explicit. Capital growth is also explicit, by courtesy of the resale assumption. At the resale point Marshall recommended capitalisation of the then rental value at the equated yield.

By implication, this ignores any growth potential in the investment after the 30 year period. This may be a convenient and realistic allowance for depreciation. However, the use of risk adjusted equated yields already assumes risk of depreciation (see chapter eight); consequently, we must reject capitalisation at the resale point at the equated yield. Implied rental growth analysis is based on a presumption of perpetual growth in a freehold: this must be reflected in the resale price projection. The resale price is therefore arrived at by capitalisation of the then rental value at a rate which implies future growth; the implied rate of growth is derived from the current market capitalisation rate; so the same rate should be used at the point of resale (but see chapter eight for development of the model to deal with the depreciation problem).

Thus valuation by a shortened explicit cash flow model requires three inputs:

equated yield (e);
market capitalisation rate (k); and

review period (t).

From e and k, implied growth (g) can be calculated.

EXAMPLE 5.3

Value the freehold interest in a shop property to be let on a 25 year lease with 5 year reviews at its current net rental value of £10 000 p.a. Use an equated yield of 13%; market capitalisation rates are around 5%. Assume a holding period of 30 years.

Implied rental growth: 8.712% from the following.

$$k = e - (SF \times p)$$

where $SF =$ annual sinking fund over t at e

$p = (1 + g)^t - 1$; implied rental growth over the review period.

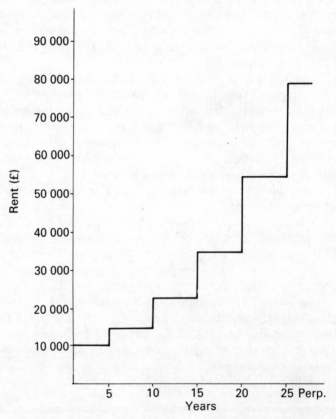

Figure 5.1   Income profile (example 5.3)

Valuation

Years	Current ERV p.a. (£)	A £1 at 8.712%	Projected income (£)	YP 5 years at 13%	PV at 13%	Present value (£)
0– 5	10 000	1.0000	10 000	3.5172	1.0000	35 172
6–10	10 000	1.5184	15 184	3.5172	0.5428	28 987
11–15	10 000	2.3056	23 056	3.5172	0.2946	23 889
16–20	10 000	3.5009	35 009	3.5172	0.1599	19 688
21–25	10 000	5.3156	53 158	3.5172	0.0868	16 226
26–30	10 000	8.0716	80 716	3.5172	0.0471	13 372
30	10 000	12.2562	122 562	20.0000*	0.0256	62 666
						£200 000

* YP perp. at 5%

A different holding period does not change the result. Assume a sale after 15 years.

Years	Current ERV p.a. (£)	A £1 at 8.712%	Projected income (£)	YP 5 yrs at 13%	PV at 13%	Present value (£)
0– 5	10 000	1.0000	10 000	3.5172	1.0000	35 172
6–10	10 000	1.5184	15 184	3.5172	0.5428	28 987
11–15	10 000	2.3056	23 056	3.5172	0.2946	23 889
15	10 000	3.5009	35 009	20.0000*	0.1599	111 952
						£200 000

* YP perp. at 5%

Note that either valuation reconciles with the conventional valuation:

$$\frac{ERV}{k} = \frac{£10\ 000}{0.05} = \underline{£200\ 000}$$

As stated in chapter four, the fully let freehold (of all investment types) is least prone to inaccurate valuation by the implicit conventional technique. The advantage offered by a DCF valuation in the above format is not that (as long as growth forecasts are linked to the market by an implied rental growth formula) a more accurate valuation will result, but that

(a) more information is provided for future analysis purposes;
(b) the yield used enables cross-investment comparisons; and
(c) specific problems affecting the cash flow of the investment can be incorporated. Hence depreciation as evidenced by repair costs,

ment expenses or redevelopment can be explicitly and accurately accounted for.

A DCF solution need not, therefore, be laborious. An equally convenient but alternative solution is provided by a summation formula.

5.3.3   DCF by formula

The capital value is the summation of the discounted value of each block of income.

$$\text{YP 5 years at } 13\% + \left[(1.08712)^5 \times \text{YP 5 years at } 13\% \times \frac{1}{(1.13)^5}\right] \cdots$$

$$
\begin{array}{lll}
\text{where} & \text{income} & = £1 \\
& \text{total term} & = n \\
& \text{term of review} & = t \\
& \text{equated yield} & = e \\
& \text{growth rate} & = g
\end{array}
$$

$$\text{YP of whole} = \text{YP } t \text{ at } e + \left[(1 + g)^t \times \text{YP } t \text{ at } e \times \frac{1}{(1 + e)^t}\right] \cdots$$

$$= \text{YP } t \text{ at } e \left[1 + \frac{(1 + g)^t}{(1 + e)^t} + \frac{(1 + g)^{2t}}{(1 + e)^{2t}} \cdots\right]$$

The final block of income has grown for the term (n years) less one review period (t years).

(1)   YP of whole (Σ) =

$$\text{YP } t \text{ at } e \left[1 + \frac{(1 + g)^t}{(1 + e)^t} + \frac{(1 + g)^{2t}}{(1 + e)^{2t}} \cdots + \frac{(1 + g)^{n-t}}{(1 + e)^{n-t}}\right]$$

Multiplying through by $\dfrac{(1 + g)^t}{(1 + e)^t}$,

(2)

$$\Sigma \frac{(1 + g)^t}{(1 + e)^t} = \text{YP } t \text{ at } e \left[\frac{(1 + g)^t}{(1 + e)^t} + \frac{(1 + g)^{2t}}{(1 + e)^{2t}} \cdots + \frac{(1 + g)^n}{(1 + e)^n}\right]$$

Subtracting (2) from (1),

$$\Sigma - \Sigma \frac{(1 + g)^t}{(1 + e)^t} = \text{YP } t \text{ at } e \left(1 - \frac{(1 + g)^n}{(1 + e)^n}\right)$$

$$\Sigma \left[1 - \frac{(1 + g)^t}{(1 + e)^t}\right] = \text{YP } t \text{ at } e \left[1 - \frac{(1 + g)^n}{(1 + e)^n}\right]$$

$$\Sigma = \text{YP } t \text{ at } e \left[\frac{1 - \dfrac{(1 + g)^n}{(1 + e)^n}}{1 - \dfrac{(1 + g)^t}{(1 + e)^t}} \right]$$

$$\text{YP } t \text{ at } e = \left[\frac{1 - \dfrac{1}{(1 + e)^t}}{e} \right] \quad \text{so } \Sigma = \left[\frac{1 - \dfrac{1}{(1 + e)^t}}{e} \right] \left[\frac{1 - \dfrac{(1 + g)^n}{(1 + e)^n}}{1 - \dfrac{(1 + g)^t}{(1 + e)^t}} \right]$$

This formula represents the summation of the DCF model to create a multiplier for use with the current rental value. The solution to the problem is as follows:

EXAMPLE 5.4

As example 5.3.

ERV £10 000 p.a.; $e = 13\%$; $g = 8.712\%$; $t = 5$ years; $n = $ perpetuity.

$$\text{As } n = \text{perpetuity,} \left[1 - \frac{(1 + g)^n}{(1 + e)^n} \right] = 1 - 0 = 1$$

$$\text{YP perp.} = \text{YP 5 years at } 13\% \times \left[\frac{1}{1 - \dfrac{(1.08712)^5}{(1.13)^5}} \right] = 3.52 \times \frac{1}{0.17587}$$

$$\text{YP perp.} = 20.00 : \quad k = 5\%$$

The solution is: ERV   £10 000 p.a.
YP whole term is 5%   20.00

Valuation   £200 000

Thus both shortened DCF and DCF by formula valuations are straight-forward and reconcile with conventional techniques in the case of the fully let freehold. This is not, however, necessarily true of reversionary freeholds or of leaseholds (see chapter six).

5.3.4 The 'rational model'

A third variation on the shortened DCF approach is the rational model of Sykes (1981), the basis of which Greaves had already established (1972). The basis of the model mirrors the approach of Norris (1884) and is best illustrated using a reversionary freehold. The capitalisation of a rack rented property let on a normal review pattern is undertaken at the appropriate capitalisation rate (k) found from market analysis. This capitalisation rate is a surrogate for an increasing rental value (at each review date) discounted at the opportunity cost of capital (risk adjusted), that is the equated yield. The capitalisation of a current rent fixed under a lease is at the equated yield, although this is shown as a capitalisation in perpetuity of the current rent less the value of the current rent after reversion. The model unfortunately becomes cumbersome in its application to more complex reversionary freeholds and leaseholds.

The rational model, in the simple case of a reversionary freehold, can be simplified to two parts:
(a) the fixed initial income before reversion; and
(b) the resale price at the date of reversion.

Following the rationale so far established it is clear that a fixed rent should be capitalised at the required target rate or equated yield; and the resale price should be the predicted inflated price deferred over the period to reversion at the equated yield. In this format it is identical to our presentation of the equated yield valuation with a holding period determined not artificially but by the first reversion or review. The model suffers because no concise device for the YP of a terminable rising income has been established, although Greaves presented such a device in 1972 (Greaves, 1972b and 1985). If for example an income of £1 p.a. was expected to last for 20 years and to be reviewed at 5 yearly intervals, the valuation approach would be to capitalise the £1 p.a. in perpetuity and then deduct the resale price at year 20. This creates problems in all but the most elementary of appraisals and attempts to suggest solutions to various applications (Sykes and McIntosh, 1983; McIntosh, 1983b) have only served to highlight these problems, which are well documented. Any reader wishing to investigate this model further should refer to Bowcock, 1983b; Baum, 1984; Baum and Yu, 1985; Crosby, 1985; Crosby, 1986a; Fraser, 1985a; and Greaves, 1985 (all consolidated in Crosby, 1987).

As a result of the criticisms made by these authors we pay no further attention to this work as published although we recognise its contribution to a wholly desirable progress towards DCF based appraisals and present an example at page 143.

An alternative to equated yield, DCF or rational models – all of which are expressions of the same explicit cash flow projection and capitalisation process – is the real value model of Wood (Wood, 1972), which can be amended and reconciled with the equated yield approach (Mason, 1978; Crosby, 1983).

5.4 REAL VALUE MODELS

5.4.1 Real value theory

The real value model was formed by Wood as part of his PhD research (Wood, 1972) and subsequently published (Wood, 1973). It has gained little acceptance in its published form and was dismissed by the RICS research project interim report: 'It is considered that Dr Wood's 'real value' approach is too complex for most practitioners to use in their day to day work' (Trott, 1980).

No indication is given regarding whether this relates to the valuation or analysis role.

The real value approach of Wood starts from the simplifying premise that an income can be reviewed at each rent payment date to a new rental which matches inflation over the intervening period. The investor has as a result an inflation proof investment. A rent paid annually in arrears, however, would always be worth less than an inflation proof rent and would decline in real value over each year, while the inflation proof rent would have a static real value profile into perpetuity.

The rate of return required on such an income is the interest rate required for giving up the capital, taking into account all risks attached to the investment but excluding any extra return for the effects of future inflation. Wood termed this real return the inflation risk free yield (IRFY).

Fisher (1930) broke down the yield into a reward for three factors (see page 47); time preference or impatience (i), expected inflation (d) and risk (r). Wood's IRFY is a combination of i and r such that IRFY $= (1 + i) (1 + r) - 1$.

The valuation of a fixed income should not be carried out on the same basis. The rate of return must reflect the fact that on each rent payment date the same sum of money would be paid, regardless of the fact that, if inflation was present, the purchasing power of the last payment would be less than the previous payment. This inflation prone income would not have the ability to retain its purchasing power and the real value of the income would decline. The investor would require not only a real return to match his inflation proofed counterpart, but also an added return to make up for the decline in purchasing power (that is $(1 + i) (1 + d) (1 + r) - 1$).

The yield differential between fixed interest and index-linked gilts illustrates the difference between an inflation prone yield and an inflation risk free yield (i).

The valuation of an inflation proofed income would be undertaken at the IRFY (i). If the income was receivable in one year's time, the valuation would be:

$$\text{PV £1 in 1 year at } i = 1/(1 + i)$$

The valuation of an inflation prone income receivable at the end of the year would be at a higher rate of return. The IRFY would be supplemented by the inflation rate: the two incomes differ only insofar as in one case the income can amend itself for inflation, while the fixed income cannot (see Figure 5.2). The real return is adjusted for the inflation rate (d), and the fixed income is discounted in the usual way:–

PV £1 in 1 year at $(1 + i)(1 + d)(1 + r) = 1/(1 + i)(1 + d)(1 + r)$.

Assuming inflation and growth are the same, the different profiles of the equated yield and real value approaches can be compared for an inflation proofed and a more normal property income, subject to a periodic review.

The periodically reviewed income compounds downwards in real terms until a review where the purchasing power is returned. In money terms the rent is reviewed to a higher level and will be able to be used to purchase goods which have also increased in value. In money terms the income is increased to $(1 + d)$ at the review while it remains static between reviews. In real terms the income is static at each review, but between reviews the income declines by $(1 + d)$. See Figure 5.3.

In valuation terms, the term rent between reviews is capitalised as shown opposite on page 127.

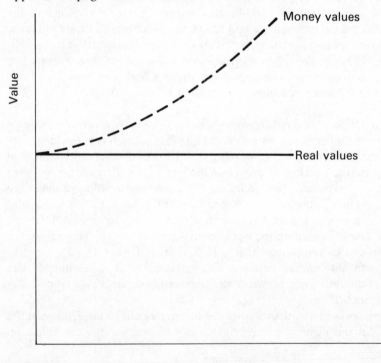

Figure 5.2 Proofed income

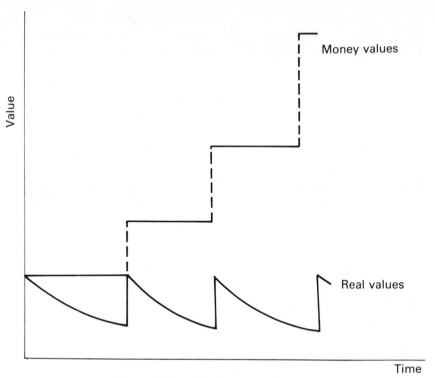

Figure 5.3 Periodically reviewed income

$$\text{Income} \times \left(\frac{1}{(1 + d)}\right) = \text{real value of year 1 rent}$$

This rent has now been adjusted for inflation and is equivalent to an inflation proofed rent, and can now be discounted at the *IRFY* (i):

$$\text{Income} \times \frac{1}{(1 + d)} \times \frac{1}{(1 + i)} = \text{Income} \times \frac{1}{(1 + d)(1 + i)}$$

The valuation of a proofed income $= 1/(1 + i)$.

The valuation of a prone income $= 1/(1 + d)(1 + i)$.

The determination of yields for the proofed and prone incomes are then incorporated into the valuation of a periodic rental flow. Assuming t is the rent review term and n the whole term (assume perpetuity for a freehold) the valuation can be built up in blocks of the review pattern term. The present value of £1 p.a. formula

$$\frac{1 - PV}{i}$$

can be substituted for the PV £1 formula when the rent is to remain static in money terms, but declining in real value. When the rent is assumed static even though it is declining in real terms the yield is adjusted as for the PV of £1.

$$\text{Thus, PV of £1 p.a. at } i \text{ adjusted for } d = \frac{1 - \left[\dfrac{1}{(1 + i)(1 + d)}\right]}{(1 + i)(1 + d) - 1}$$

The rent is assumed to remain static at review in real terms and the capital value of each block is discounted at the IRFY. The valuation of a periodically reviewed rent is undertaken by constructing a series and summating to obtain the real value formula of Wood for the YP of a rising income.

Ist t years rent: £R p.a.

$$\text{YP } t \text{ years (prone): } \quad \frac{1 - \left[\dfrac{1}{(1 + i)(1 + d)^t}\right]}{(1 + i)(1 + d) - 1}$$

2nd t years' rent: £R p.a.
YP t years (prone):   As above
PV t years (proofed): $= 1/(1 + i)^t$

3rd t years' rent: £R p.a.
YP t years (prone):   as above
PV 2t years (proofed): $= 1/(1 + i)^{2t}$

Up to and including
last t years' rent: £R p.a.
YP t years (prone):   as above
PV n-t years (proofed) $= 1/(1 + i)^{n-t}$

Summating:

$$\text{Value} = R \; \frac{1 - \left[\dfrac{1}{(1 + i)(1 + d)^t}\right]}{(1 + i)(1 + d) - 1} \left[1 + \frac{1}{(1 + i)^t} \;...+\; \frac{1}{(1 + i)^{n-t}}\right]$$

For the YP, R can be removed from the series:

$$\text{YP} = \frac{1 - \left[\dfrac{1}{(1 + i)(1 + d)^t}\right]}{(1 + i)(1 + d) - 1} \left[1 + \frac{1}{(1 + i)^t} \;...\; \frac{1}{(1 + i)^{n-t}}\right] \qquad (1)$$

Multiplying both sides by $1/(1 + i)^t$,

$$\text{YP} \left(\frac{1}{(i + i)^t} \right) = \frac{1 - \left[\dfrac{1}{(1 + i)(1 + d)^t} \right]}{(1 + i)(1 + d) - 1} \left[\frac{1}{(1 + i)^t} + \frac{1}{(1 + i)^{2t}} \right.$$

$$\left. \ldots + \frac{1}{(1 + i)^n} \right]$$

Taking (2) from (1),

$$\text{YP} - \text{YP} \frac{1}{(1 + i)^t} = \frac{1 - \left[\dfrac{1}{(1 + i)(1 + d)^t} \right]}{(1 + i)(1 + d) - 1} \left[1 - \frac{1}{(1 + i)^n} \right]$$

$$\text{YP} \left(1 - \frac{1}{(1 + i)^t} \right) = \text{as above}$$

$$\text{YP} = \frac{1 - \left[\dfrac{1}{(1 + i)(1 + d)^t} \right]}{(1 + i)(1 + d) - 1} \left[\frac{1 - \dfrac{1}{(1 + i)^n}}{1 - \dfrac{1}{(1 + i)^t}} \right]$$

The valuation of a rising income can be undertaken using the above formula. The valuer needs to determine i, d, t and n. Trott (1980) comments:

> The method has suffered from its complexity. A valuation technique, if it is to be accepted by the profession, must be easily understood and easy to use. Its theoretical soundness must be matched by a practical application. Unlike the later, and theoretically similar, equated yield analysis, Dr Wood's method is difficult to use. For instance, to obtain the years' purchase in perpetuity from Wood's tables the valuer must know: (i) the inflation risk free yield (i), (ii) the inflation risk rate per cent (d) and (iii) the rent review period (t).

These criticisms can be countered. Index-linked investments could provide suitable measures of comparative real returns. The typical rent review period is something all valuers are aware of. The analysis of future inflation rates would be the necessary subject of research; the distinction between real and inflationary growth would become a consideration.

As an analysis model, the extra inputs necessary can be subjectively assessed. However, the static real value assumption could usefully be dropped in favour of separate assessments of inflation and rental growth for an initial yield determination. Using the model for valuations, it would be necessary to make assumptions about expected inflation rates to assess implied real rental growth or loss. The model instigated by Wood therefore appears to have more use in the determination of real returns, as opposed to fixed income returns, for comparative investment appraisal. The real value model is better equipped in this respect than the equated yield approach.

While most investment portfolio performance measurement concentrates on the use of total returns rather than real returns for comparison purposes (property performance measurement is no exception), this is changing with the growing influence of index-linked investments. The evaluation of real returns and real and inflationary growth or loss is increasingly demanded, and in this context Wood's real value model may yet be shown to be of greater significance.

Although the criticisms of complexity when compared with equated yield models for investment appraisal seem unfounded, difficulties in application to market valuation are apparent. These difficulties can be overcome by simplifying the real value model and adapting it to the same basis as the equated yield model. The advantages of this move will be examined after some amendments are made and after the resulting model has been reconciled with the equated yield models.

5.4.2 A real value/equated yield hybrid

The main discrepancy between real value theory and equated yield techniques is the definition of growth. The equated yield models define the growth in rents in money terms as g while the real value theory discounts the fixed income by a yield made up of real return (IRFY) and inflation (d). If a static real value profile is assumed then d and g are the same: the level of rental growth (g) is equal to the level of inflation (d). In these circumstances the two models can be reconciled by substituting g for d in the real value formula. The equated yield model requires a choice of equated yield (e) while the real value model relies on a choice of inflation risk free yield (i).

Real value theory suggests that a fixed income and a totally reviewable income can be distinguished by the rate of inflation, the fixed income being worse by the inflation rate compounded downwards. The difference between the two types of income could be viewed as being the rental growth that the reviewable income can exploit; or the rate of rental growth forgone by the fixed income recipient. The effect of this view would be to discount the fixed income by an additional factor of g or to increase the reviewable income by a factor of g. These two alternatives represent the two different methods. The additional discount by g represents the basis of approach for a real value hybrid; the increase in the reviewable rent by g has already been seen to be the basis of the equated yield technique.

The real value hybrid starts from the basis of discounting a proofed income at a real return (IRFY).

The valuation of a proofed income of £1 at the end of one year is given by:

$$£1 \times \text{PV £1 in 1 year at i} = \frac{1}{(1 + i)}$$

The valuation of a fixed income of £1 at the end of one year is again undertaken on the basis that it is declining in real value by the rate of rental growth. The rent can be discounted at g before being discounted at i or the discount rate can be made up of both i and g.

Either: $£1 \times \dfrac{1}{(1 + g)} \times \text{PV £1 in 1 year at } i = \dfrac{1}{(1 + g)} \times \dfrac{1}{(1 + i)}$

or: $£1 \times \text{PV £1 in 1 year at } i \text{ (adj. g)} = \dfrac{1}{(1 + g)(1 + i)}$

The reconciliation of the real value and equated yield models can now be undertaken. The equated yield model requires a choice of e, while the real value model requires a choice of i. They both use g. The real value model does not require the selection of i. Consider the valuation of a fixed income of £1 for one year by both techniques.

Method (a): equated yield

$$£1 \times \text{PV of £1 in 1 year at } e = \frac{1}{(1 + e)}$$

Method (b): real value

$$£1 \times \text{PV of £1 in 1 year at } i \text{ (adj. g)} = \frac{1}{(1 + i)(1 + g)}$$

On the assumption that the same valuation should be found by either method, the inflation prone capital value of £1 is:

$$\frac{1}{(1 + e)} \quad \text{or} \quad \frac{1}{(1 + i)(1 + g)} \quad \therefore \quad \frac{1}{(1 + e)} = \frac{1}{(1 + i)(1 + g)}.$$

Solving the equation gives

(i) $i = \dfrac{(1 + e)}{(1 + g)} - 1$

(ii) $g = \dfrac{(1 + e)}{(1 + i)} - 1$

(iii) $e = (1 + i)(1 + g) - 1$

This mathematical relationship has already been noted in chapter one (see page 11) in the context of fixed income and index-linked gilts.

To reconcile the methods, the equated yield approach requires a choice of e and g. The real value approach requires i, but i can be a product of e and g. So, given e and g, i can be calculated. The reverse is true (e from i and g) but as the widest acceptance of contemporary techniques has been for methods based on an assumption of e, the former is taken as a basis for the application of the model. If future trends move the emphasis to the selection of real returns for property investment the real value model can change to the latter basis.

The valuation, by both techniques, of a proofed income of £1 for one year illustrates the reconciliation. The equated yield technique increases the rent by rental growth before discounting at the equated yield. The real value approach assumes a reinstatement of the rent at the end of the year, and discounts the real value of the rent at a real return.

Method (a): equated yield

$$£1 \times (1 + g) \times \text{PV £1 in 1 year at } e = \frac{(1 + g)}{(1 + e)}$$

Method (b): real value

$$£1 \times \text{PV £1 in 1 year at } i = \frac{1}{(1 + i)}$$

To reconcile, the assumption of the same valuation by both methods is taken:

$$\frac{(1 + g)}{(1 + e)} = \frac{1}{(1 + i)}$$

This equation solves exactly as in the previous example.

The criticisms of Dr Wood's approach made by Trott concerned the choice of inputs. The valuer must know:

(i) The inflation risk free yield.
(ii) The inflation risk rate per cent.
(iii) The rent review period.

The discrepancy between Wood's inflation risk rate and rental growth has been countered in the real value hybrid. Any new approach based on explicit future value changes must either assume or know the review pattern; and the inflation risk free yield can be calculated from the equated yield and growth. The real value hybrid, therefore, enables the same inputs that are required for the equated yield model to be used and cannot therefore be dismissed on Trott's grounds.

Based on the above assumptions the model can be formulated. Using example 5.4 (equated yield 13%, rental growth 8.712% p.a., reviews every

5 years) the capital value of the right to receive an estimated rental value of £10 000 p.a. with the above inputs can be determined.

The valuation of the first five years must be the rent at an inflation prone yield $((1 + i)(1 + d)(1 + r) - 1)$. This can be represented by the equated yield.

Year 0–5	ERV	£10 000 p.a.
	YP 5 years at 13%	3.5172
	Valuation	£35 172

(This part of the valuation is the same as in the equated yield approach.)

The rent review is not treated as an increase in rent, but as a reinstatement of the real value of the rent. In real terms the rent will be returned to its existing value of £10 000 p.a.; but it will still be fixed for the next 5 years, and as it is inflation prone it is valued at the equated yield.

Years 5–10	ERV	£10 000 p.a.
	YP 5 years at 13%	3.5172
	Valuation	£35 172

The progression can be built up to form an infinite number of capital values of £35 172 for each 5 year block, at the start of each block. Figure 5.4 (overleaf) illustrates.

To complete the valuation, the capital value of each block must be discounted to present values. The yield at which to discount can be selected by determining whether the capital value is prone or proofed. The block of income from years 5 to 10 has a capital value of £35 172 at year 5. The purchasing power of that value must be ascertained. As the capital value has been assessed by capitalising a rent in real terms, not money terms, then the capital value is also in real terms. It is apparent that if rents rose by 9% p.a. then the rent on review would be £15 184 (the amount of £1 in 5 years at 8.712% = $(1 + g)^5$), not £10 000. The capital value of the right to receive £15 184 p.a. for years 5 to 10 (in year 5) would also be higher, £53 406.

The amount stated in the valuation (£35 172) represents the purchasing power of the right to receive the next 5 years' rent, not the actual money value (£53 406). The capital value of £35 172 is completely proofed against inflation and can rise continuously during the waiting period. It must therefore be discounted at an inflation risk free yield.

$$\text{IRFY } (i) = \frac{(1 + e)}{(1 + g)} - 1 = \frac{1.13}{1.08712} - 1 = .03944$$
$$= 3.944\%$$

The valuation of the interest is therefore a succession of rents of £10 000 p.a., capitalised every 5 years at an equated yield, and then discounted at the inflation risk free yield for the appropriate number of years.

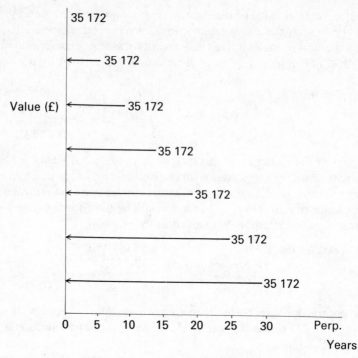

Figure 5.4 Capital values in real terms

Years 0–5		£10 000 p.a.
	YP 5 years at 13%	3.5172
		£35 172

5–10		£10 000 p.a.
	YP 5 years at 13%	3.5172
	PV 5 years at 3.944%	0.824
		£28 987

10–15		£10 000 p.a.
	YP 5 years at 13%	3.5172
	PV 10 years at 3.944%	0.679
		£23 889

The above forms a geometric progression which can be summated into a formula.

The constants are rent and the YP 5 years at 13%; the only change is the discount factor.

Assuming rent = £1, then capital value = years' purchase. The last term will have a PV of the number of years less 1 term. Thus, the value of the last tranche is:

$$PV \text{ (whole term} - t \text{ years)} = \frac{1}{(1 + i)^{n-t}}$$

The summation (S) is:

(1) $$S = YP \ t \ at \ e \left[1 + \frac{1}{(1 + i)^t} + \frac{1}{(1 + i)^{2t}} + \dots \frac{1}{(1 + i)^{n-t}} \right] \quad (1)$$

Multiplying both sides by $\dfrac{1}{(1 + i)^t}$:

(2) $$S \ \frac{1}{(1 + i)^t} = YP \ t \ at \ e \left[\frac{1}{(1 + i)^t} + \dots \frac{1}{(1 + i)^n} \right] \quad (2)$$

Deducting (2) from (1):

$$S - S \left[\frac{1}{(1 + i)^t} \right] = YP \ t \ at \ e \left[1 - \frac{1}{(1 + i)^n} \right]$$

$$S \left[1 - \frac{1}{(1 + i)^t} \right] = YP \ t \ at \ e \left[1 - \frac{1}{(1 + i)^n} \right]$$

$$S = (YP \ t \ at \ e) \times \left[\frac{\left[1 - \frac{1}{(1 + i)^n} \right]}{\left[1 - \frac{1}{(1 + i)^t} \right]} \right]$$

The advantage of the real value approach is that the latter term can be amended from

$$1 - \frac{1}{(1 + i)^n} \bigg/ 1 - \frac{1}{(1 + i)^t}$$

to

$$\frac{1 - \frac{1}{(1 + i)^n}}{i} \bigg/ \frac{1 - \frac{1}{(1 + i)^t}}{i}$$

which constitutes

$$\frac{YP \ n \ at \ i}{YP \ t \ at \ i}$$

Including the first term, the formula becomes:

$$YP \text{ of the whole} = YP \ t \ at \ e \times \frac{YP \ n \ at \ i}{YP \ t \ at \ i}$$

To determine the capital value of the right to receive a rent of £10 000 p.a. in perpetuity growing at 8.712% p.a. reviewable every 5 years (see example 5.4), and to obtain an equated yield of 13%, the valuation proceeds as follows:

$$\text{Preliminary calculation}: i = \frac{(1 + e)}{(1 + g)} - 1$$

$$\frac{1.13}{1.08712} - 1 = 0.3944 = 3.944\%$$

Valuation: ERV   £10 000 p.a.

$$\text{YP} = \text{YP 5 years at 13\%} \times \frac{\text{YP perp. at 3.944\%}}{\text{YP perp. at 3.944\%}}$$

$$= 3.52 \times \frac{25.354}{4.459} = \underline{20.000}$$

Valuation   £200 000
                                                              ‾‾‾‾‾‾‾‾

The underlying assumptions have already been reconciled and the answer is consistent with previous results.

5.5 SUMMARY

Real value approaches have been heavily criticised and have not gained any acceptance within the property valuation profession. Yet the appraisal of property investment by comparison with expected real returns has no more problems associated with it, in theoretical terms, than comparative appraisal using fixed income returns, and lends itself to comparisons with both conventional and index-linked gilts. The use of a static real value profile is unrealistic, however, and inconsistent with market analysis to calculate growth rates, as expected inflation does not necessarily equal the market's expectation of rental growth. However, the split of growth into inflation and real elements makes analysis more difficult due to the multiplicity of variables. The real value hybrid model, on the other hand, equates growth and inflation so as to employ the same variables as other DCF techniques.

DCF by formula reconciles in all cases with the real value hybrid, as they are summations of identical geometric progressions. Consequently, in order to progress towards recommendations, only explicit DCF and real value hybrid models are generally compared in the next chapter by undertaking a range of practical problems in the valuation of freehold and leasehold investment properties.

Chapter Six

CONTEMPORARY FREEHOLD AND LEASEHOLD APPRAISALS

6.1 INTRODUCTION

The equated yield and real value hybrid models, having been shown to be based on reconcilable principles, should produce identical solutions for any given example. This chapter applies the models to a number of examples of appraisals to illustrate how the models could be applied in practice.

The RICS research interim report had an objective to produce an appraisal approach which was 'useable in the day to day work of the valuation surveyor' (Trott, 1980). The authors are confident that both models will be seen to pass this test.

6.2 FULLY LET FREEHOLDS

We investigate two different problems:
(a) The valuation of property let subject to a review pattern where evidence of capitalisation rates is available for the same review pattern (example 6.1); and
(b) The valuation of property let subject to a review pattern where evidence is only available for property let on a different review pattern (example 6.2).

EXAMPLE 6.1

Value the freehold interest in a property just let at its rental value of £20 000 p.a. on a 5 year review pattern. Similar property also just let on a 5 year review pattern recently sold for a price based on a 6% capitalisation rate.

In both models no resort would need to be made to analysis for implied growth rate as a valuation direct to capitalisation rate would be undertaken. If, however, the full analysis and valuation was undertaken, assuming $e = 13\%$ and given that $k = 6\%$, and $t = 5$ years, an analysis for implied growth is necessary.

$$(1 + g)^t = \frac{\text{YP perp. at } k - \text{YP } t \text{ at } e}{\text{YP perp. at } k \times \text{PV } t \text{ at } e}$$

$$(1 + g)^5 = \frac{\text{YP perp. at 6\% } - \text{YP 5 years at 13\%}}{\text{YP perp. at 6\% } \times \text{PV 5 years at 13\%}}$$

$$(1 + g)^5 = \frac{16.667 - 3.5172}{16.667 \times 0.5428}$$

$$(1 + g)^5 = \frac{13.1494}{9.0460} = 1.4536$$

$g = (1.4536)^{1/5} - 1 = 0.0776807 = 7.76807\%$ p.a.

(i) **Explicit DCF**

Assume a 10-year holding period.

$$\begin{aligned} e &= 13\% \\ t &= 5 \text{ years} \\ g &= 7.76807 \\ k &= 6\% \end{aligned}$$

Year	Current rent p.a. (£)	A £1 5 yrs at 7.76807	Projected rent p.a. (£)	YP 5 yrs at 13%	PV at 13%	Present value (£)
1–5	20 000	1.0000	20 000	3.5172	1.0000	70 345
6–10	20 000	1.4536	29 072	3.5172	0.5428	55 500
10	20 000	2.1130	42 260	16.6667*	0.2946	207 489
						£333 334

* YP perp. at 6%

The projected rental increases are discounted at the equated yield until the deemed resale where the property is assumed to be sold at the capitalisation rate for a fully let property (k). We already know that 6% implies a growth rate of 7.76807% p.a. to achieve an equated yield at 13%.

(ii) Real value

$$i = (1 + e/1 + g) - 1 = (1.13 / 1.0776807) - 1$$
$$i = 0.0485481 = 4.85481\%$$

For a fully let freehold, the formula is:

$$\text{YP } t \text{ at } e \times \frac{\text{YP perp. at } i}{\text{YP } t \text{ at } i}$$

and the calculation becomes:

ERV   £20 000 p.a.

$$\text{YP 5 years at 13\%} \times \frac{\text{YP perp. at } 4.85481\%}{\text{YP 5 years at } 4.85481\%}$$

$$= 3.5172 \times \frac{20.5981}{4.3469} \qquad\qquad\qquad = \quad \underline{16.6667}$$

Valuation $\underline{\underline{£333\ 334}}$

In this case both methods reconcile to the conventional valuation based on a 6% capitalisation rate.

EXAMPLE 6.2

Value a rack rented freehold let on a different review pattern. Assume the same comparisons as before, but the subject property is let on a 3 year review pattern at £20 000 p.a.

The analysis for implied growth rate is as before: $g = 7.76807\%$ p.a.

(i) Explicit DCF

Assume a 9-year holding period.

$$
\begin{aligned}
e &= 13\% \\
t &= 3 \text{ years} \\
g &= 7.76807\% \\
k &= 6\%
\end{aligned}
$$

Note, however, that k is the relevant capitalisation rate where reviews are five-yearly. Where reviews are three-yearly, the potential for growth is enhanced and market capitalisation rates would be forced down. (See also solution (ii) below.)

$$k = e - (SF \times p) \text{ (see page 115) where}$$
$$k = \text{capitalisation rate}$$
$$e = \text{equated yield}$$
$$SF = \text{annual sinking fund over rent review period } t \text{ at } e$$
$$p = \text{percentage rental growth over the review period } t \text{ such}$$
$$\text{that } p = (1 + g)^t - 1 \text{ where } g = \text{annual rental growth}$$

On three-yearly reviews:

$$k = 0.13 - \left\{ \left\{ \frac{0.13}{(1 + 0.13)^3 - 1} \right\} \times (1.0776807)^3 - 1) \right\}$$

$$= 0.13 - (0.295322 \times 0.251614)$$
$$= 0.13 - 0.073854 = 0.056146$$
$$= 5.6146\%$$

Year	Current rent p.a. (£)	A £1 3 yrs at 7.76807%	Projected rent p.a. (£)	YP 3 years at 13%	PV at 13%	Present value (£)
1–3	20 000	1.0000	20 000	2.3612	1.0000	47 224
4–6	20 000	1.2516	25 032	2.3612	0.6931	40 963
7–9	20 000	1.5665	31 330	2.3612	0.4803	35 531
9	20 000	1.9607	39 214	17.8107*	0.3329	232 496
						£356 214

* YP perp. at 5.6146%

The solution is nearly £23 000 higher than in example 6.1, reflecting the advantage of three yearly reviews in a rising market.

To finish the calculation after only nine years requires an accurate choice of capitalisation rate. As this choice can be undertaken based on formula, the explicit DCF model for such a calculation is unnecessary but has the advantage of being explicit regarding the actual rental level in the future (in this case at years three, six and nine). The same solution would be obtained by assessing the capitalisation rate at 5.6146% and capitalising the current estimated rental value at this rate.

ERV   £20 000 p.a.
YP perp. at 5.6146%   17.8107

Valuation   £356 214

(ii) Real value

e (13%), g (7.76807% p.a.) and i (4.85481%) are as calculated in example 6.1 and inserted into the 3 YP formula incorporating a change of review pattern from 5 years to 3 years.

ERV £20 000 p.a.

$$\text{YP 3 years at 13\%} \times \frac{\text{YP perp. at 4.85481\%}}{\text{YP 3 years at 4.85481\%}}$$

$$= 2.3611526 \times \frac{20.598128}{2.7306738} \qquad = \underline{17.8107}$$

Valuation £356 214
_____

All solutions reconcile.

6.3 SIMPLE REVERSIONARY FREEHOLDS

EXAMPLE 6.3

Value the freehold interest in a shop property which is let on a lease with 4 years unexpired at £10 000 p.a. The estimated rental value is £20 000 p.a. based on 5-year review patterns and a similar property, as before, has just been sold at a capitalisation rate of 6%. Assume the same e (13%).

As before the following facts can be used.

$$e = 13\%$$
$$g = 7.76807\%$$
$$i = 4.85481\%$$

(i) Explicit DCF

This type of example was examined in chapter five (page 124).

In line with investors' expectations of future growth, an explicit DCF approach would be to increase the rent by the implied growth rate at each lease renewal or review and discount the total income flow at an equated yield. The yield excludes any growth potential, which is already accounted for in the income flow, and should therefore be equivalent to the fixed income yield, that is the equated yield.

Assume a 9 year holding period.

$$e = 13\%$$
$$t = 5 \text{ years}$$
$$g = 7.76807\%$$
$$k = 6\%$$

Year	Current rent p.a. (£)	A £1 at 7.76807%	Projected rent p.a. (£)	YP at 13%	PV at 13%	Present value (£)
1–4	10 000	1.0000	10 000	2.9745	1.0000	29 745
5–9	20 000	1.3488	26 976	3.5172	0.6133	58 194
9	20 000	1.9607	39 214	16.6667*	0.3329	217 562
						£305 501

* YP perp. at 6%.

(ii) Real value

The 3 YP formula which forms the basis of the real value hybrid produces a 6% capitalisation rate which is more easily derived in this case from the market, and the reversion is capitalised at this rate. The term is capitalised at 13% to take account of the fixed nature of the term income. The equated yield could be derived from $e = (1 + i)(1 + g) - 1$ but, as i was derived from e and g, 13% (e) can be used directly.

> *Valuation*
> Current rent   £10 000 p.a.
> YP 4 years at 13%   2.9745
>
>   £29 745
>
> Reversion to ERV   £20 000
> YP perp. at 6%   16.667
> PV 4 years at 4.85481%   0.8273
>
>   £275 756
>
> Valuation   £305 501

Note that both results again equate. However, the deferment of the reversion at 4.85481% and the use of the current rental value on reversion differ from the explicit DCF approach. A return to the original summation of the model in chapter five will illustrate that real value and explicit DCF models are doing the same thing in a different way. The real value approach views income profiles in real terms while the explicit DCF model views the rental flows in absolute money terms. The reversion to a rental value of £20 000 p.a. in the real value model is the expected real value of the rent on reversion while the rent of £26 977 p.a. in the DCF model represents the actual amount of rent expected. To reconcile the two different figures would mean that a commodity which cost £20 000 now would be expected to cost £26 977 in 4 years' time.

The deferments are at two different yields. The real value approach recognises the rent of £20 000 as having the ability to rise as rental values rise and can be expected to be worth more than an inflation prone sum. The deferment is at a growth implicit yield. The explicit DCF approach acknowledges the estimation of a rent in money terms in the future and discounts on the basis that the purchasing power of the estimated rent will decline as inflation increases in the four year waiting period.

The two approaches reconcile as follows. The term valuations are common; the reversions differ.

$$\text{DCF: reversion} = \text{rent } (1 + g)^4 \times \frac{1}{(1 + e)^4}$$

$$\text{Real value: reversion} = \text{rent} \times \frac{1}{(1 + i)^4}$$

As $(1 + e) = (1 + i)(1 + g)$, the DCF approach becomes:

$$\text{rent } (1 + g)^4 \times \frac{1}{(1 + i)^4 (1 + g)^4}$$

which reduces to:

$$\text{rent} \times \frac{1}{(1 + i)^4}$$

that is the real value approach. Sykes' 'Rational model' illustrates the difference in approach. This is effectively an explicit DCF valuation in conventional format, so that it compares clearly with the real value approach shown at page 142 (example 6.3).

Valuation

Current rent	£10 000 p.a.	
YP 4 years at 13%	2.9745	
		£29 745
Reversion to ERV	£20 000 p.a.	
A £1 4 years at 7.76807%	1.3488	
		£26 977 p.a.
YP perp. at 6%	16.667	
PV 4 years at 13%	0.6133	
		£275 756
		£305 501

6.4   FIXED LEASEHOLD PROFIT RENT

EXAMPLE 6.4

A property has 6 years unexpired at a ground rent of £2 000 p.a. The head lessee has sublet the property for the remainder of the term at £30 000 p.a. with no further reviews. Assuming the same equated yield of 13% as before for a freehold, assume 18% for the leasehold to reflect increased risk (but see chapters seven and eight for a consideration of risk adjustments).

(i)   Explicit DCF

Year	Rent received (£)	Rent paid (£)	Profit rent (£)
1	30 000	2 000	28 000
2	30 000	2 000	28 000
3	30 000	2 000	28 000
4	30 000	2 000	28 000
5	30 000	2 000	28 000
6	30 000	2 000	28 000

Given fixed rents received and paid, there is no advantage in a tabular layout. Capitalisation of the profit rent is possible by a YP multiplier, in this case for 6 years at 18%. A conventional layout is preferred.

Profit rent	£28 000 p.a.
YP 6 years at 18%	3.4976
Valuation	£97 933

(ii)   Real value

The real value technique would give the same solution to this fixed profit rent case, but the similarity hides a fundamental difference between the explicit DCF and real value approaches in application.

The real value approach does not necessitate the determination of profit rent but is based upon separate capitalisation of the two income flows in order that growth profiles, which may differ between the two, can be separately reflected (see page 146).

Rent received	£30 000 p.a.
YP 6 years at 18%	3.4976
	£104 928

Less rent paid	£ 2 000 p.a.	
YP 6 years at 18%	3.4976	
		£6 995
Valuation		£97 933

6.5 GEARED LEASEHOLD PROFIT RENTS

EXAMPLE 6.5

A shop property is let on ground lease with 50 years unexpired at a fixed rent of £5 000 p.a. The property has just been sublet at its estimated rental value of £30 000 p.a. on 5 year reviews. Similar freehold properties sell for 6% capitalisation rates when let on 5 year review patterns.

A fixed rent paid coupled with the perceptions and expectations of future rental growth creates a situation that pre-1950s valuers did not envisage. The expectations of a pre-reverse yield gap investment was no growth. The ability of the rent to grow was no advantage over the fixed ground rent; indeed, the lack of ability to change was seen as an advantage (the yield on ground rents being below the yield on rack rents). The valuation technique of assessing profit rent and capitalising for the unexpired term fitted these perceptions, and the expected income flow was as shown overleaf in Figure 6.1.

The obvious solution was to assess the difference in rents and capitalise at the appropriate rate, assessed as more risky than a freehold. The expected income profile takes on a different shape given current perceptions (see Figure 6.2).

Two factors are apparent. The net income is expected to grow and the growth rate is not the same as the equivalent freehold (see page 109). In addition the growth will be different depending on the ratio of the rent received to the rent paid. The problem can be illustrated by two identical profit rents based on different rents.

(1)	Rent received	£10 000	(2)	Rent received	£100 000
	Rent paid	£1 000		Rent paid	£91 000
	Profit rent	£9 000		Profit rent	£9 000

Assuming 10% p.a. growth, in case 1 a rent review in year 5 will increase the rent received to:

£10 000 × A £1 5 years at 10% (1.61051) =	£16 105 p.a.
less rent paid	£1 000 p.a.
profit rent	£15 105 p.a.

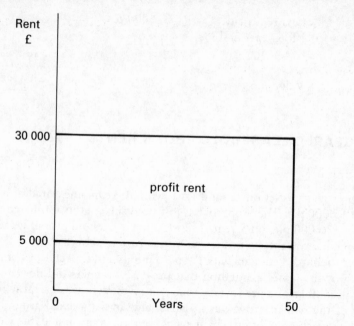

Figure 6.1 Fixed profit rent

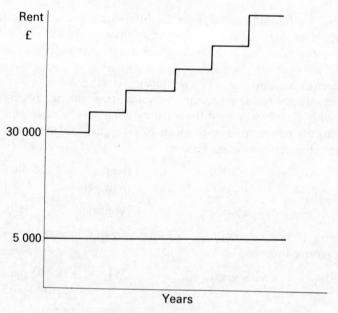

Figure 6.2 Geared profit rent

In case 1, the increase from £9 000 to £15 105 represents an increase of 67.8% or 10.9% p.a.

In case 2 the same assumptions produce a review rent of:

£100 000 × A £1 5 years at 10% (1.6105)   = £161 051 p.a.
less rent paid   £91 000 p.a.

profit rent   £70 051 p.a.

The increase from £9 000 to £70 051 represents an increase of 678% or 50.7% p.a.

In the following 5 years the increases are:

	Freehold	Leasehold (1)	Leasehold (2)
Growth in ERV	61.05%	61.05%	61.05%
Growth in net income	61.05%	65.09%	140.36%
Increase p.a.	10.00%	10.55%	19.17%

The gearing effects are as follows.

(a) Except where the rent paid is a peppercorn, the rental growth is at a greater rate for a leasehold than for an equivalent freehold.
(b) The rate of growth is dependent on the ratio of the rent received to the rent paid.
(c) The rate of growth diminishes at each subsequent review and tends towards the rate of growth in the ERV in perpetuity.

The lack of a constant growth rate in net income combined with the individuality of each interest depending on the lease structure and ratio of rent received to rent paid leads to the conclusion that a valuation model which makes no attempt to isolate any of these factors lacks a logical base. Any contemporary technique which ignores these factors is, therefore, open to the same charge.

(i) Explicit DCF

In an explicit DCF approach all future rent changes are incorporated in the income flow so that the gearing effects are taken into account. Assuming the same freehold analysis as before ($e = 13\%$, $k = 6\%$), this leads to a growth rate of 7.76807% p.a. Assuming the same risk adjustment (+5%), the equated yield model is based on the following inputs:

$$e = 18\%$$
$$g = 7.76807\% \text{ p.a.}$$

Years	Current rent (£)	A £1 at 7.76807%	Projected rent (£)	Less GR (£)	Net Income (£)	YP at 18%	PV at 18%	Present value (£)
0– 5	30 000	1.0000	30 000	5 000	25 000	3.1272	1.0000	78 179
6–10	30 000	1.4536	43 609	5 000	38 609	3.1272	0.4371	52 775
11–15	30 000	2.1130	63 390	5 000	58 390	3.1272	0.1911	34 888
16–20	30 000	3.0715	92 145	5 000	87 145	3.1272	0.0835	22 760
21–25	30 000	4.4648	133 944	5 000	128 944	3.1272	0.0365	14 720
26–30	30 000	6.4901	194 704	5 000	189 704	3.1272	0.0160	9 466
31–35	30 000	9.4342	283 025	5 000	278 025	3.1272	0.0070	6 064
36–40	30 000	13.7137	411 410	5 000	406 410	3.1272	0.0031	3 875
41–45	30 000	19.9344	598 034	5 000	593 034	3.1272	0.0013	2 471
46–50	30 000	28.9771	869 314	5 000	864 314	3.1272	0.0006	1 574
Valuation								£226 773

(ii) Real value

The income flow is capitalised in two parts. The capital value of the right to receive the rent from the sub lessee is found and the capital value of the liability to pay the ground rent is then deducted. The remainder is the capital value of the net income to the head lessee. The risk rate used in both parts of the calculation is the risk rate for the head lessee's net income. In this case the whole of the rental value is capitalised at 18% and the liability to pay the ground rent is also capitalised at 18%, to leave a residue of the head lessee's interest, by implication valued using an 18% target rate.

$$i = (1.18/1.0776807) - 1 = 9.4944\%$$

Rent received $£30\ 000$ p.a.

$$\text{YP 5 years at 18\%} \times \frac{\text{YP 50 years at 9.4944\%}}{\text{YP 5 years at 9.4944\%}}$$

$$= 3.1272 \times \frac{10.4196}{3.8403} = \underline{8.4848}$$

$£254\ 544$

Less rent paid $£5\ 000$ p.a.

YP 50 years at 18% $\quad$ 5.5541

$\underline{£27\ 771}$

Valuation $\underline{£226\ 773}$

6.6 COMPLEX INCOME FLOWS

It is possible to extend the range of examples and test the contemporary models against more complicated income flow structures (Crosby, 1985). In this examination the explicit DCF approach and the real value hybrid reconcile in all cases except one: the valuation of a terminable income subject to rent reviews in the term where the total term is not an exact multiplier of the review pattern (for example, a 14 year term with a review every 5 years). The discrepancy is caused by the DCF approach not adjusting the rent at the final review for the reduced term (4 years instead of 5 years) whereas the real value hybrid (and other formulae) automatically undertake an equated rent adjustment within the formulae.

It is, however, inadvisable to use short cut techniques where leasehold income flows are based on reviews to proportions of rents paid or received rather than based on reviews to rental values (Novi, 1985).

In part three we look at the application of the contemporary models to the determination of price (market valuation) and in the analysis of price (investment analysis) before reaching our conclusions in the final chapter.

Part Three

APPLICATIONS

Chapter Seven

PROPERTY INVESTMENT VALUATION

7.1 INTRODUCTION

In chapter one, the distinction between the two different types of appraisal, valuation and analysis, was introduced and discussed. This chapter relates to the valuation role, in other words the assessment of price in the market place. It has been suggested that the last thing an irrational market needs is a rational model (Fraser, 1985a); but we have challenged this view (in chapter one). Taken to its logical extreme, this approach would result in retention of the status quo for all time. The analysis contained in chapters three and four suggests that valuation techniques can and do change, albeit slowly, usually provoked by a sustained period of debate often initiated by changes in market conditions. If techniques are seen to be illogical, the use of alternatives will have an increasing influence on the level of prices. This is already happening where DCF techniques are used in the analysis role (see chapter eight). It has been suggested in chapter four that this type of analysis of worth may not be confined to the individual, but may influence a number of purchasers similarly: it is then a short step to market valuation.

This book is predicated on the basis that, if the evidence suggests that one technique is more appropriate than another, a movement towards this technique will slowly occur. Arguments such as the current non-use by the majority making the alternatives irrelevant are ignored in favour of a more detailed investigation of the merits of each technique on the assumption that a combination of time and logic must and will move the profession towards the best techniques.

7.2 FREEHOLD MARKET VALUATION

7.2.1 The defence of conventional techniques

The change in the perceptions of investors outlined in chapter four should naturally and logically lead to a change in the valuation model. Our examination of the typical income profile incorporating a growth expectation illustrated that the new model should be based upon an explicit DCF format employing the target rate or equated yield. Why then, 25 years after the appearance of the reverse yield gap, has the technique of valuers remained largely unchanged?

The change in perception led to a model which incorporated three extra variables: the equated yield, the growth rate and the timing of rent increases in the future. Although the timing of future rent increases is based on current or actual review patterns, the equated yield and growth rate are not so simple to estimate.

It has been illustrated in chapter five that if the equated yield is assumed the growth rate can be calculated using market analysis. This leaves the problem of subjective equated yield choice.

DCF models which rely on the calculation of implied growth accept, by implication, reliance on the major basis of market valuation: comparable evidence. Logic has been suggested as a major criterion for a valuation model (see chapter one): objectivity in the use of comparable evidence becomes another major criterion. The defence of conventional techniques relies on objectivity to a greater extent than it does upon logic. The defence of traditional models in practice relies on the following argument:

(i) the contemporary models have an inherent flaw in assuming an equated yield subjectively; and

(ii) the crux of a valuation is comparable evidence, and if the comparables are good then the valuer does not have to be subjective in his use of them.

The argument, put simply, is that objectivity is not present in the contemporary models' choice of equated yield, while objectivity is present in the conventional models' use of comparisons. This argument can now be examined.

7.2.2 Equated yield choice

The first part of the argument relates to the subjective choice of equated yield in DCF based models. Most published comment suggests that:

(i) conventional gilt-edged stock gross redemption yields should be the major comparison for the property target rate; and

(ii) a margin of 2% above gilts allows for the additional risks of property (see chapter two).

The reasons for using conventional gilts are a natural consequence of a supposition that gilts are a substitute for a risk free investment (ignoring interest rate and inflation risks). The risk margin has no other basis than the historical relationship between prime property yields and gilt yields prior to the reverse yield gap (see Table 3.1, page 69). A detailed investigation of the historical relationship (Crosby, 1985) has concluded that a margin of 2% was the investor's perception of the risk differential between shop property and gilts prior to the reverse yield gap. However, this historical analysis of yield choice would suggest a different margin for different sectors (industrials, offices) and classes (prime, secondary) of property.

Table 7.1   Gilt and property yield differentials, 1929–1955

	Prime shops	Secondary shops	Prime offices	Ground rents
Yield gap	2.25%	3.03%	3.03%	0.73%

Source: Senior (1975).

This historical perspective shows a range of margins for different types of property resulting from initial yield differences between those property types. The 2% margin is confirmed for prime shops but is different for offices, ground rents and secondary shops. If a historical basis is valid for equated yield choice then equated yields will vary for each type of property. If that is the case, the implied growth rate will appear to be the same for each property type, as the equated yield will rise as the initial yield rises. This is too simplistic. Equated yield choice in modern times cannot be based on historical analysis: a rational basis must be found.

This basis could be founded upon the qualitative differences between the comparable (gilts) and property. The risks of property have been examined in chapter two; the possibility of diversifying these risks has also been considered. In the valuation context the difficulties of assessing each risk factor for an individual property has led to a choice of yields which imply these risks. Equated yields in practice are no exception, the only difference being that the rental growth rate and timing of reviews have been explicitly dealt with. The incidence of other risk factors will vary from property to property.

To include a detailed isolation of factors within a market valuation is not, we suggest, a realistic proposition given that each comparable property must be subjected to the same scrutiny. The problems of identifying and quantifying these differences in the market valuation context leaves the valuer to choose a suitable equated yield for each property type and confirms the charge of subjectivity. Although attempts to quantify the 'risk' of property investments is a relevant area of study in the context of the analysis role (see chapter eight) there seems little advantage to be gained in the market valuation context (see Crosby, 1985).

Equated yield choice is therefore a subjective element in the DCF-based valuation process and to that extent the defence of conventional techniques is sound. However, is the valuation sensitive to equated yield choice?

To investigate this, an analysis of fully let freehold and reversionary freehold valuations folllows.

7.2.3 Fully let freeholds

Although the contemporary models appear to mirror the change in investors' perceptions since the 1960s the extra variables necessitated in DCF models introduce an element of subjectivity. The previous discussion indicates that subjective equated yield choice impacts upon implied growth rates and hence the valuation. But is this important? We examined the effect of varying the equated yield by undertaking an analysis of valuation ranges produced by a wide variation in equated yields. In the following analysis a range of equated yields between 10% and 20% is utilised and the resulting valuations are compared.

EXAMPLE 7.1

Value the freehold interest in a property just let at its rental value of £20 000 p.a. on a 5 year review pattern. A similar property has also just been let on a 5 year review pattern and recently sold for a price based on a capitalisation rate of 6%.

Conventional analysis and valuation

Analysis:	$k = 6\%$	
Valuation:	ERV	£20 000 p.a.
	YP perp. at 6%	16.6667
	Valuation	£333 333

Contemporary analysis and valuation

Assume: (1) $e = 10\%$; (2) $e = 20\%$

$$\text{Analysis: } (1 + g)^t = \frac{\text{YP perp. at } k - \text{YP } t \text{ years at } e}{\text{YP perp. at } k \times \text{PV } t \text{ years at } e}$$

(1) at $e = 10\%$, $g = 4.4668\%$ p.a., $i = 5.2966\%$
(2) at $e = 20\%$, $g = 15.3463\%$ p.a., $i = 4.0346\%$

Valuation (1): $e = 10\%$

ERV		£20 000 p.a.

$$\text{YP perp. at } 5.2966\% \times \frac{\text{YP 5 years at } 10\%}{\text{YP 5 years at } 5.2966\%} = \underline{16.6667}$$

Valuation	£333 333

Valuation (2): $e = 20\%$

ERV		£20 000 p.a.

$$\text{YP perp. at } 4.0345\% \times \frac{\text{YP 5 years at } 20\%}{\text{YP 5 years at } 4.0345\%} = \underline{16.6667}$$

Valuation	£333 333

These two valuations by the real value method are of course short cuts to a full DCF valuation at the equated yield. An explicit DCF approach confirms these valuations.

(1) Equated yield 10%
    Growth at 4.4668%

Years	Income (£)	YP	PV	Present value (£)
1– 5	20 000	3.7908	1.0000	75 816
6–10	24 884	3.7908	0.6209	58 572
11–15	30 961	3.7908	0.3855	45 250
16–20	38 522	3.7908	0.2394	34 958
21–25	47 929	3.7908	0.1486	27 007
26–30	59 633	3.7908	0.0923	20 864
31–35	74 196	3.7908	0.0573	16 119
36–40	92 315	3.7908	0.0356	12 452
41–45	114 858	3.7908	0.0221	9 620
46–50	142 907	3.7908	0.0137	7 432

	£308 089

Plus:	Rental value year 50	£177 806 p.a.
	YP perp. at 6.00%	16.6667
	PV 50 years at 10%	0.0085

	£ 25 244

Valuation	£333 333

(2) Equated yield 20%
    Growth at 15.3463%

Income (£)	YP	PV	Present value (£)
20 000	2.9906	1.0000	59 812
40 836	2.9906	0.4019	49 080
83 381	2.9906	0.1615	40 273
170 249	2.9906	0.0649	33 047
347 619	2.9906	0.0261	27 117
709 776	2.9906	0.0105	22 251
1 449 238	2.9906	0.0042	18 258
2 959 090	2.9906	0.0017	14 982
6 041 940	2.9906	0.0007	12 294
12 336 578	2.9906	0.0003	10 088

£287 202

Rental value year 50	£25 189 122
YP perp. at 6.00%	16.6667
PV 50 years at 20%	0.0001

£46 132

Valuation   £333 333

The use of a real value hybrid shows a number of interesting points. Although the valuations all reconcile, the variables are extremely diverse. The increase in the equated yield from 10% to 20% obviously shows that a much higher growth rate is required to justify the initial return of 6%. The real return (i) shows the opposite effect in this case, as a result of the review period. As the equated yield choice rises, the real return decreases. At a 10% e, i = 5.3%. At a 20% e, i = 4.03%.

The influence of these variations is insignificant when perfect comparables are present. In example 7.1, the comparable is perfect (the equated yield result could therefore have been quickly achieved by conventional techniques: see chapter 6, example 6.1 at page 138).

In the following example, the comparable is let on a different review pattern to the property to be valued.

EXAMPLE 7.2

Assuming the same comparison, value the following properties:

(a) ERV £20 000 p.a. on an inflation proof basis (indexed rents, for example).

(b) ERV £20 000 p.a. on 3 year reviews
(c) ERV £20 000 p.a. on 7 year reviews.

EXAMPLE 7.2(A)

The inflation proofed rent assumes a review at each rent payment date. The capitalisation can be undertaken at the real return (i).

(1) e at 10%, i at 5.2966%

ERV	£20 000 p.a.
YP perp. at 5.2966%	18.8679
Valuation	£377 358

(2) e at 20%. i, at 4.0345%

ERV	£20 000 p.a.
YP perp. at 4.0345%	24.8139
Valuation	£496 278

The range in answers is very wide. At an e of 10% the valuation is 76% of the valuation at an e of 20%.

EXAMPLE 7.2(B)

(1) e at 10%, reviews 3 years

ERV £20 000 p.a.

$$\text{YP perp. at } 5.2966\% \times \frac{\text{YP 3 years at } 10\%}{\text{YP 3 years at } 5.2966\%} = 17.3270$$

Valuation £346 540

(2) e at 20%, reviews 3 years

ERV £20 000 p.a.

$$\text{YP perp. at } 4.0345\% \times \frac{\text{YP 3 years at } 20\%}{\text{YP 3 years at } 4.0345\%} = 18.8461$$

Valuation £376 923

The e at 20% valuation is still higher but the e at 10% valuation is now 92% of the higher equated yield solution.

EXAMPLE 7.2(C)

(1) e at 10%, reviews 7 years

ERV £20 000 p.a.

$$\text{YP perp. at } 5.2966\% \times \frac{\text{YP 7 years at } 10\%}{\text{YP 7 years at } 5.2966\%} = 16.0477$$

Valuation   £320 955

(2) *e* at 20%, reviews 7 years
ERV   £20 000 p.a.

$$\text{YP perp. at } 4.0345\% \times \frac{\text{YP 7 years at } 20\%}{\text{YP 7 years at } 4.0345\%} = 14.9187$$

Valuation   £298 375

In this case the 20% equated yield choice produces the *lower* valuation, the *e* at 10% valuation being 7.6% higher.

When the comparable is on the same review pattern as the property to be valued, there is no discrepancy in the contemporary valuations. Where the comparables are not perfect, discrepancies occur. The greater the divergence of review patterns between comparable and subject properties, the greater the range of valuations produced. It may be thought that a higher discount rate would always produce a lower valuation but this is not the case. A high equated yield choice produces a higher valuation if the property to be valued has a shorter review pattern than the comparable, while the effect is reversed when the review pattern of the comparable is shorter than the property to be valued.

All the solutions are controlled by the consistent relationship between the equated yield, the growth rate and the real return. Table 7.2 sets out implied growth rates and real returns derived from equated yields of between 10% and 20% and capitalisation rates of 4%, 6% and 8%, all based on comparables with 5 year review patterns.

The table illustrates the slightly higher growth rate required each year to offset the fact that increases in rent are only obtainable every 5 years. It also illustrates the reducing real return as the equated yield increases.

The ranges in valuations shown above are perhaps enough to cast doubts on a method which relies on a subjective choice of equated yield. The wider the review patterns, the more significant the effect of equated yield choice: this is of importance, for example, in the evaluation of constant or equated rents (Crosby, 1983).

We are left, then, with the problem that subjective equated yield choice can affect the valuation of unusual fully let freeholds (those for which no perfect comparables exist) and no easy rule can be adopted in that choice.

However, we have demonstrated this problem over a very large range: note that a more realistic range of equated yields would result in very little difference in result. It should also be emphasised that the DCF-based model is much less sensitive to a change in yield than the conventional model.

Table 7.2   Implied rental growth rates and real returns

	Capitalisation rates on 5 year reviews (%)					
	4.0		6.0		8.0	
Equated yield (%)	g	i	g	i	g	i
10	6.44	3.34	4.47	5.30	2.33	7.49
11	7.50	3.25	5.57	5.14	3.49	7.26
12	8.57	3.16	6.67	4.92	4.63	7.04
13	9.62	3.08	7.77	4.85	5.77	6.83
14	10.68	3.00	8.86	4.72	6.91	6.63
15	11.74	2.92	9.95	4.59	8.04	6.44
16	12.79	2.85	11.03	4.47	9.16	6.26
17	13.84	2.78	12.12	4.36	10.28	6.09
18	14.89	2.71	13.20	4.24	11.40	5.93
19	15.94	2.64	14.27	4.14	12.51	5.77
20	16.98	2.58	15.35	4.03	13.61	5.62
Average	11.73	2.94	9.93	4.61	8.01	6.49
Range	10.54	0.76	10.88	1.27	11.28	1.33

Doubling the capitalisation rate will halve the conventional valuation of a fully let freehold; doubling the equated yield in a contemporary approach to the same problem has already been shown (at page 159) to have a much reduced effect. The choice is therefore between conventional models, which are intuitive concerning choice of capitalisation rate within which all investment qualities are implicit, and contemporary DCF-based models which are intuitive concerning choice of equated yield/target rate, albeit with a partial self-correction (the implied growth rate), within which some investment qualities are implicit (for example risk) and others may be made explicit (for example growth). We accept that neither contemporary nor conventional models are wholly objective. But which are the most logical?

7.2.4 Reversionary freeholds

The valuation of reversionary freeholds is more complex than the valuation of fully let freeholds. The perfect comparison is harder to find because of the effect of the existing lease. The valuations of fully let freeholds are based on finding comparables which are on the same review term as the property to be valued. For reversionary freehold investments, the property is let on an existing lease at a rent which is often at less than the estimated rental value. The perfect comparable is a property which has not only the right physical and locational characteristics but also the same unexpired term and rent received to rental value ratio. Differences in these factors will cause properties to have different growth prospects regardless of future growth in rental values. It would be useful at this stage to reiterate the defence of conventional techniques.

(a) The need for subjective equated yield choice is an inherent flaw in contemporary models. (This has been examined and illustrated to cause variation in the valuation of fully let freeholds when the review patterns are different.)

(b) The objectivity of conventional models is ensured by their use of comparables. (This has been seen to be nonsense, as it relies upon having the perfect comparable.)

A third factor should also be considered. A single capitalisation rate used in the conventional model has to reflect the growth potential of the property as a whole rather than the parts of the valuation. This is the basis of the equivalent yield model (the least dangerous conventional approach, which we use for illustration purposes in the remainder of this chapter in preference to term and reversion or layer methods (see chapter four)).

The availability and use of comparables and the effect of equated yield choice in the valuation of reversionary freeholds can now be examined to determine whether any of the models pass the tests of rationality and objectivity. The availability and analysis of comparables is examined first.

(i)   The availability and analysis of comparables

In the context of the debate regarding conventional or contemporary techniques for market valuation of reversionary freeholds Fraser (1984b) comments:

> The answer to this evergreen debate ultimately rests on the quality of the sales evidence from comparable property. In any particular instance the choice of valuation method should depend on whether market evidence is sufficient to enable the valuer accurately to identify the appropriate capitalisation rate.

Fraser then suggests that sufficient evidence is usually available for short unexpired terms, where the property is let subject to a standard review pattern. He restricts evidence to comparables with a similar income flow pattern and a similar ratio of rent received to current rental value. In accordance with normal valuation practice he also indicates comparisons should be similar in their locational and physical characteristics.

These arguments do not revolve around logic. The defence of the conventional technique relies solely on the fact that the technique has only one variable as against the greater number of variables inherent in the contemporary models. It is accepted by Fraser that the term income possesses no growth potential and that the use of a low capitalisation factor over-values the term; the defence relies on ease of use rather than an accurate reflection of investors' expectations. The investors' expectations are included globally in the overall capitalisation rate rather than in the separate parts of the valuation. Fraser's conclusion is:

> In market valuation, the greater the proportion of the figure which derives from objective market evidence and the smaller the proportion which results from the valuer's own estimate, the greater will be the accuracy of the valuation.

The equivalent yield model's use of one overall capitalisation rate helps objectivity in the analysis of comparables, as no assumption has to be made regarding the split of yields on different parts of the valuation (as there is in layer and term and reversion). The following example of equivalent yield and equated yield approaches to the analysis of comparables is therefore a fair illustration of the techniques involved.

EXAMPLE 7.3

A property is let at a current rent of £15 000 p.a. with 3 years unexpired. The estimated rental value is £20 000 p.a. and the property has just been sold for £375 000.

Conventional analysis

Income flow: Years 1–3	£15 000 p.a.	
Reversion	£20 000 p.a.	

Find equivalent yield (IRR on current income estimates):

Trial rate 5%

Current rent	£15 000 p.a.	
YP 3 years at 5%	2.7232	
		£ 40 849
ERV	£20 000 p.a.	
YP perp. at 5% ⎫		
PV 3 years at 5% ⎭	17.2768	
		£345 535
Valuation		£386 384

Trial rate 5.5%

Current rent	£15 000 p.a.	
YP 3 years at 5.5%	2.6979	
		£ 40 469

ERV   £20 000 p.a.
YP perp. at 5.5% ⎫
PV 3 years at 5.5% ⎭   15.4839

£309 678

Valuation   £350 147

Net present value at 5%   = £386 384 − £375 000 = + £11 384
Net present value at 5.5% = £350 147 − £375 000 = − £24 853

$$\text{IRR} = 5\% + \left\{ 0.5 \times \left\{ \frac{11\ 384}{36\ 237} \right\} \right\} = .157077 + 5 = \underline{5.16\%}$$

Equivalent yield = 5.16%

Contemporary analysis
This requires a subjective assumption to be made regarding equated yield choice.

(1) Assuming an equated yield of 10%

Current rent   £15 000 p.a.
YP 3 years at 10%

ERV   £20 000 p.a.
YP perp. at k
PV 3 years at i

The valuation of the term can be assessed but the valuation of the reversion requires two unknowns to be assessed. This can again only be undertaken by trial and error.
The term value is:

Current rent   £15 000 p.a.
YP 3 years at 10%   2.4869

£37 303

The reversion has a value of:

£375 000 − £37 303 = £337 697
k = 5.20%; given that e = 10%, g = 5.28%, and i = 4.48%

(2) At an assumed equated yield of 20% the term value is:

£15 000 × YP 3 years at 20% = £31 597

The reversion has a value of:

$$£375\ 000 - £31\ 597 = £343\ 403$$
$$k = 5.25\%; \text{given that } e = 20\%, g = 15.97\%, i = 3.48\%$$

It can be seen from these analyses that the conventional technique requires no subjective assumption, whereas the contemporary analysis requires an assumption of equated yield. This may produce some valuation error unless a narrow range of appropriate equated yields can be identified.

However, it can be seen that there is no problem or error in either contemporary or conventional analysis/valuation where the perfect comparable exists. To be perfect, the comparable must be similar in location and physical characteristics. It must also have the same ERV to rent received under the existing lease ratio and the same unexpired term.

EXAMPLE 7.4

Rent passing £10 000 p.a. with 3 years unexpired. ERV £20 000 p.a.; sold for £372 500.
Conventional analysis produces an equivalent yield of 5.0034%.
Contemporary analysis:

(1) at 10% equated yield:

$$g = 5.4105\% \text{ p.a.}; k = 5.0627\%; i = 4.3539\%$$

(2) at 20% equated yield:

$$g = 16.0540\% \text{ p.a.}; k = 5.1478\%; i = 3.4001\%$$

Although the equivalent yield model produces one answer only, the equated yield model produces a multiplicity of possible solutions. But if the comparison is perfect then the errors do not exist. Example 7.5 illustrates.

EXAMPLE 7.5

Value an identical property let with 3 years unexpired at £15 000 p.a., ERV £30 000 p.a. (this is the same unexpired term and ERV/rent received ratio).

Conventional valuation

Term	£15 000 p.a.	
YP 3 years at 5.0034%	2.7231	
		£ 40 846
ERV	£30 000 p.a.	
YP perp. at 5.0034%	19.9865	
PV 3 years at 5.0034%	0.8638	
		£517 904
Valuation		£558 750

Contemporary valuation

(1) at 10% equated yield

Term	£15 000	p.a.
YP 3 years at 10%	2.4869	
		£ 37 303
ERV	£30 000	p.a.
YP perp. 5.0627%	19.7522	
PV 3 years at 4.3539%	0.8800	
		£521 447
Valuation		£558 750

(2) at 20% equated yield

Term	£15 000	p.a.
YP 3 years at 20%	2.1065	
		£ 31 597
ERV	£30 000	p.a.
YP perp. at 5.1478%	19.4258	
PV 3 years at 3.4001%	0.9046	
		£527 153
Valuation		£558 750

The valuations are identical. The rent passing and the ERV are both one and a half times as much as the comparable, so the solution should be £372 500 multiplied by 1½ = £558 750. Where the perfect comparison exists, no investment valuation is necessary: the direct comparison method is far better.

The debate regarding investment valuation technique is therefore focused upon the use of imperfect comparables. This is a major problem. Generally, the quality and quantity of suitable evidence is open to doubt.

The prudent valuer is active in the investment market and is well aware that exactly comparable investment transactions are rarely available at the time of valuation, and the skill of valuation lies in interpreting the evidence available in the market place (Healey and Baker, 1985).

This view is also held by Sykes (1983a) who believes that the unique nature of each lease structure leads to a lack of good comparable evidence. The level of turnover ratios in institutional property ranged between 1.5% and 2.8% of insurance company holdings and 1.5% and 1.8% of pension fund holdings between 1978 and 1982. The level of secrecy in the market would ensure that a valuer would not have knowledge of every transaction. If valuers only need to interpret the capitalisation rate for a rack rented income, there may be enough information regarding yield levels in a locality: but if they must also bear in mind the term length and the estimated rental value to rent received ratio, then Sykes's view appears to be confirmed. Fraser admits that the choice of method depends on comparisons; the evidence suggests that the quality of comparison rarely exists.

Sykes described the conventional process of analysis and valuation as follows:

> The valuer has assessed the market yield for the property, if rack rented, as 7%. He therefore uses his intuitive judgement when dealing with a reversionary situation to arrive at an equivalent yield. This is somewhat greater than the rack rented initial yield (say 8%) and is used to value both the current income stream and the future estimated increase in income (in current rental value terms) (Sykes, 1983a).

Other evidence also leads the authors to surmise that the equivalent yield is manipulated upwards when the unexpired term is greater than the comparison. This is illogical: it has been shown that the rack rented equivalent yield should be *lower* than the capitalisation rate when the unexpired term is less than the normal review period (Fraser, 1984b; Crosby, 1985). It has also been illustrated that the equivalent yield technique has an inherent assumption within it, an implication of no growth in the future (Crosby, 1986b). The manipulation of yields by the valuer is necessary to offset this deficiency in the conventional model.

To illustrate the latter point the next example assumes that the rent received to ERV ratio of the property to be valued is different to the comparison.

EXAMPLE 7.6

Rent passing £3 000 p.a. with 3 years unexpired; ERV £30 000. (The example differs from example 7.5 in one respect only: the amount of the rent passing has been reduced from £15 000 p.a. to £3 000 p.a.)

The analysis of example 7.4 gave an equivalent yield of 5%. Using this yield in the valuation 7.6 gives the following solution:

Term	£ 3 000	p.a.
YP 3 years at 5%	2.7233	
	£8 170	

Reversion to ERV   £30 000 p.a.
YP perp at 5% ⎫
PV 3 years at 5% ⎭   17.2768

£518 303

Valuation   £526 473

The comparison property and the property with a rent passing of £15 000 p.a. and an ERV of £30 000 p.a. would show an identical future performance irrespective of whether there was any future growth in rents and capital values, and, if growth was obtained, irrespective of the amount of growth.

Assume three different growth rates, 0 per cent, 5 per cent and 10 per cent each year. If the comparison (example 7.4) is compared to the property which was valued (example 7.5), the internal rates of return earned by both are identical at the same growth rate (assuming a sale at the end of year three).

Growth	Example 7.4: Internal rate of return	Example 7.5: Internal rate of return
0%	5.00%	5.00%
5%	10.00%	10.00%
10%	14.99%	14.99%

The property with the rent passing of only £3 000 p.a. (example 7.6) shows a different performance at anything other than nil growth.

Growth	Example 7.6: Internal rate of return
0%	5.00%
5%	10.19%
10%	15.40%

This analysis indicates that if no distinction is made between a property with a rent passing of £15 000 p.a. and one with a rent passing of £3 000 p.a. (that is, they are both deemed to warrant the same equivalent yield) the performance will differ assuming positive growth. Although the properties are identical in all respects except for the rent passing, this one difference is enough to indicate that the property investment of example 7.6 is a better investment than an equivalent investment in example 7.5, if growth is expected.

The reason for this discrepancy can be easily seen within a comparison of examples 7.5 and 7.6. In example 7.5 the term rent is £15 000 while in example 7.6 it is only £3 000.

The £12 000 difference is discounted at 5%, the equivalent yield, which is a growth implicit yield. The extra £12 000 p.a. income is implied to be a growth income over the next three years but, of course, it is not, as the rent of £15 000 p.a. is fixed under the lease. The solution to the problem requires a subjective manipulation to the equivalent yield of example 7.6 in a downward direction. Unless this is done, the comparable has been utilised incorrectly (again assuming positive growth).

This illustrates that the equivalent yield model operates under a no growth assumption; but low initial yields imply growth, so the model is irrational. The lack of a logical basis requires the valuer to manipulate equivalent yields in the valuation stage for the non perfect comparison. The manipulations necessary are difficult intuitively and become increasingly difficult as the comparables get less perfect. Without manipulation, the equivalent yield model gives almost no help to the valuer.

For example, how should the following valuations be differentiated? Property (a) is let at the current ERV of £30 000 p.a. with 3 years unexpired. Property (b) is let at the same rent with the same ERV but has 50 years unexpired.

The comparison property (c) is identical to properties (a) and (b) but is fully let and has been sold for £600 000, showing an equivalent yield of 5%. Valuation (a) would be as follows:

Term	£30 000 p.a.	
YP 3 years at 5%	2.7232	
		£ 81 697
ERV	£30 000 p.a.	
YP perp. 5%	20	
PV 3 years at 5%	0.8638	
		£518 303
		£600 000

Valuation (b):

Term	£30 000 p.a.	
YP 50 years at 5%	18.2559	
		£547 678

ERV	£30 000 p.a.
YP perp. at 5%	20
PV 50 years at 5%	0.0872

£52 322

Valuation   £600 000

Using an equivalent yield of 5% valuation (b) equates with valuation (a). As the property investment in (a) is greatly superior to that in (b), to use an equivalent yield of 5% in both is inappropriate: but what is correct? In order to manipulate the valuation for the long fixed term, the equivalent yield must be adjusted. By how much is a matter for the valuer's intuition. The claims for the objectivity of the equivalent yield model rest solely on the finding of near-perfect comparables, yet if comparisons of that quality are available, a yield analysis should not be necessary. A model which relies totally on comparables obviously cannot function when those comparables do not exist. Fraser has suggested that such near-perfect comparables do exist for reversionary property with up to ten years unexpired, but are sparse for longer unexpired terms and leasehold interests. Given the very low turnover levels of institutional property, secrecy in the market place, and the qualities necessary for good comparables, this seems an optimistic assumption.

Surely what is needed is a model which helps the valuer to reconcile non perfect comparables with a degree of objectivity and a logical base which, in the last resort, can utilise any property comparable which has locational and physical similarities. Contemporary techniques offer an alternative which may satisfy these requirements. However, it has already been noted that the analysis process for contemporary equated yield or real value techniques requires a subjective estimate of equated yield choice.

When the process of market analysis by contemporary techniques was undertaken a variation in results was found, dependent upon the equated yield choice. The comparison was analysed assuming both 10% and 20% equated yields and the results were as follows:

e	$= 10\%$	e	$= 20\%$
k	$= 5.06\%$	k	$= 5.15\%$
g	$= 5.41\%$	g	$= 16.05\%$
i	$= 4.35\%$	i	$= 3.40\%$

The results can be incorporated into the valuation of the reversionary property with an unexpired term of three years, a rent passing of £3 000 p.a. and an ERV of £30 000 p.a. (example 7.6).

EXAMPLE 7.6 (real value solution)

(1) *e* at 10%

Term	£3 000 p.a.	
YP 3 years at 10%	4.4869	
		£7 461
Reversion	£30 000 p.a.	
YP perp. at 5.06% ⎱		
PV 3 years at 4.35% ⎰	17.3929	
		£521 787
		£529 248

(2) *e* at 20%

Term	£3 000 p.a.	
YP 3 years at 20%	2.1065	
		£6 320
Reversion	£30 000 p.a.	
YP perp. at 5.15% ⎱		
PV 3 years at 3.4% ⎰	17.5643	
		£526 929
		£533 249

The valuations of the subject property in example 7.6 by the equivalent yield technique and the equated yield technique at assumed equated yields of 10% and 20% are:

Equivalent yield at 5%	£526 473 (see page 168)
Assumed equated yield at 10%	£529 248
Assumed equated yield at 20%	£533 249

Previous analysis suggested that the equivalent yield technique under-valued the property in example 7.6; both equated yield assumptions have produced increased valuations. Whether they are any more accurate depends on how close the actual growth rate in the future matches the implied growth rate of the valuation. The growth rates expressly accounted for in the three different valuations are:

Equivalent yield	0%	p.a.
Assumed equated yield at 10%	5.41%	p.a.
Assumed equated yield at 20%	16.05%	p.a.

The prospective internal rates of return of the comparable (example 7.4) were:

Growth	IRR
0.00%	5.00%
5.00%	10.00%
10.00%	14.99%

The prospective internal rates of return of the subject investment in example 7.6 at each of the three valuations and at the two different growth rates are:

Growth	Equivalent yield	Equated yield 10%	Equated yield 20%
5%	10.19%	10.00%	9.72%
10%	15.40%	15.20%	14.91%

The closest result is obtained when, at the growth rate of 5%, the internal rate of return of example 7.4 is compared with the 10% equated yield valuation.

If growth is 5% p.a., this is very close to the implication of the 10% equated yield valuation and therefore this valuation (with the benefit of hindsight) reflected the comparable most accurately. As the growth gets greater the valuation with the highest implication of growth becomes more accurate.

The supporters of equivalent yield techniques may object to the no growth implication for the model suggested above. However, although they may appreciate the growth implication within the equivalent yield, the model cannot adjust itself. The equivalent yield would have to be adjusted by the valuer to account for differences between the subject and the comparable. If any future growth is expected the adjustment would have to be downwards. How many valuers would make any adjustment, particularly in a downwards direction?

The contemporary model does not necessarily display any more accuracy than the equivalent yield model in this case but the factors to be adjusted are at least made explicit. The implied growth rate has to be judged against the actual growth rate expected, a far easier task than the manipulations of equivalent yield, especially for short term reversions. The valuer's estimates are focused on the crucial issue rather than upon a subjective manipulation of equivalent yield.

(ii)   The effect of equated yield choice

The previous analysis of fully let freeholds revealed that equated yield methods produce a significant range of valuations from the same comparable when a range of equated yields are assumed. For example, when a comparison of a fully let freehold based on a 5 year review pattern was analysed to value a similar property on 3 year reviews, a market analysis and valuation at 10% equated yield produced a result 8% lower than a market analysis and valuation at 20% equated yield (example 7.2(b)). When the analysis of comparables is based on subjective equated yield assumptions, it was also apparent that a high equated yield choice produced a higher implied growth rate but a lower real return than a lower equated yield choice. Although it might be expected that a higher discount rate (equated yield) would produce a lower valuation, this is not always the case. A high equated yield choice produced an increased valuation where the property being valued was subject to more frequent rent reviews than the comparable.

In the previous section, the property in example 7.6 was valued at two different equated yields and yet the range of valuations produced was only £529 248 to £533 249, less than 1%. Example 7.7 extends this comparison by examining the solution to a typical term and reversion valuation assuming a fully let freehold sells at a 5% capitalisation rate when let on 5 year reviews.

EXAMPLE 7.7

A property let on lease with 3 years unexpired at £15 000 p.a. ERV based on 5 year reviews is £30 000 p.a.; rack rented capitalisation rate is 5% (5 year reviews).
Assume equated yields to be:

(1)10%;   (2) 15%;   (3) 20%
(1) Analysis for rental growth: $e = 10\%$

$$(1 + g)^5 = \frac{\text{YP perp. at 5\%} - \text{YP 5 years at 10\%}}{\text{YP perp. at 5\%} \times \text{PV 5 years at 10\%}}$$

$$= \frac{20 - 3.7908}{20 \times 0.6209} = \frac{16.2092}{12.4184} = 1.305$$

$$g = 5\ \sqrt{1.305} - 1 = 0.0547 = 5.47\% \text{ p.a.}$$
$$i = (1.1/1.0547) - 1 = 0.0429 = 4.29\% \text{ p.a.}$$

$$\therefore e = 10\%; \quad i = 4.29\%; \quad g = 5.47\% \text{ p.a.}$$

Repeating the analysis at equated yields of 15% and 20% produces solutions of:

(2) $e = 15\%$; $i = 3.74\%$, $g = 10.86\%$ p.a.
(3) $e = 20\%$; $i = 3.29\%$, $g = 16.18\%$ p.a.

Valuations

(1) : 10% equated yield

Term	£15 000	
YP 3 years at 10%	2.4869	
		£37 303
Reversion	£30 000	
YP perp. at 5%	20	
PV 3 years at 4.29%	0.8815	
		£528 920
Total		£566 233

(2) : 15% equated yield

Term	£15 000	
YP 3 years at 15%	2.2832	
		£ 34 248
Reversion	£30 000	
YP perp. at 5%	20	
PV 3 years at 3.74%	0.8958	
		£537 462
Total		£571 710

(3) : 20% equated yield

Term	£15 000	
YP 3 years at 20%	2.1065	
		£31 597
Reversion	£30 000	
YP perp. 5%	20	
PV 3 years at 3.29%	0.9074	
		£544 436
Total		£576 033

As the equated yield is increased, the term value is reduced. The opposing effect is apparent in the reversion, and a cancelling out of the differences leads to valuations which have small errors. The valuation at 20% equated yield is 1.73% higher than the valuation at 10% equated yield.

The extent of the cancelling out process is dependent on the relative ratios of values of term and reversion, which in turn are dependent on the ratio of the term rent to ERV and the unexpired term of the lease. In order to study this effect, an examination of a number of different capitalisation rates and ratios of ERV to current rent received was undertaken with the following ranges:

Capitalisation rates	3.5% to 8% (step 0.5%)
ERV/rent ratios	25%, 50%, 75%, 100%
Review pattern	5 years
Unexpired term	1–10, 15, 20, 25, 50
Equated yields	10% to 20% (step 1%)

We tested 560 permutations and 11 valuations were carried out for each permutation making a total of 6 160 valuations. The results were then analysed to show the excess of the highest valuation in each case over the lowest valuation on in each case. These results are illustrated in Tables 7.3 to 7.6 on pages 176–9.

A further analysis was undertaken to assess at what unexpired term the higher equated yield choice did not exhibit the highest valuation for each situation. This represented the point at which the increase in value in the reversion caused by a higher equated yield choice was compensated by the reduction in the term value. At this changeover point the range in values is at a minimum and the choice of equated yield practically irrelevant (see Table 7.7).

The analyses provided a generalised picture. For unexpired terms of ten years and less, the range in valuation solutions is very low at 2.2187%. The range increases as the unexpired term increases, and the range also increases as the capitalisation rate increases. Therefore the valuation of prime property would appear to be more objective by contemporary techniques than valuations of higher yielding secondary property. The smallest ranges in value are when the rent passing to ERV ratio is high. As the unexpired term increases beyond ten years, the ranges increase, except where the changeover points illustrated in Table 7.7 are reached. The values for the 160 permutations analysed for over ten years unexpired show an average range of 15 per cent. (For a more detailed explanation and analysis of Table 7.7, see Crosby, 1985.)

7.2.5 Conclusions

Much comment has been made regarding the individuality of leasehold income flows and the need for a more logical model to appraise these

Table 7.3 Range of valuations – EY 10% to 20%, rent received/ERV ratio 25%

Unexpired term (yrs)	Capitalisation rate (%)										Average	SD
	3.5	4.0	4.5	5.0	5.5	6.0	6.5	7.0	7.5	8.0		
1	0.54	0.66	0.79	0.88	0.96	1.06	1.15	1.32	1.42	1.52	1.030	0.309
2	1.09	1.26	1.47	1.65	1.82	2.00	2.26	2.53	2.73	3.02	1.983	0.611
3	1.53	1.80	2.05	2.30	2.62	2.89	3.24	3.52	3.90	4.21	2.806	0.859
4	1.94	2.25	2.56	2.94	3.28	3.69	4.06	4.43	4.82	5.32	3.529	1.073
5	2.339	2.71	3.10	3.50	3.91	4.34	4.78	5.24	5.72	6.21	4.184	1.236
6	2.70	3.15	3.61	4.03	4.52	4.95	5.24	5.93	6.49	6.96	4.782	1.360
7	3.05	3.51	3.98	4.47	5.02	5.53	6.05	6.58	7.11	7.77	5.307	1.497
8	3.36	3.89	4.38	4.93	5.50	6.07	6.56	7.06	7.66	8.14	5.755	1.537
9	3.69	4.24	4.79	5.35	5.83	6.47	6.92	7.57	8.12	8.67	6.165	1.589
10	3.99	4.61	5.17	5.73	6.26	6.88	7.40	7.89	8.36	8.94	6.523	1.568
15	5.50	6.17	6.79	7.33	7.78	8.24	8.48	8.72	8.84	8.81	7.666	1.123
20	6.99	7.69	8.23	8.55	8.86	8.67	8.60	8.11	7.28	6.51	7.949	0.758
25	8.47	9.05	9.37	9.50	9.09	8.45	7.49	6.60	5.51	4.49	7.802	1.649
50	14.42	12.72	10.75	8.32	5.71	9.04	14.53	20.38	28.26	36.89	16.102	9.285
Average (1st 10 yrs)	2.422	2.808	3.190	3.578	3.972	4.379	4.790	5.207	5.633	6.076		
SD	1.085	1.242	1.383	1.537	1.686	1.861	1.987	2.106	2.247	2.387		
Average (total)	4.257	4.551	4.788	4.963	5.083	5.585	6.214	6.849	7.587	8.384		
SD	3.540	3.221	2.891	2.579	2.372	2.477	3.174	4.306	6.106	8.179		

Table 7.4 Range of valuations – EY 10% to 20%, rent received/ERV ratio 50%

Unexpired term (yrs)	Capitalisation rate (%)										Average	SD
	3.5	4.0	4.5	5.0	5.5	6.0	6.5	7.0	7.5	8.0		
1	0.50	0.57	0.69	0.76	0.84	0.98	1.06	1.15	1.24	1.41	0.920	0.283
2	0.86	0.99	1.16	1.30	1.43	1.64	1.78	2.00	2.24	2.40	1.58	0.497
3	1.13	1.34	1.52	1.75	1.94	2.19	2.39	2.59	2.88	3.09	2.082	0.626
4	1.37	1.57	1.79	2.00	2.28	2.51	2.82	2.98	3.31	3.56	2.419	0.706
5	1.50	1.73	1.97	2.21	2.46	2.71	2.97	3.23	3.50	3.77	2.605	0.725
6	1.60	1.85	2.11	2.31	2.58	2.78	3.05	3.32	3.51	3.79	2.690	0.693
7	1.70	1.93	2.10	2.31	2.57	2.78	2.97	3.16	3.43	3.61	2.656	0.613
8	1.73	1.97	2.14	2.30	2.57	2.63	2.89	2.99	3.15	3.20	2.557	0.483
9	1.76	1.96	2.13	2.29	2.36	2.55	2.56	2.71	2.75	2.77	2.384	0.330
10	1.75	1.90	2.07	2.16	2.28	2.30	2.29	2.32	2.22	2.08	2.137	0.180
15	1.78	1.73	1.64	1.53	1.33	1.23	1.07	1.50	2.12	2.82	1.675	0.475
20	1.96	1.81	1.57	1.34	1.88	2.82	3.95	5.38	6.90	8.76	3.638	2.439
25	2.32	2.08	1.69	2.76	4.09	5.92	7.95	10.47	13.18	16.43	6.689	4.909
50	3.90	5.72	9.69	14.91	21.78	29.31	37.47	45.34	52.96	59.82	28.090	19.105
Average (1st 10 yrs)	1.390	1.581	1.768	1.939	2.131	2.307	2.478	2.645	2.823	2.968		
SD	0.409	0.452	0.471	0.499	0.546	0.551	0.604	0.637	0.697	0.757		
Average (total)	1.704	1.939	2.305	2.852	3.599	4.454	5.373	6.367	7.385	8.394		
SD	0.753	1.124	2.087	3.383	5.095	6.980	9.043	11.029	12.960	14.737		

Table 7.5   Range of valuations – EY 10% to 20%, rent received/ERV ratio 75%

Unexpired term (yrs)	Capitalisation rate (%)										Average	SD
	3.5	4.0	4.5	5.0	5.5	6.0	6.5	7.0	7.5	8.0		
1	0.42	0.52	0.54	0.65	0.72	0.85	0.92	1.06	1.14	1.22	0.804	0.264
2	0.67	0.77	0.91	1.02	1.18	1.29	1.46	1.58	1.70	1.90	1.248	0.389
3	0.78	0.90	1.06	1.18	1.30	1.49	1.62	1.82	2.04	2.18	1.437	0.452
4	0.79	0.91	1.07	1.19	1.32	1.44	1.57	1.77	1.91	2.13	1.410	0.416
5	0.72	0.83	0.94	1.05	1.16	1.27	1.39	1.50	1.61	1.73	1.220	0.322
6	0.62	0.67	0.76	0.80	0.88	0.97	0.98	1.07	1.07	1.14	0.896	0.169
7	0.44	0.47	0.48	0.54	0.48	0.52	0.50	0.46	0.42	0.36	0.467	0.049
8	0.26	0.26	0.20	0.16	0.18	0.20	0.22	0.32	0.51	0.55	0.286	0.129
9	0.15	0.17	0.30	0.39	0.56	0.68	0.82	1.13	1.40	1.69	0.729	0.502
10	0.31	0.44	0.61	0.80	1.07	1.32	1.68	2.07	2.42	2.89	1.461	0.836
15	1.46	1.99	2.62	3.42	4.32	5.27	6.41	7.57	8.84	10.21	5.211	2.834
20	2.55	3.64	4.84	6.30	7.99	9.90	12.04	14.18	16.51	19.01	9.696	5.334
25	3.63	5.14	7.10	9.44	12.15	14.93	18.14	21.43	24.80	28.41	14.517	8.079
50	9.15	14.26	20.80	28.15	35.95	43.56	51.09	58.32	64.79	70.39	36.23	18.552
Average (1st 10 yrs)	0.516	0.594	0.687	0.778	0.885	1.003	1.116	1.278	1.422	1.579		
SD	0.218	0.249	0.293	0.327	0.367	0.411	0.479	0.548	0.614	0.734		
Average (total)	1.568	2.212	3.016	3.935	4.947	5.978	7.060	8.163	9.226	10.272		
SD	2.303	3.612	5.288	7.187	9.216	11.205	13.208	15.131	16.894	18.479		

Table 7.6 Range of valuations – EY 10% to 20%, rent received/ERV ratio 100%

Unexpired term (yrs)	Capitalisation rate (%)										Average	SD
	3.5	4.0	4.5	5.0	5.5	6.0	6.5	7.0	7.5	8.0		
1	0.35	0.40	0.45	0.55	0.60	0.66	0.78	0.84	0.97	1.04	0.664	0.225
2	0.45	0.60	0.63	0.76	0.87	0.95	1.10	1.18	1.27	1.43	0.924	0.303
3	0.42	0.52	0.58	0.65	0.77	0.89	0.97	1.04	1.12	1.27	0.823	0.266
4	0.24	0.32	0.36	0.45	0.49	0.54	0.58	0.70	0.75	0.80	0.523	0.178
5	0	0	0	0	0	0	0	0	0	0	0	0
6	0.32	0.40	0.45	0.56	0.61	0.67	0.79	0.85	0.91	1.05	0.661	0.225
7	0.71	0.86	0.97	1.13	1.30	1.48	1.67	1.80	2.08	2.31	1.431	0.505
8	1.12	1.32	1.58	1.82	2.06	2.38	2.72	3.00	3.30	3.69	2.299	0.822
9	1.53	1.84	2.22	2.58	2.91	3.31	3.37	4.26	4.73	5.23	3.234	1.180
10	1.99	2.42	2.83	3.32	3.85	4.41	4.94	5.56	6.22	6.82	4.236	1.555
15	4.25	5.25	6.29	7.48	8.70	10.16	11.56	13.03	14.59	16.21	9.752	3.848
20	6.24	7.89	9.81	11.81	13.98	16.25	18.68	21.24	23.81	26.49	15.620	6.521
25	8.04	10.40	13.16	16.03	19.19	22.51	26.06	29.59	33.26	36.90	21.514	9.337
50	16.18	22.94	30.27	37.95	45.69	52.94	59.82	66.19	71.57	76.42	47.997	19.797
Average (1st 10 yrs)	0.713	0.868	1.007	1.182	1.346	1.529	1.728	1.923	2.135	2.364		
SD	0.603	0.724	0.866	1.006	1.159	1.332	1.495	1.694	1.894	2.083		
Average (total)	2.989	3.940	4.971	6.078	7.2157	8.368	9.5286	10.663	11.756	12.833		
SD	4.368	6.092	8.004	9.998	12.040	13.983	15.859	17.630	19.189	20.632		

Table 7.7 Unexpired term at which highest equated yield does not give highest value

Capitalisation rate (%)	Rent received/ERV ratio			
	25%	50%	75%	100%
	Years			
3.5	50+	50+	10	5
4.0	50+	25/50	9	5
4.5	50+	25	9	5
5.0	50+	20	9	5
5.5	50+	15/20	9	5
6.0	25/50	15/20	8	5
6.5	25/50	10/15	8	5
7.0	25/50	10/15	8	5
7.5	25/50	10/15	8	5
8.0	25/50	10/15	8	5

complex flows. The flows from freehold reversionary property are also individualistic and require a logical approach which helps the valuer in his use of non-perfect comparisons. The charge of subjectivity is not unfounded when applied to contemporary models but the effect of the subjectivity is minimal for reversionary property with under ten years unexpired. Given the range of equated yields used in the analysis, which should be reduced by future research (10 per cent is an excessive range given today's knowledge of comparative investment appraisal), the reliability of valuation can be improved.

The charge of subjectivity should also be addressed to equivalent yield models, which have an unbridled degree of manipulation in the valuation stage. The claim for objectivity is a mirage, unless the number of transactions in the market is enough to give almost perfect comparisons every time.

A logical market valuation model which helps the valuer to manipulate the non perfect comparison while retaining as much objectivity as possible is needed. The equivalent yield model does not pass the test, while the equated yield model can pass the test especially if a more rigorous basis for equated yield choice is found. Even if a more rigorous basis is not available, the compensating effects inherent within freehold reversionary valuation by contemporary techniques would lead to more consistent valuations in practice.

7.3 LEASEHOLD MARKET VALUATION

7.3.1 Use of capitalisation rates

Our critique of leasehold valuation by conventional techniques illustrated in chapter four that changes in investors' perceptions in the 1950s and 1960s introduced a variety of problems which led to the conclusion that a rational and logical basis for appraisal had been lost.

Any defence of the continued use of years' purchase dual rate, tax adjusted, capitalisation factors applied to current profit rents must, as in a defence of freehold appraisals, be based on objectivity, such objectivity to be based on the analysis of similar transactions.

While a debate exists regarding whether a sufficient quantity and quality of comparables exists for the typical freehold valuation, there is no doubt that good leasehold investment comparisons are usually very hard to find. To be a perfect comparison, a leasehold investment must be similar in terms of a wide variety of criteria.

These criteria change depending on the nature of the subject leasehold investment. The fixed income leasehold, where the head lease and the sub lease have no more reviews and expire at the same time, creates a property investment where the property characteristics (location and so on) are of very little importance compared to the quality of tenant (see Baum and Butler, 1986). The investment comprises a fixed income stream and can be valued by direct comparison or by reference to other fixed income investments. It has been termed the 'property gilt'.

When rising rents are introduced in either lease the criteria for a good comparison change. The usual characteristics of a similar tenant, a similar position, a similar physical condition, and so on, are necessary, but similarity in this situation also requires the same unexpired term, the same relationship between rent passing and ERV in the sub lease, and the same relationship between rents received and rents paid to the superior landlord.

The use of initial yields in order to effect a comparison of unidentical leasehold investments is, in the authors' opinion, highly dangerous.

It was suggested in chapter four that the common use of a 1% higher initial yield for a leasehold implied a higher risk rate rather than a different implied growth rate. Our investigation of gearing (see chapter four, page 109) shows that a different growth rate can occur in the net income of freehold and leasehold investments in the same property. Even if gearing does not produce a different growth rate, the use of a perpetual capitalisation rate analysed from a freehold to value a leasehold is misleading. It assumes that the capitalisation rate for a perpetual income implies the same growth rate as for a terminable income. This is false.

EXAMPLE 7.8

Value the leasehold interest in property held at a peppercorn rent for the next 15 years. The property is sub-let for the remainder of the term at the estimated rental value of £10 000 p.a. with reviews in years 5 and 10. A similar freehold fully let on a 5 year review pattern has just sold on the basis of a 6% capitalisation rate.

It might be assumed, as the profit rent would grow at the same rate as the ERV, that a direct comparison could be made between freehold and leasehold. Assuming no risk adjustment is required to distinguish between freehold and leasehold in this case, and that a 13% equated yield is required, the growth rate needed to increase an initial 6% to an equated yield of 13%, assuming 5 year reviews, is 7.768% p.a. in perpetuity.

The conventional application of the comparable to the leasehold using a capitalisation rate of 6% would produce a gross single rate valuation as follows:

Profit rent	£10 000 p.a.
YP 15 years at 6%	9.7122
Valuation	£97 122

If, as suggested, the 6% capitalisation rate is a short cut to assuming 7.768% p.a. rental growth, receivable every 5 years, then the internal rate of return over the 15 years should be 13%, as it would be for the freehold. Unfortunately this is not the case. A DCF approach does not produce the same answer. Using the real value 3 YP formula to illustrate:

$$(i = (1.13/1.07768) - 1 = 0.04855)$$

Profit rent   £10 000 p.a.

$$\text{YP 15 years at 4.855\%} \times \frac{\text{YP 5 years at 13\%}}{\text{YP 5 years at 4.855\%}}$$

$$= 10.48196 \times \frac{3.5172}{4.3469} = 8.4813$$

Valuation   £84 813

As the direct use of the capitalisation rate gives a solution nearly 15% higher than the equated yield approach (which is explicit regarding the growth rate) the capitalisation rate of 6% must imply a much higher growth rate than 7.768% to produce an internal rate of return of 13%. The growth rate implied by a 6% capitalisation rate for 15 years to produce an IRR of 13% is in fact 11.1% p.a. To add to the confusion, the capitalisation rate of 6% implies completely different growth rates for every different unexpired term. Table 7.8 and Figure 7.1 illustrate the manipulation of a perpetual

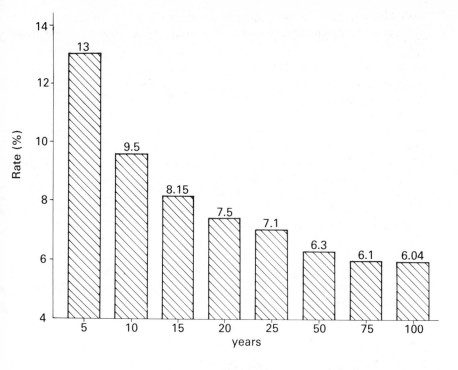

Figure 7.1 Terminal capitalisation rates

Table 7.8 Terminal capitalisation rates

Years	YP at 6%	3 YPs (Correct multiplier)	Required yield to equate with 3 YPs
	YPs at $k = 6\%$, $e = 13\%$, $g = 7.76807\%$ p.a., $t = 5$ years		
5	4.2124	3.5172	13.00%
10	7.3601	6.2922	9.50%
15	9.7122	8.4816	8.15%
20	11.4699	10.2088	7.50%
25	12.7834	11.5716	7.10%
50	15.7619	15.1091	6.30%
75	16.4558	16.1904	6.10%
100	16.6175	16.5217	6.04%
Perp.	16.6667	16.6667	6.00%

capitalisation rate of 6% for terminable incomes on 5 year reviews. Example 7.8 required the use of a capitalisation rate of 8.15% applied to the 15 year term to imply the same growth rate as 6% on a perpetual income, or 6.3% on a 50 year term, or 7.1% for a 25 year term. The use of comparisons which do not have the same unexpired term therefore invalidates growth implicit capitalisation rate comparisons.

Our examination of leasehold valuation in chapter four indicates that the conventional leasehold model does not have a logical framework in the modern context and, as in freehold valuation, relies on the concept of similar comparisons. The particular problems of finding perfect leasehold comparisons indicate that conventional leasehold valuation has more conceptual difficulties than its freehold counterparts.

However, although contemporary equated yield and real value models do address these conceptual problems, the necessity of a subjective assumption of equated yield still exists. Which imperfect method is best?

A choice between conventional or contemporary model should be made after examining the application of each. To this end the ways in which both conventional and contemporary models use the information available in the market is examined in the next section.

7.3.2 The analysis of comparables

In order to illustrate the possible use of comparisons, it is assumed that a similar property in terms of physical and locational characteristics is available.

EXAMPLE 7.9

A leasehold interest has sold for £73 600. The rent paid to the freeholder is £10 000 p.a. on a lease with 10 years unexpired and with no further reviews. The lessee has just sub-let for the remainder of the term, with a review in 5 years, at the estimated rental value of £20 000 p.a.

A conventional analysis (on a single rate gross of tax basis) would simply be to find the capitalisation rate on the basis of a 10 year term at the current profit rent.

Profit rent	£10 000 p.a.	
YP 10 years at ?%	x	
Sale price		£73 600

£73 600 = £10 000 × x; x = 7.3600;
YP 10 years at 6% = 7.3600;
Capitalisation rate = 6%.

The use of this information in practice is to apply the capitalisation rate direct to any property of similar locational and physical characteristics, regardless of lease structure, or to amend the capitalisation rate intuitively to reflect perceived differences.

The contemporary analysis is more complex. In order to find the equated yield of the investment the valuer must either assume a growth rate or assess an implied growth rate by using freehold comparisons. Assuming the first alternative, an assumption of a growth rate of 5% p.a. would produce an equated yield of 10.25% by trial and error (see below).

Current profit rent	£10 000 p.a.	
YP 5 years at 10.25%	3.7667	
		£37 667
ERV	£20 000 p.a.	
A £1 in 5 years at 5%	1.2763	
Inflated rent	£25 526 p.a.	
Less rent paid	£10 000 p.a.	
Profit rent	£15 526 p.a.	
YP 5 years at 10.25%		
PV 5 years at 10.25%	2.3124	
		£35 903
Valuation		£73 570

(Sale price £73 600)

The analysis is based on a pure speculation of the anticipated growth rate. It could alternatively have been based on an assumption of an equated yield from which a growth rate could have been assessed.

Freeholds provide much more market evidence. For example, assume that the freehold interest in a property similar to the subject of example 7.9, recently let on a lease with 5 year reviews at its estimated rental value, has been sold on the basis of a capitalisation rate of 4%.

The analysis for implied growth rate gives the following growth rates, depending upon the equated yield selected.

(1) Equated yield 10%: rental growth 6.44% p.a.
(2) Equated yield 20%: rental growth 16.98% p.a.

The application of the information to the valuation of a leasehold investment can now be considered.

EXAMPLE 7.10

The leasehold interest in a property similar to the subject of example 7.9 (in terms of locational and physical factors) is let on a lease with 20 years unexpired at a fixed rent of £20 000 p.a. The property has just been let at its estimated rental value of £30 000 p.a. on a 20 year lease with 5 year reviews.

The conventional valuation is likely to be undertaken with no intuitive adjustment of yield.

Profit rent	£10 000 p.a.	
YP 20 years at 6%	11.4699	
Valuation		£114 699

Contemporary analysis produces two alternative implied growth rates at the freehold equated yields of 10% and 20%. These are 6.44% and 16.98% respectively. These are appropriate indicators, given that what is needed is the market perception of the rate at which the property's ERV is expected to increase, a factor quite independent of tenure. The analysis for leasehold equated yield can therefore be repeated at these two growth rates.

The analysis of the comparison by trial and error shows that at a growth of 6.44% p.a. the equated yield is 11.4%, and at a growth of 16.98% p.a. the equated yield is 19.1%.

The valuation can then be attempted using each of these sets of results.

(1) $e = 11.4\%$, $g = 6.44\%$, $i = 4.66\%$

Rent received   £30 000 p.a.

$$\text{YP 20 years at 4.66\%} \times \frac{\text{YP 5 years at 11.4\%}}{\text{YP 5 years at 4.66\%}}$$

$$= 12.8295 \times \frac{3.6590}{4.3705} = \qquad 10.7409$$

		£322 323
Less rent paid	p.a. £20 000 p.a.	
YP 20 years at 11.4%	7.7594	
		£155 189
Valuation		£167 134

(2) $e = 19.10\%$, $g = 16.89\%$, $i = 1.81\%$
Valuation: £220 363

The valuation results show a considerable variation between the two contemporary approaches; but note that both the contemporary solutions are in excess of the conventional approach. To compare the results, the results, the internal rates of return of the comparable and the property to be valued are assessed for each solution at different prospective growth rates (Table 7.9).

The results show that the valuations are true to their assumptions. The conventional valuation reconciles with the comparison with a no growth assumption, while the two contemporary valuations reconcile with the comparison at the growth rates implied from the relevant equated yield assumption for the freehold.

The use of comparisons for both conventional and contemporary models is subject to difficulty. The contemporary models are true to their inputs but the subjective input of equated yield causes some variation in answers (but note the wide range of inputs illustrated). The conventional model on the other hand is simply illogical. The analysis of leasehold comparables is made complex by the inadequacies of the model, and its use of a capitalisation rate in an inflationary market is meaningless and misleading. For comparisons to be useful they must have the same unexpired term and the same gearing.

However, a consideration of which model creates the greater problems in the use of comparables is superfluous. By far the greater issue in the valuation of leaseholds is the availability of comparisons.

Table 7.9 Comparison of the performance of the comparable property and the subject property at different rental growth rates

IRRs Rental growth	0% p.a.	6.44% p.a.	16.98% p.a.
Valuations			
Comparison £73 600	6%	11.4%	19.1%
Conventional £114 700	6%	15.5%	28.0%
Equated yield at 10% £167 141	1.8%	11.4%	23.6%
Equated yield at 20% £220 363	negative	8.7%	19.1%

7.3.3 Conclusions

Given the much greater problem encountered in the conventional model for leaseholds, the reliance on comparison is of even greater importance than for the freehold model and the availability of comparisons is the major issue.

Contemporary leasehold valuations may be based partially on the analysis of freehold transactions: this is a major argument in their favour. However, this involves a subjective choice of equated yield, already investigated in this chapter. The range of values created by this subjective estimate is then compounded by risk adjustments which may differ between freehold and leasehold. In freehold valuation the effect of the choice of equated yield was compensated for by a corresponding opposite effect of a change in the implied growth rate. In leasehold valuation, however, the subsequent risk adjustment has an unbridled effect on the solutions obtained.

In a market place consisting of a number of unique leasehold investments, with few or no good comparables, the choice of method is therefore a conceptual decision based upon rationality. The problem of equated yield choice illustrates that although the contemporary models are conceptually more positive in taking into account the perceptions of investors they do not make valuations accurate. Accuracy is an unobtainable goal in an attempt to analyse property markets (see chapter one). Contemporary models do, however, enable the valuer to make reasoned qualitative decisions and translate those decisions into a rational mathematical model. The conventional model does not enable this process to take place. The model is seen to rely totally on comparable evidence. If the evidence is not available the model gives no basis for the valuer to translate his qualitative judgements into a mathematical solution. The leasehold valuation model is beset with conceptual problems and, in the absence of the perfect comparison, gives no aid to the valuer. It could be argued that it is worse than using no model at all, as it obscures some of the major influences on prospective income flow and price.

7.4 TAXATION

7.4.1 Freeholds

The effects of taxation on the future flows of income and/or capital are mainly ignored in the market valuation of freehold interests. Whether this should be so is open to debate (see, for example, Baum and Mackmin, 1981).

The structure of leases within the property investment market can produce a wide variety of taxation implications. The market is made up of a variety of groups or individuals, all having unique exposures to taxation. No two groups of purchasers will be exactly alike; it is thus beyond dispute that taxation is a crucial part of an investment appraisal for an individual purchaser (see chapter eight). But what of market valuation?

The two main taxes are those on income (Income and Corporation Tax) and capital gain (Capital Gains Tax) and frequent changes in legislation will alter an individual's incidence of taxation. Recent examples of change are the demise of investment surcharges and the indexing of capital gains.

Conventional appraisal techniques assume that investors make a gross of tax comparison with other investment opportunities and returns on capital are therefore assessed on this basis. Using the conventional model for a rack rented freehold investment, and the pre 1960 assumptions of no growth, a gross of tax or net of tax comparison becomes immaterial, as example 7.11 shows.

EXAMPLE 7.11

Capitalisation rate	6%
Tax rate	40%
ERV	£6 000 p.a.

Valuation (1): Gross of tax

ERV	£6 000	p.a.
YP perp. at 6%	16.6667	
Valuation	£100 000	

On a net of tax basis, the required return (based on opportunity cost) falls by 40% to 3.6%. The income after tax also falls by 40% to £3 600 p.a.

Valuation (2): Net of tax

Net ERV	£3 600	p.a.
YP perp. at 3.6%	27.7778	
Valuation	£100 000	

In times of growth, this conventional approach can become misleading. It suggests that the investor's return is reduced by the tax rate, but this is not the case. A contemporary technique can be used to illustrate that the equated yield is not reduced by 40%.

A 6% capitalisation rate implies a growth rate of 5.57142% p.a. to achieve a return of 11%, assuming 5 year reviews. Yet a purchase at £100 000 does not give a net of tax return of (11% × 0.6) 6.6% if a gross return of 11% is achieved. A valuation on a net of tax basis to show 6.6% would be far in excess of £100 000, as the valuation below shows.

$e = 6.6\%$ net, $g = 5.57142\%$ p.a., ERV £3 600 net.

The YP formula for the capitalisation of an income subject to rent reviews (t) when the required return (e) is achieved via a constant growth rate (g), is:

$$YP = \left\{ \frac{1 - \dfrac{1}{(1 + e)t}}{e} \right\} \times \left\{ \frac{1 - \dfrac{(1 + g)^n}{(1 + e)^n}}{1 - \dfrac{(1 + g)^t}{(1 + e)^t}} \right\} :$$

(When n = perp, $\left\{ 1 - \dfrac{(1 + g)^n}{(1 + e)^n} \right\}$ = 1; in this case, YP = 4.1445 × 21.1311 = 87.574

ERV (net)	£3 600 p.a.
YP perp.	87.574
Valuation	£315 274

This seemingly ridiculous solution (compare £100,000) is produced by a calculation which increases the rents at the same growth rate as for the gross of tax valuation, but discounts the future flows at a net of tax discount rate. The real return is assessed by:

$$i = (1 + e/1 + g) - 1$$

Gross of tax $i = (1.11/1.0557) - 1 = 5.14\%$

Net of tax $i = (1.066/1.0557) - 1 = 0.97\%$

The 40% reduction in equated yield has produced a relatively much greater reduction in the real return, and therefore the real values of the future flow are discounted at over 5% gross, but at less than 1% net.

Assume that the gross rent of £6 000 does increase by 5.57% p.a. up to the first review in 5 years' time. The rent on review will be:

$$£6\,000 \times (1.0557)^5 = £7\,868 \text{ p.a.}$$

After deducting 40% for tax the net ERV at year 5 is:

ERV	£7 868 p.a.
less 40%	£3 147 p.a.
net ERV	£4 721 p.a.

The current net of tax income is £3 600 p.a. The increase in rent also represents 5.57% p.a.

$$£3\,600 \times (1.0557)^5 = £4\,721 \text{ p.a.}$$

The net of tax ERV grows at the same rate as the gross of tax ERV: so it is not the assumption of rental growth which creates the problem.

The problem lies in the choice of the net of tax equated yield. The equated yield does not fall by the tax rate: it can, however, be correctly assessed by using a real value approach. Tax should be deducted from the real return rather than the fixed income return, that is the IRFY rather than the equated yield.

$$\text{net IRFY} = 5.14\% \times .6 = 3.085\%$$

The equated yield net of tax can be found by a rearrangement of the formula $i = (1 + e/1 + g) - 1$ to $e = (1 + i)(1 + g) - 1$. As the growth rate is held at its original level of 5.57% p.a. the equation becomes

$$e = (1.03085)(1.0557) - 1 = 8.829\%$$

The 3YP formula can now be used to reconcile with the net of tax capitalisation rate.

$$\text{YP} = \text{YP 5 years at } 8.829\% \times \frac{\text{YP perp. at } 3.085\%}{\text{YP 5 years at } 3.085\%}$$

$$\text{YP} = 3.90760 \times (32.4121/4.5686) = 27.186$$

ERV (net)	£3 600 p.a.	
YP perp.	27.7186	
Valuation		£99 787

$$k = \frac{£3\ 600}{£99\ 787} = 3.6\%$$

Only the rounding of yields in the preliminary analysis stage caused the valuation to miss £100 000. This approach can therefore be used to appraise the net of tax equated yield for an individual by:

(1) analysing the implied growth rate from the gross of tax capitalisation rate;
(2) calculating the gross of tax real return (i);
(3) reducing the real return by the investor's rate of tax; and
(4) calculating the net of tax equated yield using $e = (1 + g)(1 + i) - 1$.

The holding period will only affect the return if Capital Gains Tax has a differential impact. The above valuation assumes the property is held into perpetuity; but often a valuation will take into account the time horizons of a typical investor in the market.

Assuming the market investor will keep the property for ten years, any growth in capital value should be exempt from tax on account of Capital Gains Tax indexing provisions (this assumes a static real value, inflation and growth being equal). Only if rental growth does not match inflation will a discrepancy arise. An explicit DCF valuation is used below to compare the real value approach above. The two valuations – one perpetual, one for ten years – equate.

On the basis of a ten year holding period, the purchase price of £100 000 will produce a fixed rent of £3 600 net for the next five years, a reversion to £4 721 net in years five to ten and a sale price of £171 951 in year ten (assuming the growth rate of 5.57% p.a. is achieved and capitalisation rates remain static).

The net of tax flow is:

Years	Outflow (£)	Inflow (£)	PV at 8.829%	PV (£)
0	(100 000)		1.0000	(100 000)
1		3 600	0.9189	3 308
2		3 600	0.8444	3 040
3		3 600	0.7759	2 794
4		3 600	0.7130	2 567
5		3 600	0.6552	2 359
6		4 721	0.6020	2 843
7		4 721	0.5532	2 612
8		4 721	0.5084	2 401
9		4 721	0.4671	2 206
10		4 721 + 171 951	0.4293	75 854
				£0

Reversionary freehold investments are however more difficult to value on a net-of-tax basis. Reversionary properties enjoy an inherent real growth produced by the lease structure. As the reversion to a higher rent gets closer, the capital value increases even if the ERV does not increase, and a CGT liability will arise.

EXAMPLE 7.12

Current rent £1 000 p.a., unexpired term 10 years, ERV £10 000 p.a., tax 60%.

The conventional valuation of the reversionary freehold at a 6% equivalent yield is as follows:

Current rent	£1 000 p.a.
YP 10 years at 6%	7.3601

£7 360

Reversion to ERV	£10 000 p.a.	
YP perp. at 6%	16.6667	
PV 10 years at 6%	0.5584	
	£93 066	
Valuation		£100 426

In one year's time the capital value will have risen to £105 452 on account of the approach of the reversion. In ten years' time the capital value will have risen to £166 667 (ERV × YP perp. at 6%) on the reversion to the ERV of £10 000 p.a. This assumes no rental growth. The increase in value would be subject to Capital Gains Tax, as it is a real rather than an inflationary gain.

Net of tax flows

Income years 1–10	£	1 000 p.a.
less tax at 60%	£	600 p.a.
net of tax income	£	400 p.a.
sale price on lease renewal in year 10	£166 667	
less purchase price	£100 000	
gain	£ 66 667	
tax at 30%	= £ 19 872	
Sale price	= £166 667	
less tax	£ 19 872	
net proceeds of disposal	£146 795	

Inflows

Years 1–10	£	400 p.a.
Year 10	£146 795	

The net of tax internal rate of return is 4.2%, but 60% reduction from the gross of tax yield would give a net of tax yield of 2.4%. However, a conventional valuation carried out on the net of tax basis would give an incorrect result.

Current rent	£400 p.a.	
YP 10 years at 2.4%	8.7975	
		£ 3 519
ERV	£4 000 p.a.	
YP perp. at 2.4%	41.6667	
PV 10 years at 2.4%	0.7889	
	£131 484	
Valuation		£135 002

Introducing the growth element implicit in current market conditions complicates the valuation process still further. The same example of a reversionary freehold was assessed at a 6% gross capitalisation rate because of the implied future growth. A real value or equated yield valuation to show an equated yield of 11% and a rack rented capitalisation rate of 6% would have produced a slightly different gross of tax solution.

$$k = 6\%, \; e = 11\%, \; g = 5.57\% \text{ p.a.}, \; i = 5.14\%$$

Current rent	£ 1 000 p.a.	
YP 10 years at 11%	5.8892	
		£ 5 889
ERV	£10 000 p.a.	
YP perp at 6%	16.6667	
PV 10 years at 5.14%	0.6058	
		£100 944
Valuation		£106 833

Adopting a net of tax approach by real value the IRFY would be reduced to 2.056% assuming a 60% tax rate. The equated yield can be assessed by $e = ((1 + i)(1 + g)-1)$, that is $((1.0256 \times 1.0557)-1) = 0.0774$, or 7.74%. The valuation becomes (at a net of tax equated yield of 7.74% and a net of tax IRFY of 2.056%):

Current rent (net of tax)	£400 p.a.	
YP 10 years at 7.74%	6.7895	
		£ 2 716
ERV (net)	£4 000 p.a.	
YP perp. at 2.056%		
$\times \dfrac{\text{YP 5 years at 7.74\%}}{\text{YP 5 years at 2.056\%}}$	= 41.5521	
PV 10 years at 2.056%	0.8159	
		£135 602
Valuation		£138 319

The different rates of tax on income and capital and the different Capital Gains Tax treatment of real and inflationary gain make the use of 'short cut' valuation models extremely dangerous when the complexities of taxation are involved. Practices such as assessing a gross of tax redemption yield (equated yield) and then reducing this to a net of tax redemption yield by deducting the income tax rate are fraught with danger. The danger becomes extreme in certain cases. For example, growth explicit models which discount at net of tax equated yields based on a simplistic reduction from gross equated yields will produce valuations which suggest investments have infinite values when the net of tax equated yield is lower than the growth rate.

Given the difficulties of carrying out market valuations on a net of tax basis it is not surprising that gross of tax comparisons are commonplace. If all income flows were taxed similarly then the problem would be a minor one. In essence initial incomes are taxed at the investor's own marginal income tax rate, inflationary capital gains are exempt from tax, and real capital gains are taxed at the CGT rate. A gross equated yield is made up of real return and growth, and growth can be made up of real growth/loss and inflationary growth. The initial return can be made up of all ranges of these elements; so generalising on the taxation incidence of a particular investment property for the typical purchaser is dangerous. This is not to say that an individual purchaser should not consider the taxation implications of a purchase: this is the role of analysis and is a crucial element in an appraisal for investment worth fully covered in the following chapter. At this point, let it suffice to say that contemporary models are of infinitely greater value than conventional models in this role.

It has already been established that, when using the conventional basis, comparisons should have similar lease structures, locational and physical similarities, similar unexpired terms and ERV/rent received ratios. Added to this list is similar taxation profiles (although the last factor flows from the preceeding). A consideration of the effect of tax reinforces the need for quality comparisons.

Contemporary models, on the other hand, require a subjective equated yield choice based on other investments (probably conventional gilts). Part of the yield differential should be the product of different taxation implications. Freehold property has advantages over gilts. Although the capital gain from gilts is exempt from tax, prime properties invariably produce lower initial returns than gilts. This implies greater capital gains for prime property, and, given that such gains may be largely or wholly exempt from capital gains tax as a result of index-linking, net of tax prime property returns may be relatively higher for the same gross of tax return. This problem is mitigated by the influence of non-taxpaying institutions on both gilt and property prices.

Our suggested approach to tax in freehold valuations is to ignore taxation and to make comparisons on a gross of tax basis, undertaking the valuation using a DCF approach. Taxation is nonetheless a crucial factor in the analysis of investments (see chapter eight), where contemporary models become infinitely superior.

7.4.2 Leaseholds

Leasehold initial yields are high to make up for disadvantages, in comparison with freeholds, such as:

(1) no capital gain to redemption through asset appreciation as a result of inflation;
(2) loss of the historic cost as a result of the wasting nature of the asset.

Given higher initial yields, more income is produced for a given outlay. This extra income is taxed. Freehold property investments, largely free of capital taxes and providing low income yields, are generally subject to a low tax incidence. In the leasehold market, on the other hand, high tax-payers have to obtain a massive equated yield gross of tax to compensate for its decimation by taxation (see example 8.1 at page 206). It is not surprising therefore that high taxpayers do not participate to a great extent in the leasehold investment market (especially short leaseholds): this reinforces the view that taxation should not be a consideration in leasehold market valuation, but as for freeholds is a crucial element in an analysis for individual worth.

However, where it is possible to identify a group of potential purchasers subject to a common tax incidence, so that tax implications become relevant in market valuation, the following approach may be utilised.

EXAMPLE 7.13

Value the head leasehold interest in property held on a lease with 20 years unexpired at a fixed rent of £5 000 p.a. The property has just been sub-let for the remaining 20 years, with 5 year reviews, at the ERV of £20 000 p.a. Assume $e = 15\%$, growth = 6%, income tax = 40%.

The real net yield should not be the net of tax equated yield, (see page 191), but should instead be the net of tax real return.

The gross of tax real return is $(1 + e)/(1 + g) - 1$; $= (1.15)/(1.06) - 1 = 8.4906\%$, which at 40% tax gives a net real return of 5.0943%. The net of tax equated yield is therefore the product of the net of tax i and the growth rate $(1 + g)(1 + i) - 1$.

$$\text{Net of tax EY} = (1.06)(1.050943) - 1 = 11.40\%$$

Net of tax IRFY approach

Rent received	£12 000 p.a.
YP 20 years at 5.0934%	

$$\times \frac{\text{YP 5 years at } 11.40\%}{\text{YP 5 years at } 5.0934\%} = 10.4758$$

£125 710

less rent paid	£ 3 000 p.a.	
YP 20 years at 11.4%	7.7594	
		£ 23 278
Valuation		£102 432

Most valuers would argue that the identification of the tax position of a dominant group of purchasers in a sub-market is unlikely and difficult unless the group concerned is the gross fund (the tax-exempt pension funds and charities). The effect of tax upon market valuation techniques is therefore debatable, whether conventional or contemporary methods are employed.

The same is not true in analysis, which is dealt with in the following chapter.

Chapter Eight

PROPERTY INVESTMENT ANALYSIS

8.1 INTRODUCTION: A MODEL FOR ANALYSIS

Property investment analysis was explained in chapter one as an exercise differentiated from property investment valuation by its subjectivity. It is the estimation of the worth of a property investment to an investor. For our purposes, the investor is likely to be a fund or a property company.

Worth may be expressed in three forms. Where the price of an investment is known, for example in a retrospective analysis after a sale, or where negotiations for a purchase by private treaty have neared completion, then the worth of the investment must be expressed either as a *rate of return* or as an excess value over the price (*net present value*) at a given target rate. Where the price is unknown, for example where an investment is to be sold by auction, the analysis is aimed at an assessment of the *capital value* of the investment, or the maximum price that can be paid, given a target rate of return.

We utilise a single model for all types of analysis. Such a model may be more explicit than that used in market valuation (see Baum, 1984b), because it is no longer necessary to generalise. For example, the tax implications of an investment purchase to a particular investor may be ascertained, while net of tax appraisals in market valuation are usually avoided because a market tax rate cannot be generalised. In fact, the model should be absolutely explicit in order that the assumptions upon which the net present value or internal rate of return are predicated are exposed.

In order to be accurate, the rate of return needs to be an overall rate of return based upon an explicit projection of the cash flow likely to be produced by the investment. This rate of return has appeared throughout this book as the internal rate of return, the equated yield or the redemption yield.

We need to be careful to stress, however, that we are aiming at analyses of *net* returns, that is returns remaining after all expenses have been stripped away. This is not always the case when terms of overall return are used: for example, redemption yield as used by the *Financial Times* for the analysis of gilts is gross of tax and gross of transaction costs. Consequently, given that the purpose of property investment analysis is to facilitate investment comparison, and therefore decision making, the analyst must be careful to adjust such measures to the same, absolutely net, terms in pursuit of accurate comparisons.

We do not, however, base our analysis upon the estimation of *real* returns, that is returns remaining after the effects of inflation have been stripped away. We recognise that real return analysis (to produce real return estimates or to estimate capital value given a target real return) is increasingly desirable and possible since the introduction of index-linked gilts and given the practices of several investment management companies. However, real return analysis requires a projection of expected inflation, and for reasons we have already stated in part one the concentration of this book is upon monetary returns.

We have no doubt that in the near future this may have to be reconsidered. In pursuit of this, the models presented in this chapter and throughout this book are immediately adaptable to real return analysis and the analyst can amend the outlines presented herein accordingly.

Property investment analysis has been particularly aided by the popularisation of small computers in recent years and the introduction of spreadsheet software. Our own work has developed in this way. Consequently our model has taken shape as an explicit cash flow projection in monetary terms and in spreadsheet (row and column) format. We see the goal as an analysis of risk against return (see page 212): but before considering using our model for this purpose, we need to build it.

8.2   THE VARIABLES

The return from a property investment is a function of income, capital return and psychic income (see chapter two). We make no attempt to measure the latter, and for shorter leaseholds we may not expect a capital return. Thus our gross cash flow will be made up of income and (perhaps) capital. The income may increase at reviews. Estimation of a capital return depends upon timing of a sale; therefore, we need to estimate a likely holding period. Holding costs will be incurred during the period of ownership, and these will need to be estimated. Purchase and sale transfer costs will be payable; at each rent review a fee will be payable; letting or re-letting costs may have to be faced; and management fees may be incurred. Taxes on income and capital gain will be charged. Leaseholders may be faced with dilapidations claims. The income may be inclusive, so that (unusually) the investor pays rates out of the rent received; and a service charge may not cover the cost of service provision. Properties have to be repaired and refurbished: even then the impact of building depreciation may have to be faced.

The estimation of each of these factors will help us to reach an explicit net cash flow projection. If the price is known, the rate of return becomes the dependent variable in the analysis. If the price is not known, the target rate has to be added to the above list of independent variables, the capital value becoming the dependent variable. The same spreadsheet model can accommodate either variation.

All variables will now be briefly considered.

8.2.1   The holding period

For purely technical reasons – that is, to avoid an infinitely long cash flow projection in a freehold analysis – a finite holding period must be utilised in the analysis model. For freeholds, this implies the assumption of a resale. For leaseholds, the holding period will usually equate with the remaining term.

The overriding concern in the choice of holding period must be the intentions of the investor. Discussions with the investor might reveal his likely or intended period of ownership. Where no intention to sell is apparent, the holding period becomes arbitrary.

In either case, there are reasons for coinciding the resale date with the end of an occupation lease or a rent review period. This reflects likely practice, as a suspicion that fuller and fairer prices are achieved immediately after review or with a tenant under a new lease in harness appears to be common. (It is clear from earlier chapters that conventional valuation techniques may contribute to this policy, although risk aversion is a mighty influence.)

While the holding period is of no effect upon a market valuation in explicit DCF form, the introduction of costs, taxes and so on in investment analysis will destroy this consistency. Consequently, while periods of 10 or 15 years are often settled on for convenience, it should be noted that slight changes in holding period return may be achieved by shortening or lengthening the holding period, and this type of exercise is one of several uses of the model. Our analyses utilise holding periods which coincide with rent reviews or lease ends and usually fall in the 10–20 year range.

8.2.2   Resale price

In the cases of freeholds and long leaseholds the selection of a holding period will trigger the assumption of a resale at that date. The resale price has to be projected as the most likely selling price at that date. If the most common method of market pricing is the years' purchase method, and given that the sale will usually coincide with a review, the freehold resale price is given by:

Estimated rental value (ERV) $\times$ YP in perpetuity
or:

$$\frac{ERV}{\text{Capitalisation rate } (k)}$$

This requires the projection of two variables: ERV at the resale and k at resale.

Estimated rental value

A projection of rental value to the point of resale in property investment analysis need not, of course, be based upon a market-implied growth rate (see chapter five). While this may be a guide, it should be remembered that the implied growth rate is an *average* rate in perpetuity; it is also *net of depreciation*. In analysis an attempt should be made to forecast rental growth in some cases at a changing rate, and depreciation should be explicitly accounted for. This is further discussed and illustrated from page 202 onwards.

Capitalisation rate

The prediction of a capitalisation rate for the subject property 10 or 15 years hence requires the estimation of two distinct trend lines. Firstly, yields for the type of property under consideration may be expected to change over the period. If so, the extent to which the market yield will change must be estimated. However, it may be hypothesised that the expectations of the property investment market over the past century have been of generally stable prime yields (see chapters three and four), so that this may not be as large a task as it appears. Secondly, the movement in yield of the subject property against an index of yields for such properties in a frozen state over the holding period needs to be estimated. In other words, the extent of depreciation likely to be suffered by an ageing building (see also (d) below) needs to be estimated. A cross-section analysis may facilitate this process: if the subject property is 10 years old, and the appropriate capitalisation rate is 7%, given an expectation of stable yields over time the best estimate of the resale capitalisation rate after a 10 year holding period is the current yield on similar but 20-year old buildings.

8.2.3   Gross income flow

Forecasting rental growth over the holding period is important both in the estimation of the rental flow and in the prediction of the resale price. Again, a two-tier approach is necessary. Firstly, the rental value of the frozen property over time is to be forecast.

Forecasting a variable such as this might be based upon any of three methods.

(1) Extrapolation of time series data

A time series is a series of figures, for example rental values, over time. From the time series it may be possible to identify a long term trend in rental values, but a cyclical pattern will almost certainly obscure this to some extent. In addition there may be non-recurring influences – rent freezes, for example – which need to be smoothed away. Extrapolation involves continuation of the time series line into the future, reflecting both cyclical variations and the long term trend.

(2) Identifying causal relationships

Analysis of past relationships can often give a clue to the future and forecasting the future by statistical analysis of these relationships is an integral forecasting tool used, for example, by economists. The analyst forms a hypothesis relating to causal relationships and tests that hypothesis by using statistical tests of data analyses. For example, the lagged impact of interest rates (the independent variable) upon property yields (the dependent variable) might be tested by comparing the two factors over time and measuring the correlation between the two. If correlation is high, a simple prediction may be made.

The ideal situation for the forecaster would be where the independent variables are seen to move in advance of the dependent variable. Analysis of the business cycle is often undertaken to find indicators which lead the economy and those leading indicators form the basis of models which predict changes in the economy.

(3) A combined approach

The most common method of forecasting utilised in the property market is an approach which combines extrapolation with a causal analysis, almost certainly in an informal framework. Gilt yields might be used as an indicator of prime property yields: when they fall, property yields might follow. However, this is not always the case. At the time of writing, falling gilt yields coincided with rising prime property yields, so that an extrapolated forecast would conflict with a simple causal forecast based only on gilt yields.

In such circumstances the analyst is likely to base projections primarily on extrapolation coloured by causal influences (the forthcoming supply of new property in the sector, for example). If such an approach is used, the cyclical and long term trends in a time series should be differentiated.

Whatever the method used, the science of forecasting in the property market has far to go, and the rewards to a professional approach are likely to be high. Nonetheless the long term view of many property investors influences a reluctance to take on board these techniques. There is, however, an increasing acceptance of short term forecasting, which is likely to be much more accurate than long term projections. For example Hillier Parker's *Forecast of Shop Rents* (Hillier Parker Research, annually) identifies a relationship between (*inter alia*) retail profits and shop rents. This study identifies a causal relationship where movements in shop rents follow movement in retail profits.

Forecasts within a year ahead can be undertaken using actual movements in retail profits. Longer term forecasts require forecasts of the independent variables to produce a forecast of the dependent variable. While a property investor with a long term view, aware of the difficulties of producing accurate long term forecasts, is not likely to be impressed with such a technique, to dismiss the method out of hand may be a grave error. Given that the economy is subject to increasing scrutiny, property investors may find that greater research into causal relationships coupled with increasing accuracy of economic forecasts gives rewards to those who are influenced in their decision-making by forecast-based analytical techniques.

Rental values

The estimation of gross income flow requires the estimation of rental values for the subject property as it ages in comparison to the projected value of the 'frozen' property. Again, this allows for building depreciation resulting from the ageing process (see page 204), and is again possible by means of a cross-section analysis.

In this type of analysis, the rent of the subject is expressed as a percentage of its frozen equivalent over time. To continue the example begun at page 201 above, the current ERV of the subject 10-year old building is £25 per square foot. A rental growth estimate of 6% p.a. over the 10 year holding period is projected. 15 year old similar buildings let at £22 per square foot: 20 year old buildings let at £18 per square foot.

The projected rental values are as follows:

Year 1–5: £25.00

$$6\text{--}10\text{:} \quad £22 \times (1.06)^5 \quad = \quad £29.44$$

$$10 \text{ (resale):} \quad £18 \times (1.06)^{10} \quad = \quad £32.24$$

As the resale capitalisation rate is predicted as 8%, the resale price is therefore:

$$\frac{\text{Rent}}{\text{Yield}} = \frac{£32.24}{0.08} \quad \text{per square foot}$$

$$= £402.94 \quad \text{per square foot}$$

At current yields of 7%, the price is $\dfrac{£25}{0.07} = £357.14$ per square foot. The gross cash flow is therefore:

Years	Outlay (£)	Income (£)	Realisation (£)
0	(357.14)		
1–5		25.00	
6–10		29.44	
10			402.94

The internal rate of return of this investment – gross of all costs – is 8.37%.

The gross income flow is termed gross effective income in North American texts (see, for example, Greer and Farrell, 1984) to distinguish between maximum potential income when the property is fully let and the actual income likely to remain after voids. In this projection of income flow, an assumption has been made that 100% occupancy is achieved. If voids in a multi-let building are expected, the gross income flow should be reduced to a gross effective income flow by deducting an allowance for voids.

8.2.4 Depreciation

Allowances for depreciation have been referred to above. Both rental value and resale capitalisation rate are adjusted in the example used to effect a loss of value caused by ageing.

Note that the complexity of property depreciation is illustrated by an ageing building producing a rising rental income. This may be explained by the split of investment into site and building (see chapter two): while the site may appreciate or depreciate in value in real terms, the building must depreciate. It is, however, impossible to test this effect accurately without abundant evidence of the rental value of bare sites, which is rare in the UK.

Thus, while the depreciation in real terms of a property investment may be attributable to site or building factors, typically it is the latter which is primarily responsible for the income pattern declining in comparison to a 'frozen' index of values. The cross-section analysis referred to at page 201 is recommended as an accessible method of estimating a depreciation-prone investment income pattern.

Acceptance of differential building and site value performance over time leads to a necessary check in the analysis of a property investment. Given an ageing and declining building on an inflation-proof or improving site, the time will come when the net value of the site (after demolition and clearance) exceeds the value of the developed property. This may happen within the holding period, and if so the analysis must reflect that fact, subject to legal considerations (the tenant may not be removable until the lease end).

In the example, assume the net site value is initially 50% of the total value and is expected to grow at the same rate as the 'frozen' rent index (6%). At the resale date it is worth £12.50 $(1.06)^{10}$ = £319.79. This is exceeded by the property resale value (£403): but in different circumstances, especially where a longer holding period is used, this may not be the case, and a check needs to be built into the model. Estimates of the current net site value and the rate at which it will increase are therefore needed. The latter should equate with the rate at which newly prime property rental values are expected to increase: the former requires comparable evidence.

8.2.5   Regular expenses

Implicit within the gross cash flow from a property investment is a series of regularly recurring expenses. These include management costs, either fees charged by an agent or the time of staff. In the former case they may be based upon a percentage of gross rents; in the latter, they need more careful estimation, and may have to be increased over time. Repairs and maintenance will normally be covered, like insurance, by the tenant's obligations under a full repairing and insuring (FRI) lease; if not, they must be accounted for, as must the exceptional burden of rates.

While the investor who provides services, for example to the common parts of a multi-tenanted office building or shopping centre, will usually expect to recover these expenses in a service charge, the amount received may not quite match the cost of provision through a lagging effect or other causes, in which case an allowance needs to be made.

All expenses not tied to rent must be subject to an allowance for anticipated cost inflation.

8.2.6   Periodic expenses

While FRI leases place the burden of normal repairs upon tenants, dilapidations claims are not always met with the required response; in addition to this, improvements may be necessary to make the property marketable.

Thus at the end of an occupation lease the investor will be faced with the prospect of redeveloping, refurbishing, repairing or redecorating the property. If the lease end falls within the holding period, the prospect must be allowed for, again with an inflation factor.

8.2.7 Fees

In order to strip out all costs to leave a net return estimate, acquisition fees and sale fees at the end of the holding period need to be removed from the cash flow. These will normally be based upon the purchase and sale prices.

Rent review fees, based upon the new rent agreed, need to be allowed for at each review, and re-leasing fees, again based on the new rent agreed, have to be provided for at the lease end. Advertising costs may be additional to both sale and re-leasing fees. VAT should be added to all expenses where appropriate.

8.2.8 Taxes

Property investment analysis for the individual investor or fund can, and should, be absolutely specific regarding the tax implications of the purchase. Thus capital and writing down allowances should be taken into account where appropriate. Income or corporation tax should be removed from the income flow. Capital gains tax payable upon resale can be precisely projected by the model's insistence upon estimation of purchase price, sale price, intervening expenditure, holding period and intervening inflation.

The effect of tax upon return is illustrated by example 8.1.

8.2.9 Examples

EXAMPLE 8.1

A leasehold investment property has just been sold for £750 000. It is held from the freeholder on a lease with 10 years unexpired at a fixed rent of £47 500 p.a. The property has just been sub let on a lease which expires at the same time as the head lease at a rent of £200 000 p.a. with one review in 5 years' time.

The analysis of similar freehold properties implies a future rental growth rate of 8.71% p.a.

Analysis for gross of tax IRR

Cost:	£750 000		
Income:	Years 0–5	£152 500 p.a.	(i.e. £200 000 − £47 5000)
	Yrs 6–10	£200 000 p.a.	$\times (1.0871)^5$
		= £303 653	
		less £ 47 500	
		= £256 153	

Analysis shows an internal rate of return of 20.48%.

Analysis for net of tax IRR (assuming the investor pays tax on income at 60%.)

Cost:	£750 000	
Income:	Yrs 0–5	£152 500 × 0.4= £ 61 000
	Yrs 6–10	£256 153 × 0.4= £102 461

Analysis shows an internal rate of return of 1.42%. Note the vital effect of tax on return.

Of course, a large sector of the property market is dominated by the tax-exempt purchaser, and this can greatly simplify the analysis process, as demonstrated below.

Example 8.2 is presented in annual format, with all income and expenses assumed to be received at the year end. This is unrealistic in the UK market, and the model applied in practice must be amended to reflect the actual timing of expenses.

The client, a potential purchaser, is assumed to be tax-exempt; the property is a single-tenanted building where no voids are expected; and no periodic expenses are anticipated.

EXAMPLE 8.2

Property investment analysis: 10 year model

Data

Price	£357.14
Cap rate (year 0)	0.07
Cap rate (year 10)	0.08
ERV (year 0)	£25.00
ERV (year 5)	£22.00
ERV (year 10)	£18.00
Rental growth	0.06
Site value %	0.50
Resale site value	£319.79
Resale property value	£402.94
Expected realisation	£402.94
Management %	0.10
Voids %	0.00
Periodic expenses	See Schedule
Inflation	0.05
Purchase fees	0.03
Review fees	0.07

Letting fees	0.15
Sale fees	0.0275
Income Tax	0.00
CGT	0.00
Target rate	0.13

Periodic expenses: schedule

Year	Cost (£)
0	0
1	0
2	0
3	0
4	0
5	0
6	0
7	0
8	0
9	0
10	0

Cash flow

Year	Rent (£)	Voids (£)	GEI (£)*	Outlay/ resale (£)	Expenses (£)	Fees (£)	Periodic outlays (£)	Net cash (£)
0	0	0	0	−357.14	0	10.71	0	−367.85
1	25	0	25		2.5		0	22.5
2	25	0	25		2.5		0	22.5
3	25	0	25		2.5		0	22.5
4	25	0	25		2.5		0	22.5
5	25	0	25		2.5	2.06	0	20.44
6	29.44	0	29.44		2.94		0	26.50
7	29.44	0	29.44		2.94		0	26.50
8	29.44	0	29.44		2.94		0	26.50
9	29.44	0	29.44		2.94		0	26.50
10	29.44	0	29.44	402.94	2.94	11.08	0	418.36

*Gross effective income

Analysis 1		*Analysis 2*	
Price	£ 357.14	Price	£357.14
Target rate	0.13	Target rate	0.065
NPV	£−123.8	NPV	£ 13.267
IRR	0.0698	IRR	0.0698

The decision depends on choice of target rate. The IRR produced is 6.98%. Compare this with the gross IRR of 8.37% (see page 204). At any target rate less than 6.98%, a positive NPV is produced, and the decision is to accept, or purchase. For example, at a target rate of 6.5%, a positive NPV of £13.27 is the result: an outlay of an extra £13.27 would still produce the target rate. However, at a target rate of 13%, a negative NPV of nearly £128 indicates that the outlay is £128 too great, and a reduction in price of this amount would be needed to tempt a purchaser.

EXAMPLE 8.3

The same example has been amended to illustrate the effect of voids, periodic outlays, tax and a price reduction on the decision.

The property is now assumed to be priced at £250, but an immediate outlay of £100 is essential (for, let us say, repairs). A further outlay of £50 at the end of the holding period, for improvements prior to a sale, is allowed for and made subject to an inflation allowance. Income tax of 30% of net income is payable. Capital gains tax of 30% on the net real gain produced by the sale price (less fees and the outlay in year 10) over the initial outlay, fees and initial improvement expenditure is provided for. In this case a net capital loss produces a tax benefit, for set-off against other profits, of £28.86.

The after tax IRR is 7.36%, which should be compared, for example, with the after tax redemption yield net of expenses (transfer costs, and so on) on gilts. At a net of tax target rate of 6.5%, the decision is to purchase at this price.

Property investment analysis: 10 year model

Data

Price	£250.00
Cap rate (year 0)	0.07
Cap rate (year 10)	0.08
ERV (year 0)	£25.00
ERV (year 5)	£22.00
ERV (year 10)	£18.00
Rental growth	0.10
Site value %	0.70
Resale site value	£453.90
Resale property value	£583.59
Expected realisation	£583.59
Management %	0.10
Voids %	0.20
Periodic expenses	See schedule
Inflation	0.05
Purchase fees	0.03
Review fees	0.07
Letting fees	0.15

Sale fees	0.0275
Income Tax	0.30
CGT	0.30
Target rate	0.065

Periodic outlays: schedule

Year	Cost (£)
0	100
1	0
2	0
3	0
4	0
5	0
6	0
7	0
8	0
9	0
10	50

Cash flow

Year	Rent (£)	Voids (£)	GEI (£)	Outlay/ resale (£)	Expenses (£)
0	0	0	0	−250	0
1	25	5	20		2
2	25	5	20		2
3	25	5	20		2
4	25	5	20		2
5	25	5	20		2
6	35.43	7.09	28.34		2.83
7	35.43	7.09	28.34		2.83
8	35.43	7.09	28.34		2.83
9	35.43	7.09	28.34		2.83
10	35.43	7.09	28.34	583.59	2.83

*After tax cash flow

Analysis

Price	£357.14
Target rate	0.065
NPV	£ 26.172
IRR	0.0736

8.2.10 The target rate of return

The principal purpose of property investment analysis in the form discussed in this chapter is the facilitation of decision making. The basic criterion for decision making in investment, risk considerations apart, is the expected or required rate of return (IRR). This is termed the *target rate* (sometimes the *hurdle rate*) of return.

The target rate has already appeared in chapter two as I. It was seen from Fisher's work (see chapter 2) that the rate of return I can be built up from three factors: expected inflation (d), risk (r) and time preference (i). $I = (1 + d)(1 + r)(1 + i) - 1$; I is a compensation for these three factors, these three deterrents to the setting aside of capital for a period.

The target rate should be based upon the return required by the investor to compensate him for the loss of capital employed in the project which could have been employed elsewhere, that is the opportunity cost of capital (for example, the redemption yield on similar maturity gilts).

It is common to see no distinction between the required return on borrowed and equity funds. This is, however, unrealistic. Financial markets cannot be assumed to be efficient. The opportunity cost of equity to an equity investor such as a pension fund and the actual cost of equity (dividends required by investors) to an equity/debt investor such as a

Fees (£)	Periodic outlays (£)	Net cash (£)	Income T (£)	CGT (£)	ATCF* (£)
7.50	100	−357.50			−357.50
	0	18	5.4		12.6
	0	18	5.4		12.6
	0	18	5.4		12.6
	0	18	5.4		12.6
2.48	0	15.52	4.66		10.86
	0	25.51	7.65		17.86
	0	25.51	7.65		17.86
	0	25.51	7.65		17.86
	0	25.51	7.65		17.86
16.05	81.44	511.61		−28.86	540.48

property company will not equate with the actual cost of borrowing capital. Consequently, the analyst should rely upon the concept of opportunity cost (and not the actual cost of capital) in the estimation of target rate.

(In certain circumstances the cost of borrowing may be taken into account by using the weighted average cost of capital. For a fuller discussion of the weighted average cost of capital see Brigham (1985) and Brealey and Myers (1985)).

The target rate will be treated in simple terms for the remainder of this chapter, which is devoted to the fundamental focus of property investment analysis: risk/return analysis.

8.3 RISK/RETURN ANALYSIS

8.3.1 Introduction

The focus of this chapter is the analysis of property investment opportunities by means of discounted cash flow (DCF) techniques. While several markets throughout the world exhibit a reluctance to abandon initial yield based analysis, consumer-led and computer-aided improvements in service have produced, and continue to produce, widespread refinements in DCF methods. Investors should now expect no less than a present value or internal rate of return analysis based upon income and expense projections. This is a first and base level of analysis. Analysts are, as a result, increasingly forced to use market analysis to predict the uncertain, or, as stated in the introduction to this chapter, to make an explicit projection of the cash flow likely to be produced by the investment.

This element of uncertainty demands another level of decision-aiding analysis. However, risk analysis, well explored in financial theory, has not yet been the subject of comprehensive examination in the real estate sector, and empirical tests of real estate risk have not yet been developed to a point which enables risk/return analysis to be widely practised in property markets. There is an absence of reported data regarding the riskiness of individual real estate investments, both in terms of quantum and source (although developments are being made: see for example the research of Brown (1985)).

Despite this vacuum, a third level of analysis is rapidly being developed, both in theoretical and empirical terms. Recognition of portfolio risk, spurred by dominance of the real estate market by institutional investors in the UK and by a similar increasing influence in the USA, has produced applications of the capital asset pricing model (see chapter two) to real estate investment in recent years. The intellectual appeal of CAPM coupled with a well documented burst of real estate buying by UK institutions aiming towards real estate/fixed interest security/equity diversification has established risk/return analysis at the portfolio level as the subject of much research interest in the UK; a similar movement is discernible in the USA (see, for example, the *American Real Estate and Urban Economics Association* (AREUEA) journal, October, 1984).

The intention in this section is to link these levels of decision aid in a logical manner, and to establish the interdependence of the underlying techniques. Each succeeding level of analysis subsumes the previous level; deficiencies at any level are therefore compounded. It is important, therefore, to identify both theoretical and practical problems in the application of each level of analysis before proceeding to the next.

All levels of decision technology for real estate investment discussed herein are based on DCF analysis and utilise a return measure. Estimation of of return may be by net present value (NPV) or internal rate of return (IRR). These alternatives are assessed briefly below.

8.3.2 NPV or IRR?

It appears clear that in the general finance area the debate concerning theoretical preference for NPV or IRR has been well settled in favour of the former. Brigham (1985) is positive enough:

> ... the NPV method exhibits all the desired decision rule properties and, as such, it is the best method for evaluating projects. Because the NPV method is better than IRR we were tempted to explain NPV only, state that it should be used as the accepted criterion, and go on to the next topic.

Brigham's only reason for not doing so is continued use of IRR in the market. This preference for NPV is dependent, of course, upon the 'desired decision rule properties', which are in essence aimed towards maximisation of shareholder wealth. In real estate terms, this translates simply to maximisation of present asset values, the normal aim of a limited-resource investor.

Greer and Farrell (1984) therefore express surprise that in real estate literature IRR continues to find favour.

> While the internal rate of return has little substantive advantage over alternative methods of applying discount rates to projected cash flows, it does have serious weaknesses not found in the alternatives. Persistent support of a favoured technique might be admirable were there no substitutes that possess equal power to discriminate between acceptable and unacceptable opportunities. Such is not the case, however, with the IRR approach. Its continued advocacy is therefore somewhat curious.

It does not seem curious to the authors that IRR continues to find favour, because it is simpler to use. This should not be a factor acting in its favour when the alternative, NPV, is almost as simple, but the intuitive appeal of return expressed in a single point return measure, with no requirement upon the analyst to assess a target or hurdle rate, is obvious. Nonetheless, Jaffe (1977) considers that IRR remains popular in real estate simply because real estate research and debate lag behind general financial literature. It will eventually be clear in real estate practice that IRR is flawed where reinvestment of returns is likely. Given that IRR incorporates a risk premium (see below), the implicit assumption where reinvestment is likely that cash flows of any amount can be reinvested to earn the same rate is unrealistic. Modified IRR and Financial Management Rate of Return techniques (see Newell, 1985; Robinson, 1985) have merit in their intended solution of this IRR defect; but, as the appeal of the accepted technique is simplicity, such modifications may be superfluous. The prospect of multiple

IRR solutions with cash flow sign changes such as are typical in a real estate investment (which may require refurbishment or repair or fall vacant at any time) is a further restriction.

Comparison of mutually exclusive projects requiring different initial outlays is more logically dealt with by NPV; in this situation incremental analysis is another example of a superfluous theoretical advance designed to enable IRR to produce the same result as NPV. In conclusion, NPV is clearly preferable as a decision aid, but IRR has attractions for practitioners.

Both NPV and IRR will be utilised in the following discussion of risk/return analysis, which will be based around the following example.

EXAMPLE 8.4

The property investment analyst has been appointed advisor to a tax-exempt investment fund which has to make a choice between two alternative property investments which it has been offered. Investment A is a leasehold shop; Investment B is a small freehold office building. Each is for sale at £130,000, and the following information is available.

Investment A
The property comprises a single shop unit which is arranged on three floors with a total net floor area of 2 875 sq. ft. The current leaseholder holds the property on a net lease for a term of 35 years expiring 5 years after the purchase is likely to be completed, at a fixed rent of £2 250 per annum. The entire property is let on a net lease to the current occupier for a term expiring two days before the head lease at a rent of £45 000 per annum, subject to a review to open market rent 2 years before the lease expires. The current open market rental value is £52 500 (net) per annum. Acquisition fees are estimated at 3% of purchase price. Rent review fees are estimated at 7.5% of the revised rent. Management costs are 10% of rent collected per annum. Rents are currently growing in this part of the UK at 5% per annum and little change is expected in the short term.

Investment B
The property is a small freehold office building with a total area of 3 000 sq.ft., let with 5 years (at likely completion date) of the current lease to run. Last year's rent was £20 000 and around 30% of this rent was lost in outgoings, including management fees. Acquisition and sale fees are estimated at 5% of price. Rents are annually reviewable in line with RPI (the retail price index). Current capitalisation rates are between 10 and 12%.

General
RPI increased by 3.5% last year. British government fixed interest securities, medium-dated, currently yield around 11% if held to maturity. Rents from each property can be assumed to be received annually in arrear. All fees can be regarded as reliable cost estimates.

A basic NPV/IRR analysis of each transaction might be presented as follows:

Investment A

Data

Current rent received	£45 000 p.a.
Head rent paid	£2 250 p.a.
Remainder of lease	5 years
Term of review	3 years
Acquisition fees	0.03
Rent review fees	0.075
Management costs	0.10
Price	£130 000
Target rate	0.11

Variables

Rental value	£52 500 p.a.
Rental growth	0.05 p.a.

Appraisal

End of year	Rent in (£)	Rent out (£)	Review fees (£)	Man. fees (£)	Outlay (£)	Acq. fees (£)	Net cash (£)
0	0	0	0	0	130 000	3 900	(133 900)
1	45 000	2 250	0	4 500	0	0	38 250
2	45 000	2 250	0	4 500	0	0	38 250
3	45 000	2 250	4 558	4 500	0	0	33 692
4	60 775	2 250	0	6 078	0	0	52 448
5	60 775	2 250	0	6 078	0	0	52 448
						NPV	£21 913
						IRR	0.169029

Investment B

Data

Current rent received	£ 20 000
Term to review	1 year
Sale fees	0.05
Acquisition fees	0.05
Rent review fees	0.00
Management costs etc	0.30
Price	£130 000
Target rate	0.11

Variables

RPI growth	0.035 p.a.
Resale cap rate	0.11 p.a.

Appraisal

End of year	Rent in (£)	Resale (£)	Man. fees (£)	Outlay (£)	Acq./sale (£)	Net cash (£)
0	0		0	130 000	6 500	(136 500)
1	20 700		6 210	0	0	14 490
2	21 425		6 427	0	0	14 997
3	22 174		6 652	0	0	15 522
4	22 950		6 885	0	0	16 065
5	23 754	215 943	7 126	0	10 797	221 773
					NPV	£42 270
					IRR	0.0182503

The results, employing the data and variables as listed, show Investment B to be preferable to Investment A by both NPV and IRR criteria. (It should be noted that NPV and IRR will not always indicate the same decision, referring us back to the conclusion that, when in doubt, NPV should always be followed.)

However, this fails to take account of the risks of these investments. In chapter two risk was defined as 'uncertainty regarding the expected rate of return from an investment'. In this case, each investment suffers from two major uncertainties. For Investment A, these are the estimated current rental value and the anticipated rate of rental growth. For Investment B, they are the resale capitalisation rate and the rate of change in the RPI. The remainder of this chapter is devoted to methods of dealing with these uncertainties.

8.3.3 Sensitivity analysis

Sensitivity analysis was developed as a means of identifying the independent variable which causes the greatest change in the dependent variable. Many other simple explorations of risk are made possible by this technique, now enjoying an explosion of employment as a result of the opportunities for rapid recalculation offered by personal computers and spreadsheet packages.

The two uncertainties (risky variables) in investments A and B may not turn out to be as expected and shown in the basic analysis above. Given this, it will be useful to know what the effect of likely changes will be upon return. Sensitivity analysis can be used to explore the question: 'what if?'

Let us assume that a reasonable margin of error in each case is determined to be plus or minus 20%. What is the effect of a 20% change in each and then both variables?

The results are as follows:

Investment A

		NPV (£)	IRR (%)
Rental value	+ 20%	34 945	19.863
Rental value	− 20%	8 882	13.563
Rental growth	+ 20%	23 793	17.351
Rental growth	− 20%	20 069	16.456
Both variables	+ 20%	37 200	20.343
Both variables	− 20%	7 406	13.156

Every outcome indicates that the investment is worthwhile at a target rate of 11%.

Investment B

		NPV (£)	IRR (%)
Resale cap. rate	− 20%	72 706	22.476
Resale cap. rate	+ 20%	21 979	15.019
RPI growth	+ 20%	47 556	19.050
RPI growth	− 20%	37 115	17.451
Resale cap. rate RPI growth	− 20% + 20%	79 035	23.305
Resale cap. rate RPI growth	+ 20% − 20%	17 501	14.241

Again, every outcome indicates that the investment is worthwhile at a target rate of 11%. The worst outcome is better than the worst outcome in A and the best is also better than the best outcome in A. It continues to appear to be the better buy.

However, this rudimentary form of sensitivity analysis has failed to consider whether a 20% increase or reduction in each variable is equally likely. Let us assume that market research shows that this is patently not the case here. While rental growth variation in the South of England may show a 20% variation from the expected, the estimated market rental may only vary from the expected by up to 5%. On the other hand, RPI changes may vary by 30% from the expected, and a thin market means that the resale capitalisation rate could lie anywhere between 8 and 14%. Revised figures on these more realistic estimates are as follows:

Investment A

		NPV (£)	IRR (%)
Rental value	+ 5%	25 171	17.674
Rental value	− 5%	18 655	16.108
Rental growth	+ 20%	23 793	17.351
Rental growth	− 20%	20 069	16.456
Best outcome		27 145	18.131
Worst outcome		16 904	15.670

Investment B

		NPV (£)	IRR (%)
Resale cap. rate	8%	87 924	24.373
Resale cap. rate	14%	16 182	14.018
RPI growth	+ 30%	50 249	19.450
RPI growth	− 30%	34 585	17.051
Best outcome		98 266	25.630
Worst outcome		9 794	12.861

This more realistic form of sensitivity analysis leaves Investment B as the better choice, but begins to raise questions. The worst outcome of A is now better than the worst outcome of B, which now complicates the decision somewhat. If the target rate were to increase to 13%, the implications are more vital: with some outcomes, Investment B should not be undertaken, while at all outcomes Investment A remains viable. Given this information, some investors would choose A, as they would not be prepared to face the slightest prospect of a loss.

Sensitivity analysis therefore allows a more informed decision to be made. It does, however, fail to address a vital point. What are the *chances* of the possible variations becoming fact? It may be, for example, that there is only the slightest of chances that RPI growth will be more than 20% in excess of the expected, whereas it is almost impossible to estimate a likely resale capitalisation rate due to a paucity of market evidence. This will surely qualify the above analysis. What is now implied is an element of qualitative or subjective judgement. The best outcome in A is less profitable than the best outcome in B: but the latter may be much less likely than the former. This element of risk must be taken into account in a full analysis. It is not enough to say what could happen; it is necessary to qualify such hypotheses by probabilities, and to some extent the next set of techniques – and certainly the mean-variance criterion (see page 226) – attempt to do this, leaving sensitivity analysis behind as a somewhat rudimentary (albeit objective) risk analysis technique.

8.3.4 Risk-adjustment techniques

Both the potential variation and the chances of variation in the outcome from the expected must be taken into account in a full risk-return analysis. Yet the decision-maker will demand as clear an indication as possible. Risk-adjustment techniques satisfy these demands. Unfortunately, they leave rather large questions unanswered *en route*. Nonetheless, they are widely practised, both consciously and unconsciously, in both wider investment markets and in real estate.

Three manifestations of risk-adjusted technique will be considered here. They are *risk-adjusted discount rates*; the *certainty equivalent technique*; and a hybrid of these, suitable for UK property investment analysis, termed here the *sliced income method*.

(i)   Risk-adjusted discount rate

Whether by NPV or IRR, the estimation of a single point return estimate has to cope with varying risks (defined here as variance of possible returns) between alternatives. Choosing on the basis of IRRs alone where risks differ presumes indifference to risk, which undermines a whole stream of accepted finance wisdom (see chapter two). Given that most investors are risk averse to a degree, a choice on the basis of IRR involves a risk adjustment.

Adjustment may be to discount rate or to income. The use of the risk-adjusted discount rate is in accord with Fisher's work, as presented in chapter two. The interest (or discount) rate I can be constructed from the function $[(1 + i) (1 + d) (1 + r) - 1]$ where i represents a return for time preference, d represents a return for expected inflation and r represents a return for risk. The risk free rate (RFR), 11% in the sensitivity example, is a function of i and d: $(1 + i) (1 + d) - 1$, so $I = (1 - \text{RFR}) (1 + r) - 1$. This is the risk-adjusted discount rate. The greater the amount of perceived risk, the higher is r.

Note that this is not the way the risk-adjusted discount rate (RADR) is normally constructed in practice. Instead, the RADR is usually found by RFR + r. The difference is usually small, and can be shown to be unimportant as the choice of r is arbitrary. For example, suppose RFR = 0.11 and $r = 0.05$. $(1 + \text{RFR}) (1 + r) - 1 = 16.55\%$; RFR + R = 16%. Such fine distinction in the RADR would normally be pointless.

The use of risk adjusted discount rates implies that more return is required to compensate for greater risk. How much more is impossible to determine objectively: this depends upon the risk–return indifference curve of the investor, a subjective matter. Figure 8.1 below illustrates this concept. Most investors – and the market, in accepted finance theory – show behaviour which is risk averse, where an increase in risk would lead to an increase in required return (see page 28). In the case of A, the proportionate increase in measured return would exceed the proportionate increase in risk; A is therefore risk averse.

So solidly entrenched in financial theory is the acceptance of risk aversion that Investor B, who requires more return in exact proportion to the increase in risk, is called in some texts (see, for example, Gitman and Joehnk (1984)) risk-indifferent! This leaves us in some confusion concerning the position of C, typically termed risk-seeking, yet still requiring more return for some more risk. In fact all three are risk averse.

The subjectivity of the risk return trade-off makes it difficult for the analyst to rank investments which are subject to risk by IRR alone (while the capital asset pricing model (see page 38) can be used to avoid this problem, its application to real estate is in question (see page 212).) By practice the analyst may be able to build up helpful experience, but marginal cases will always devalue the reliability of advice. If on the other hand NPV techniques, which are to be preferred, are relied upon, what then? The risk adjustment has necessarily to be made to the target or hurdle rate. The

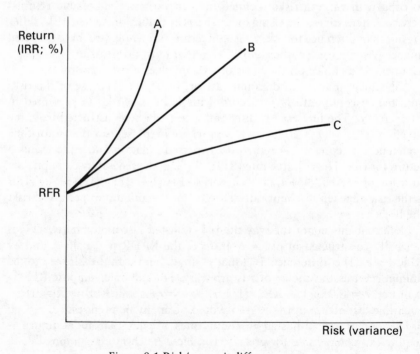

Figure 8.1 Risk/return indifference curves.

problem of quantum of adjustment to account for risk is exactly the same as for IRR. Hence the use of risk-adjustment discount rates in this first level of analysis is subject to charges of subjectivity in discount rate choice.

Nonetheless, Investment B was shown by sensitivity analysis to be riskier than Investment A. Even without the advantage of such an analysis – which does not, it should be remembered, make a decision – the experienced investor or analyst should be capable of discerning such differences and, hence, make reasonable adjustments to the RFR to produce different RADRs.

Assume 12.5% is chosen for A and 17.5% is chosen for B. The results are:

Investment A

	NPV	£15 833
	IRR	16.903%

Investment B

	NPV	£3 710
	IRR	18.250%

Note that on the basis of NPV A becomes preferable. On the basis of IRR too, A produces a greater yield margin over the target rate. Yet if RADRs of 12.5% and 15% respectively are used, the results are:

Investment A

	NPV	£15 833
	IRR	16.903%

Investment B

	NPV	£17 092
	IRR	18.250%

Now, on the NPV criterion, B should be bought. This brings to light the major problem with the RADR method. There are no objective criteria for the determination of the RADR, and relatively slight changes may reverse a decision. The analyst's perception of risk may not equate with the investor's. Who decides?

Additionally, the use of the RADR implies an increasing discount applied to future returns, and therefore that cash flows become riskier the longer the investor has to wait to receive them. The inappropriateness of such a by-product of the technique is demonstrated by the pre-let development project not subject to a fixed price building contract. The riskier cash flows are in the earlier, and not the later, years.

Finally, risk premiums have to be determined individually for each project. No two property investments are alike: risk is a complex function of gross incomes, operating expenses and capital returns.

Consequently, RADR is difficult to use reliably in practice. It continues to be used due to its simplicity and ease of application: but in property investment analysis the following method is superior.

(ii)   Certainty equivalent cash flows

At this level, avoiding the subjective adjustment of the discount rate implies facing the adjustment of the income stream. The second vital input into real estate investment analysis is the projected income flow, a function of a complex relationship of gross rental, operating expenses, financing arrangements, taxation and capital return, all of which are subject to potential variance and hence risk.

The certainty equivalent technique utilises the concept of risk aversion by theorising a single point income level which the investor would trade for the variable cash flows actually in prospect. In relation to the expected (average) income flow utilised in risk adjusted discounting, the certainty equivalent income flow for a risk averse investor will be lower. Because risk-return indifference is unique to the investor, the certainty equivalent cash flow is best determined in a process of dialogue between analyst and investor.

The selection of the certainty equivalent cash flow by way of the certainty equivalent inputs (rental growth, initial rental value, resale capitalisation rate and others) is, nonetheless, not ideally performed in this manner where the investor may, as might usually be suspected in real estate investment, suggest that the onus of analysis should fall not upon the investor but upon the analyst. An objective, analyst-performed selection of a certainty equivalent income may be produced by use of the capital asset pricing model (see Brealey and Myers, 1985, 188); we prefer a simpler route, utilising standard deviation analysis.

Our use of the standard deviation is designed to replace the best estimate of the cash flows by a certainty equivalent cash flow which there is approximately an 84% chance of bettering and only a 16% chance of failing to achieve. Assuming a normal distribution of possible cash flows, one standard deviation either side of the expected (best estimate) cash flow includes 68% of all possible outcomes. The remaining 32% includes 16% which lie below the expected cash flow less one SD, and 16% which lie above the expected cash flow plus one SD. Consequently, the use of the expected cash flow less one SD as the certainty equivalent results in the 84:16 chance of bettering it, thus reflecting a generous (but objectively determined in all cases) degree of risk aversion on behalf of the investor.

In the example, each investment has two variables. Assume that the potential outcomes and associated probabilities for each variable are represented by the following samples from a continuous distribution:

Investment A

Rental value	£49 875	£52 500	£55 125
Probability	0.2	0.6	0.2
Rental growth	0.04	0.05	0.06
Probability	0.3	0.4	0.3

Investment B

RPI growth	0.0245	0.035	0.0455
Probability	0.333	0.334	0.333
Resale cap. rate	0.08	0.11	0.14
Probability	0.3	0.4	0.3

Calculation of the standard deviation is performed as follows. (This calculation assumes, incorrectly, that the observations are derived from a finite population. See page 235 for a discussion of this problem.)

(1)   Calculate the expected value

$$\text{Expected value } (\bar{r}) = \Sigma(p \times \hat{r})$$
$$\text{where } p = \text{probability of each sample outcome}$$
$$\hat{r} = \text{each sample outcome}$$

(2)   Calculate the variance

$$\text{Variance } (\sigma^2) = \Sigma\,(p)\,(\hat{r} - \bar{r})^2$$

(3)   Calculate the standard deviation

$$\text{SD (population)} = \sqrt{\sigma^2}$$

Results are as follows:

Investment A

	Expected	Variance	SD
Rental value	£52 500	£2 756 250	£1 660.195
Rental growth	0.05	0.00006	0.007745

Investment B

	Expected	Variance	SD
RPI growth	0.035	0.000073	0.008568
Resale cap. rate	0.11	0.000540	0.023237

We can now calculate the certainty equivalents for these variables.

Investment A

	Expected value	SD	CE (rounded)
Rental value	£52 500	£1 660.195	£50 840
Rental growth	0.05	0.007745	0.04225

Investment B

RPI growth	0.035	0.008568	0.02643
Resale cap. rate	0.110	0.023237	0.13324

These values can now be fed back into the analysis model using the risk-free target rate of 11% (remember that the investments are now effectively risk-free: the values of the variables chosen represent certainty, or risk-free, equivalents of their expected values). The results are as follows:

	NPV	IRR
Investment A	£18 467	16.061%
Investment B	£15 606	13.907%

This produces the same decision as the *RADR* (NPV) method at *RADRs* of 12.5% and 17.5% respectively and suggests that the safer investment, A, should be purchased.

This interpretation of the certainty equivalent technique has the apparent advantage over RADR of objectivity. While using standard deviations to compute certainty equivalents of the variables ignores the investor's risk-return indifference function, and is only therefore of use where it is not possible to establish it, this is a major theoretical deficiency which is of little practical importance. The investor's risk-return indifference is extremely difficult to measure. Moreover, the choice of certainty equivalent need not be expected value − 1 SD: any proportion or multiple of 1 SD can be used instead to reflect the investor's risk aversion. Consequently we favour the use of this technique in preference to risk-adjusted discount rates, and suggest it as a practicable means of general risk analysis.

(iii)   The sliced income approach

While the certainty equivalent technique may represent an improvement over risk adjusted discount rates, particularly when the standardisation allowed by use of standard deviations is incorporated, the technique lends itself to further rational development in the special case of property investment analysis in the UK and other markets with rents fixed under leases. By combining risk-adjustment and certainty equivalent methods a 'sliced' view of a property investment can be moulded for use where property investment cash flows lend themselves to differential treatment.

Such cases exist wherever a minimum rental is guaranteed (certain) and an extra rental is possible (risky). Examples are (in the USA) contractually pre-determined level or stepped rents in shopping malls with extra percentage rents paid subject to retail turnover performance; or (in the UK) property let, as it typically is, subject to 5-yearly rent reviews which are upward only. In effect, a minimum rent equal to the previous contract rent is (ignoring default risk) guaranteed; any overage is a bonus.

The guaranteed income (assuming a quality tenant) should be discounted at a risk-free rate, in accordance with its certain nature. The overage, or possible bonus, is then calculated by comparing the expected – most likely – income stream (calculated exactly as per risk-adjusted discount rate techniques) with the certain (not certainty equivalent, which would typically be higher) income and producing a top-slice income which due to its leveraged nature is extremely sensitive to changes in variables (rental value, rental growth, operating expenses, etc.) and is therefore highly risky. Commensurate with this, it is discounted at a highly risk-adjusted rate.

This technique is best illustrated by Investment A. Upward only rent reviews in the sub lease will guarantee a rent on reversion equal to the current rent paid by the sub tenant. This is therefore risk-free.

The certain income is calculated in this example as the cash flow that would be received if the upward only rent review in year 3 resulted in the same rent being paid. The overage is the difference between this and the expected rent based on the expected values of the two variables of ERV and rental growth.

The resulting certain income is discounted at the RFR of 11%.

The overage is more risky than the expected income flow. Consequently, where 12.5% was the overall risk adjusted discount rate previously used to produce an NPV of £15 833, a higher rate (15% in this example) should be used in the valuation of the overage rent. A total NPV of £14 267 is produced: no IRR can be calculated, as there are two separate cash flows and only one outlay. The result is close to those produced for Investment A by both RADR and CE techniques.

Appraisal: Investment A: sliced income

End of year	Rent in (£)	Rent out (£)	Review fees (£)	Man. fees (£)
0	0	0	0	0
1	45 000	2 250	0	4 500
2	45 000	2 250	0	4 500
3	45 000	2 250	4 558	4 500
4	60 775	2 250	0	6 078
5	60 775	2 250	0	6 078

The sliced income method is inappropriate for Investment B, which is best analysed using CE techniques. The conclusion from these analyses is best based on the preferred NPV technique. Using the sliced income technique, Investment A produces an NPV of £14 267. Using the certainty equivalent technique, Investment B produces an NPV of £15 606. The decision is a marginal one.

Ideally, all three first level techniques should produce similar results. This cannot however be guaranteed. It will only happen if the subjectivity of the risk-adjusted rates in risk-adjusted discount rate and sliced analysis coincide in effect with the arbitrariness of the certainty equivalent income. It is the subjective and arbitrary nature of these techniques which harbours a wealth of criticism.

The major criticism of all techniques which incorporate risk-adjusted discount rates, that is that future returns are increasingly heavily penalised without consistent justification, remains.

This first level of analysis, however applied, has the merit of producing a single comparative decision aid: purchase if NPV is positive; where investments are mutually exclusive, purchase the investment with the higher NPV. This is a criticism as well as a merit. The decision maker may not appreciate the analyst's roughshod disregard of his individual risk-return indifference. He may therefore prefer separate measures of risk and return, and to base his decision on these two results, rather than upon the single NPV measure.

8.3.5   The mean-variance criterion

The subjectivity of the risk-return indifference function for the investor may render an objective decision-aiding analytical technique dangerous in the hands of the analyst. Risk-adjustment techniques encourage the analyst to presume to replace the subjective function by objective experience, but the sophisticated investor may not be satisfied with this. (For example, utility

Outlay (£)	Acq. fees (£)	Net cash (£)	Certain (£)	Overage (£)
130 000	3 900	−133 900		
0	0	38 250	38 250	0
0	0	38 250	38 250	0
0	0	33 692	33 692	0
0	0	52 448	38 250	14 197
0	0	52 448	38 250	14 197
		PV: £32 990	PV: £15 176	
		TOT NPV: £14 266		

(see Byrne and Cadman, 1985) may affect his position. This is largely ignored in this analysis but further reference to the point should be made by the serious reader.) He may wish to judge the merits of two alternative investments against each other by comparing their expected return and their risk in combination, represented graphically as follows. Assume Investment A is low risk, low return, and Investment B is high risk, high return.

Some investors will prefer A while others will prefer B. This will depend on their risk-aversion, as represented by risk-return indifference curves (see chapter two). Suppose investor Z is highly risk-averse, while Y is not. (It is assumed that all investors will accept the RFR for a risk-free investment.)

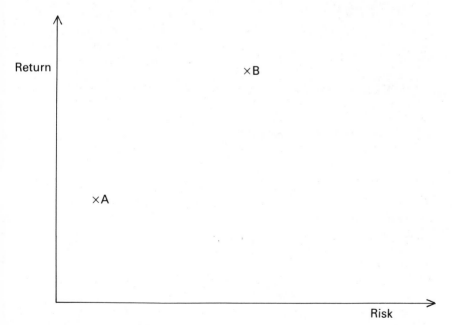

Figure 8.2 The two investment case: 1

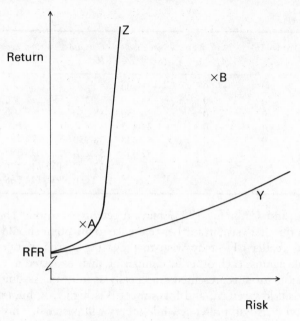

Figure 8.3 The two investment case: 2

Investor Z would buy Investment A, because the expected return is more than enough to compensate for the risk involved. He would not, however, buy B. Investor Y, on the other hand, would probably prefer B to A because the margin of return over the minimum required is higher. If, however, Investment B were riskier than A but produced less return, then any risk-averse investor would choose A (see Figure 8.4).

This leads directly to the mean-variance criterion. This is a decision rule, which states the following.

Purchase Investment A if, and only if,
    the return on A > return on B
    and the risk of A ≤ risk of B.

This applies to all risk-averse investors (thought to be the vast majority) and is therefore an objective decision rule, regardless of the risk-return indifference of the investor.

We have already concluded that return may be measured in two ways: NPV or IRR. The rule might therefore be:

Purchase investment A if, and only if,
    IRR A > IRR B or   NPV A   >   NPV B
                 at RFR   at RFR

and   the risk of A ≤ the risk of B.

Given that risk is separately measured, it follows that the NPV must be at the risk free rate (RFR). But how is risk to be measured?

It has already been shown that standard deviation (σ, or SD) offers a quantitative risk measurement device. It has been applied to variables; but now it must be applied to the return. What is the potential variability of the return from the expected return?

The following discussion continues the unrealistic presumption made to date that the observed values of the variables are part of a discrete, and not continuous, distribution. (This understates risk, and standard deviation, but may not be misleading in a comparison of similar investments.) Given this, there are nine potential *IRRs* from Investment A. These are as follows (probabilities in parentheses):

Rental value	Rental growth		
	4% (0.3)	5% (0.4)	6% (0.3)
49 875 (0.2)	15.670% (0.06)	16.108% (0.08)	16.547% (0.06)
52 500 (0.6)	16.456% (0.18)	16.903% (0.24)	17.351% (0.18)
55 125 (0.2)	17.219% (0.06)	17.674% (0.08)	18.131% (0.06)

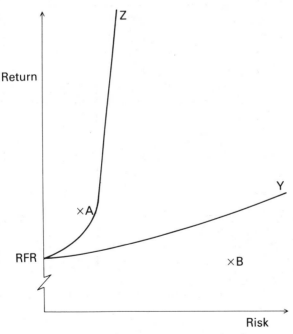

Figure 8.4 The two investment case: 3

The probabilities of these are shown in brackets. The expected (weighted average) return is given by $\Sigma\,(p \times \hat{r})$, which in this case is 16.898% (note the typical slight difference between this and the result of the most likely rental value in combination with the most likely rental growth). The standard deviation of these returns is 0.605%.

For NPV, the appropriate figures are as follows:

	Rental growth		
Rental value	4% (0.3)	5% (0.4)	6% (0.3)
49 875 (0.2)	16 904 (0.06)	18 655 (0.08)	20 441 (0.06)
52 500 (0.6)	20 069 (0.18)	21 913 (0.24)	23 793 (0.18)
55 125 (0.2)	23 235 (0.06)	25 171 (0.08)	27 145 (0.06)

$$\bar{r} = \Sigma\,(p \times \hat{r}) = \text{£}21\,924;\ \sigma = \text{£}2\,516$$

(Note that the standard deviation of NPVs is the same as the standard deviation of total values of the nine possible cash flows.)

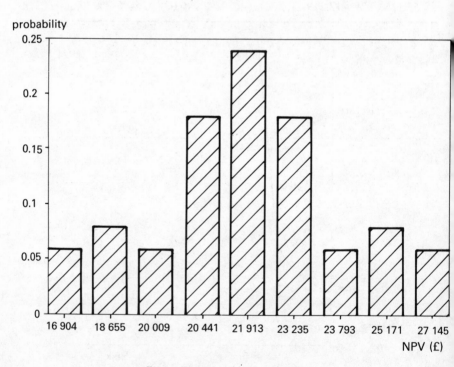

Figure 8.5 Distribution of NPVs

This computation was relatively straightforward. The assumption of a discrete distribution of cash flows in place of the more probable continuous distribution has cut down the number of possible cash flows from infinite to nine. In addition, perfect serial correlation of cash flows in years three, four and five simplifies the exercise. The combination of a particular rental growth and a particular rental value (nine in all) predicts the cash flows in each of these years, as it determines the rent review fee to be deducted in year three and the level rents received in years four and five. If this were not so the number of possible cash flows would have been 729.

The degree of simplification employed is illustrated by Investment B. There is no serial correlation between cash flows. Even assuming 3 discrete RPI growth figures – unrealistic, of course – the number of potential cash flows is $3 \times 3 \times 3 \times 3 \times 3$: combining the effect of 3 discrete resale capitalisation rates produces a total number of possible cash flows of (again, by coincidence) 729. Even a powerful small computer will take some time to produce estimates of standard deviations and expected IRR and NPV when the assumption of a discrete distribution is relaxed and this number approaches infinity.

So, for illustration purposes only, and to aid the completion of the mean-variance analysis, Investment B will be analysed making these two simplifying assumptions:

(1) Cash flows are perfectly serially correlated from year to year. For example, 3% RPI growth in year one predetermines 3% RPI growth for each year from one to five. This overstates the risk of the investment.
(2) The values of variables form a discrete distribution. This slightly understates the risk of the investment.

Analysis: Investment B

IRRs		Resale cap. rate	
	0.08	0.11	0.14
RPI growth			
0.0245	23.111% (0.06)	17.051% (0.08)	12.861% (0.06)
0.035	24.373% (0.18)	18.250% (0.24)	14.018% (0.18)
0.0455	25.635% (0.06)	19.450% (0.08)	15.175% (0.06)

$$\bar{r} = \Sigma \, (p \times \hat{r}) = 18.817\%; \ \sigma = 4.109\%$$

NPVs		Resale cap. rate	
	0.08	0.11	0.14
RPI growth			
0.0245	77 970 (0.06)	34 585 (0.08)	9 794 (0.06)
0.035	87 924 (0.18)	42 270 (0.24)	16 182 (0.18)
0.0455	98 266 (0.06)	50 249 (0.08)	22 810 (0.06)

$$\bar{r} = \Sigma \ (p \times \hat{r}) = £48\ 201; \ \sigma = £28\ 687$$

Comparative results

	IRR		NPV	
	Expected	SD	Expected	SD
Investment A	16.898%	0.605%	£21 924	£ 2 516
Investment B	18.817%	4.109%	£48 201	£28 687

The expected return of A is less than that of B: but the risks of B are higher than those of A. This means that a decision using the mean-variance criterion is impossible, and we are referred back to the risk-return indifference of the investor. The risk averse investor would choose A; the risk indifferent would choose B.

A problem to be tackled in many cases is the difference in size of investments. These are identical. But what if A cost £130 000 while B cost £220 000? While the return measures may be capable of direct comparison (NPV is preferable in such a case (see Brigham, 1985), the SD of returns from a large project would inevitably be higher than the SD of returns from a small project of identical risk. Consequently standardisation is necessary and is achieved by using the coefficient of variation, a measure of risk relative to the size of the project. This could be:

$$\frac{\text{SD of PVs}}{\text{Expected PV}} \quad \text{or} \quad \frac{\sigma \ PV}{PV} \ : \text{for Investment A, in the preceding analysis,}$$

this is $\dfrac{£2\ 516}{£155\ 824} = 0.01615.$

For Investment B, it is $\dfrac{£28\ 687}{£165\ 187} = 0.17366.$

The conclusion to be drawn from these figures is that B is over ten times riskier per unit of investment size than A.

8.3.6 The coefficient of IRR/NPV variation

Another interpretation of the coefficient of variation proposed by Reilly (1985) and Brigham has more immediate appeal and more general an application in decision-making. The mean-variance criterion will not provide a decision where the project of higher risk produces a higher return: yet this is to be expected in a competitive market for investments. An objective measure of risk per unit of return may be useful for the investor, or analyst, without a clear picture of subjective risk-return indifference.

Either NPV or IRR might be used in a coefficient of variation for measuring risk against return. The IRR version is calculated as follows:

$$\frac{\text{SD of IRR}}{\text{expected IRR}} \quad \text{or} \quad \frac{\sigma \, \text{IRR}}{\overline{\text{IRR}}}$$

For Investment A, this is: $\dfrac{0.605\%}{16.898\%} = 0.03580$

For Investment B, it is: $\dfrac{4.109\%}{18.817\%} = 0.21837$

It shows that Investment B is much riskier (around six times) than Investment A per unit of return and would prompt all but the least risk-averse investor to choose Investment A. Figures 8.6 and 8.7 illustrate the comparison.

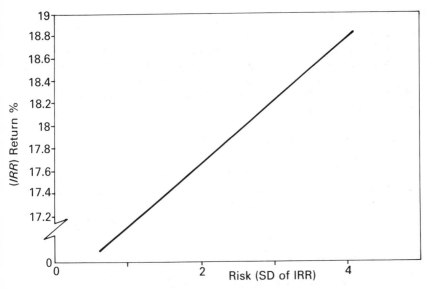

Figure 8.6 Investment A: risk/return: 1

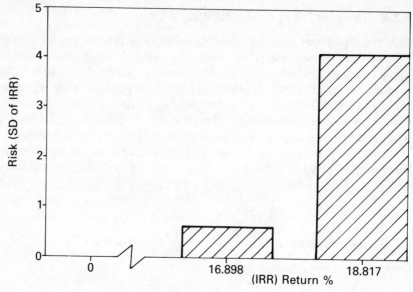

Figure 8.7 Investment A: risk/return: 2

In NPV terms, the measure is:

$$\frac{\text{SD of NPV}}{\text{expected NPV}} \quad \text{or} \quad \frac{\sigma\text{NPV}}{\overline{\text{NPV}}}$$

For Investment A, this is $\dfrac{£2\ 516}{£21\ 924} = 11.476\%$

For Investment B, this is $\dfrac{£28\ 687}{£48\ 201} = 59.515\%$

This comparison almost exactly repeats the result of the coefficient of IRR variation.

There are again reasons for preferring the NPV measure. The coefficient of IRR variation should only be used where two acceptable investments are being compared: otherwise, an apparently superior (lower risk per unit of return) investment may be preferred when it is expected to fail to produce a return equal to or exceeding the target rate (and would therefore be unacceptable). The coefficient of NPV variation does not suffer from this problem (an unacceptable project would produce a negative coefficient).

8.3.7 Standard deviations in risk analysis: some problems

Reaching this stage has only been possible with the aid of some simplifying assumptions regarding the nature of the probability distributions of the variables employed and, hence, a rather robust use of standard deviations. In this section we consider further the possible problems we have to date circumnavigated by the use of these assumptions.

Measures of investment risk are more difficult to achieve where the possible values of variables are drawn from a continuous, rather than a discrete, distribution, where the values are drawn from a skewed distribution, and where the values of variables from year to year are not perfectly serially correlated. In our property investment analysis model the first of these problems is exemplified by the fact that rental growth has to be represented as a minimum, expected and maximum value (say 4%, 5% and 6%) when average rental growth per annum could theoretically take any value between minus infinity and plus infinity to any number of decimal places. Second, the problem of lack of serial correlation is exemplified by the fact that rental growth achieved over a second rent review period may have no relationship with the equivalent value of the first review period, and so on, radically complicating the analysis.

(i) Sample standard deviation

The former problem is easily avoided by use of sample statistics. Use of the sample standard deviation puts into effect the truism that the discrete standard deviation (or standard deviation of a population, σp) understates the risk of a variable drawn from a continuous distribution. Given that the population SD = variance^2, the sample standard deviation (σs) can be found as follows:

$$\text{variance} = \sigma p^2$$
$$\sigma s = \sqrt{[(\sigma \text{ variance}) (n/(n-1))]}$$

where n = the number of samples taken from the population.

For example, assuming maximum, expected and minimum values of rental growth of 4%, 5% and 6% with probabilities of 0.2, 0.6 and 0.2 respectively, variance $= \Sigma (\hat{r} - \bar{r})^2 p$

$$
\begin{array}{ll}
\text{where } \hat{r} & = \text{observed value of the variable;} \\
\bar{r} & = \text{expected value of the variable;} \\
p & = \text{probability of occurrence of observed value.}
\end{array}
$$

$$
\begin{aligned}
V & = \Sigma(0.04 - 0.05)^2 0.2 + (0.05 - 0.05)^2(0.6) \\
& \quad + (0.06 - 0.05)^2 0.2 \\
& = (0.00002 + 0.00002) \\
& = 0.00004 \\
\\
\sigma & = \sqrt{[(\text{variance}) (n/(n-1))]}
\end{aligned}
$$

The use of n, the number of observations, is problematic. Estimates of rental growth are unlikely to be made by sampling a population. Forecasting is more likely to be undertaken by a combination of time series extrapolation and causal analysis (see page 202). However, it is possible to hypothesise that rental growth for each of the last 10 years may be taken as the population from which samples of 4%, 5% and 6% may be drawn. In that case, n is 10.

$$
\begin{aligned}
\sigma &= \sqrt{[(0.00004)\,(10/9)]} \\
&= \sqrt{(0.00004 \times 1.1111)} \\
&= \sqrt{0.00004444} \\
&= 0.006667
\end{aligned}
$$

(Note that if the sample were drawn from 100 observations, $\sigma_s = 0.006356$. As the number of samples taken increases, σ_s reduces and approaches σp. ($\sigma p = \sqrt{r}$, so that $\sqrt{0.00004} = 0.006325$).)

Of the variables listed in example 8.2 at page 207 only the scale based fees can be regarded as suitable for this type of sample analysis, and they are unlikely to be of major importance. The major variables are ERV at years 0, 5 and 10; rental growth; and the resale capitalisation rate. All samples are drawn from continuous infinite populations. The choice, therefore, between the more correct sample standard deviation, hypothesising a number of samples, and the population standard deviation is a marginal one, given the likely small difference in result.

(ii) Skewness

Skewness describes the tendency of a distribution of values of a variable to differ from the normal curve. This occurs where the median value does not equate with the mean or the mode, and the area of the curve to one side of the expected (mean) value does not equate with the area of the curve to the other side; in other words, the value of the subject variable is more likely to be higher than lower, or vice versa, than the mean value. In a normal distribution it is equally likely that a higher or a lower value will be the outcome.

The standard deviation used as the risk measure for much of this chapter may be used as a measure of dispersion in all symmetrical and even moderately skewed distributions. However, it becomes misleading as a measure of risk where the distribution is highly skewed.

This is not likely to be a large problem in property investment analysis. The variables discussed in this chapter are likely to be drawn from relatively normal distributions. However, problems may be encountered at rent reviews, which are typically 'upward-only' in the UK. In a non-inflationary context, upward-only rent reviews may significantly skew the distribution of potential rents at review, and this is a factor which must be considered within a risk-return analysis which relies upon the standard deviation measure. It is an argument in favour of the sliced income method, described at page 225.

(iii)   Serial correlation between cash flows

Where a multi-period analytical model is used, many variables have to be estimated at more than one point in time. For example, rent review fees may be 7% in the current market, and it would usually be presumed that they would continue at that level. Perfect serial correlation between succeeding levels of rent review fee percentages is thereby assumed. However, average rental growth per annum between years zero and five is unlikely to predict, except in an extremely complex manner, average rental growth per annum between years six and ten. In other words, there is unlikely to be strong serial correlation between succeeding values of expected rental growth (for empirical evidence of this, see Brown, 1985, 257).

Even allowing for the effect of the UK five-yearly rent review stabiliser, this is a considerable problem. Given a simple model with three major variables (ERV, resale capitalisation rate and rental growth) the extension of the time period for analysis beyond five years to a typical fifteen increases the number of cash flow possibilities (even taking only three values of what are continuously distributed variables from infinite ranges) from 27 to 6 561. A mean/variance analysis of the type presented for purposes of comprehension in this chapter is thereby made unworkable.

There are four possible solutions to this problem.

(a) Assuming serial correlation

The first is the method adopted to date in this chapter, and that is to assume perfect serial correlation between cash flows. This confines the number of possible cash flows in this case to 27, but overstates the riskiness of the project. Given that the purpose of the analysis may be a relative judgement rather than an absolute measure of risk, this need not be a problem. However, it will be misleading where the shapes of the distributions of the variables in the two projects are considerably different: the riskier project may be excessively penalised. Wider comparisons (for example with alternative investments) may also become invalid as a result of this simplification.

(b) Interpolation

Robinson (1987) suggests a simple robust solution: interpolation of the standard deviation or coefficient of variation, measured between the extremes of perfect serial correlation and independence between cash flows (see example at (c) below, page 238).

The advantages and disadvantages of such an approach are relatively self-evident: accuracy is not guaranteed, but a solution is attainable within a reasonable time.

(c) Hillier and Sykes

A third solution is the type of algebraic approach adapted from the work of Hillier (1963) to real estate by Sykes (1983b).

As Robinson (1987) shows, a maximum value for a project's risk is given by the standard deviation measure where the values of variables over time are independent of their preceeding values, and a minimum value of the same project's risk is given by the standard deviation measure where each variable is perfectly serially correlated.

EXAMPLE 8.5

Cost of project:	£1 000
Return in year 1:	£50 (.5p) or £75 (.5p)
Return in year 2:	£1 500 (.5p) or £1 750 (.5p)

Possible net cash flows: perfectly independent

Year 0	(£1 000)	(£1 000)	(£1 000)	(£1 000)
1	£50	£50	£75	£75
2	£1 500	£1 750	£1 500	£1 750
NPV at 10%	£285.12	£491.74	£307.85	£514.46
SD of NPVs	£103.93			

Possible cash flows: perfectly serially correlated (so that an income of £75 in year 1 predicts the larger return in year 2).

Year 0	(£1 000)	(£1 000)
1	£50	£75
2	£1 500	£1 750
NPV at 10%	£285.12	£514.46
SD of NPVs	£114.67	

Within these two extremes lies the possibility that cash flows are partially correlated. The above cash flow might represent the result of the interplay of many variables, some of which are independent of their preceding values (repair expenses, for example) and some of which are perfectly serially correlated (gross rent between reviews, for example). If there is partial correlation between the cash flows above, the standard deviation of the NPVs lies between £103.93 and £114.67; beyond this it is only possible to say that a precise measure would be extremely difficult, necessitating the estimation of partial correlation coefficients between all the cash flows. (Robinson's approach, however, is simple interpolation: use (say) £109.30 as a midpoint standard deviation measure.)

Sykes suggests that the fortunate aspect of property investment analysis in this respect is the fact that cash flows are either perfectly correlated or independent, and not partially correlated. (This ignores the complex effects of expenses, fees and so on.) Thus, while rents between reviews are perfectly correlated, Sykes posits that rents immediately before and after review are, in an inflationary environment and given normal depreciation, independent.

Hillier's equation for the standard deviation of independent cash flows and perfectly correlated cash flows respectively are as follows:

$$\sigma^2 \text{ NPV} = \sum_{j=1}^{\wedge} \frac{\sigma^2 j}{(1+i)^{2j}}$$

$$\sigma^2 \text{ NPV} = \left\{ \sum_{j=1}^{\wedge} \frac{\sigma j}{(1+i)^j} \right\}^2$$

Sykes then derives a formula for establishing the standard deviation of a property investment (ignoring outgoings) as follows. Assuming a 10 year holding period, the cash flow is made up of 5 variables. These are:

(i) The outlay

The outlay is known and risk-free. The standard deviation of the NPV is identical to that of the total present value of a cash flow. Thus, in estimating the risk of an investment where the outlay is risk-free, the outlay may be ignored.

(ii) Rent, years 0–5

This will usually already have been negotiated at the time analysis is carried out and is thus risk-free, in the absence of default risk. The standard deviation is nil, and this variable may be ignored in a combined expression of the risk of the investment.

(iii) Rent, years 6–10 and 11–15

These are perfectly correlated, although the two expressions are independent of each other and of the starting rent.

Thus the expression for the standard deviation of the present value of the rent between years 6 and 10 is:

$$\sigma^2 = \sigma \left\{ \sum_{j=6}^{10} \frac{1}{(1+i)^j} \right\}^2$$

where j = number of years
i = target rate

The equivalent for years 11–15 is:

$$\sigma^2 = \sigma \left\{ \sum_{j=11}^{15} \frac{1}{(1+i)^j} \right\}^2$$

(iv) Resale price

This is an independent risky variable (c). The total expression is therefore

$$\sigma^2 \text{ NPV} = \sigma \left\{ \sum_{j=6}^{10} \frac{1}{(1+i)^j} \right\}^2 + \left\{ \sum_{j=11}^{15} \left\{ \frac{1}{(1+i)^j} \right\} \right\}^2$$

$$+ \left\{ \frac{\sigma^c}{(1+i)^{15}} \right\}^2$$

This is the expression for total risk of an investment with perfect correlation within reviews and assuming no correlation between different period review rents and resale price.

As Sykes points out, the resale price presents a problem, as it represents the result of resale capitalisation rate (independent) and ERV at the resale date. This complicates the estimation of standard deviation by formula, but Sykes suggests formulae employing partial derivatives (see Sykes 1983b).

Sykes' adaptation of Hillier's work to UK property is a useful advance. It is questioned by Brown (1985) who is critical of its assumption of complete independence of rents between review, ignoring as it does the many complications created by outgoings and upward-only reviews. It is of necessity, therefore, a short cut. The same is only true to a much reduced extent in the case of the following, fourth, solution to the problem of independence cash flows.

(d) Simulation

We referred earlier in this chapter to 6 561 potential cash flows from a simple property investment.

It would be quite possible to program a modern computer to estimate the NPV of all 6 561 cash flows and to calculate the standard deviation of the results. It would, however, be difficult to program a small computer to do this in a reasonable amount of time; and in any event, 6 561 is a small number of potential cash flows.

A solution to this is (Monte Carlo) simulation. Given estimates of the worst, expected and best outcomes of all variables and the associated probabilities, many programs are available to select, at random, combinations of variables, calculating and storing the NPV produced by the resultant cash flow, and repeating the exercise strictly in accordance with the probabilities given. If the analyst specified a 60% chance of repairs being necessary at a cost of £5 000 at the lease end, then six times out of ten the cash flow thrown out by the simulation will include this expense. Simulation programs run this exercise repeatedly, calculate NPVs and may be made to produce the standard deviation of the results. It is to be expected that the shape of the curve of a distribution of a high number of simulations will be identical to the shape of the curve of the population, so that the standard deviation measure will be accurate.

The advantage of the numeric simulation technique is its ability to accurately take into account all variables, unlike the adaptation of the algebraic Hillier technique described above. It can also deal with the problems of serial correlation (or lack of it) within a variable and a divergence between sample and population standard deviation measures. Care must be taken where there is a suspicion of interdependence (correlation) between variables, for example where a high rate of RPI growth might imply rises in capitalisation rates, in which case a simple simulation exercise would understate risk to some extent. On balance, however, simulation is of considerable aid in the decision.

Simulation is therefore now used to compare Investments A and B.

Simulation in practice

Using the mean-variance criterion for investment decision making necessitated the estimation of possible values for each of two variables in each case.

For Investment A, the variables were rental value and average rental growth. Pessimistic, expected and optimistic values for these variables were as follows, with associated probabilities.

Rental value	p
49 875	0.2
52 500	0.6
55 125	0.2

Rental growth	p
4%	0.3
5%	0.4
6%	0.3

For Investment B, the variables were the average increase in RPI and the resale capitalisation rate. Pessimistic, expected and optimistic values for these variables, with probabilities, were as follows:

RPI growth	p
2.45%	0.2
3.5%	0.6
4.55%	0.2

Resale cap. rate	p
0.14	0.3
0.11	0.4
0.08	0.3

In a simulation program, the analyst need not be restricted to pessimistic, expected and optimistic values, depending upon the parameters established in the program used. Any number of value bands for each variable may be employed.

In the simulation program we constructed upon a spreadsheet, we chose five value bands for each variable. The value bands used (which are broadly consistent with previous pessimistic, expected and optimistic values for the two variables in Investment A) are as follows:

Investment A

Rental value (p)

Pessimistic	49 875 (0.2)
Expected	52 500 (0.6)
Optimistic	55 125 (0.2)
Band 1	49 219 − 50 531 (0.1)
Band 2	50 532 − 51 844 (0.2)
Band 3	51 845 − 53 156 (0.4)
Band 4	53 157 − 54 469 (0.2)
Band 5	54 470 − 55 781 (0.1)

Rental growth (p)

Pessimistic	0.04 (0.3)
Expected	0.05 (0.4)
Optimistic	0.06 (0.3)
Band 1	0.0375 − 0.0425 (0.15)
Band 2	0.0426 − 0.0475 (0.2)
Band 3	0.0476 − 0.0525 (0.3)
Band 4	0.0526 − 0.0575 (0.2)
Band 5	0.0576 − 0.0625 (0.15)

(New subjective probability estimates for these value ranges have been assigned (strictly, the possibilities of rents below £49 219 and above £55 781 should be included in the outlying ranges).)

Simulation programs work by generating random numbers within the chosen value bands in a frequency determined by the probability assumptions made. Hence, given sufficient cycles, 40% of all simulated cash flows will be on the basis that the rental value will be between £51 845 and £53 156; 20% of all simulated cash flows will be on the basis of growth of between 4.26% and 4.75%. Random number generation selects any value within these ranges and not a finite central point.

The first ten results in our simulation exercise were as follows:

Cycle	ERV (£)	Growth (%)	NPV (£)	IRR (%)
1	51 770	5.96	22 788	17.11
2	50 736	5.90	21 365	16.77
3	55 381	4.44	24 388	17.49
4	52 355	6.23	24 045	17.41
5	53 962	4.14	22 099	16.95
6	49 828	5.70	19 837	16.40
7	51 854	4.63	20 437	16.55
8	51 977	4.84	20 966	16.67
9	52 958	5.64	23 689	17.33
10	52 650	5.18	22 428	17.03

Already, the probability distribution of variables is being reflected in the random generation of values. The average ERV is £52 347, close to the expected £52 500; the average growth is 5.27%, close to the expected 5%, but likely to become much closer to it over 200 cycles (see page 245: it becomes 5.06%).

Investment B
For Investment B, the appropriate value bands with new probabilities are as follows:

RPI growth (%) (p)	
Pessimistic	2.45 (0.2)
Expected	3.5 (0.6)
Optimistic	4.55 (0.2)
Band 1	2.1875 − 2.7125 (0.1)
Band 2	2.7126 − 3.2375 (0.2)
Band 3	3.2376 − 3.7625 (0.4)
Band 4	3.7626 − 4.2875 (0.2)
Band 5	4.2876 − 4.8125 (0.1)

Resale cap. rate (p)	
Pessimistic	0.14 (0.3)
Expected	0.11 (0.4)
Optimistic	0.08 (0.3)
Band 1	13.26 − 14.75 (0.15)
Band 2	11.76 − 13.25 (0.2)
Band 3	10.26 − 11.75 (0.3)
Band 4	8.76 − 10.25 (0.2)
Band 5	7.26 − 8.75 (0.15)

The first ten results were as follows:

Cycle	Cap. Rate (%)	RPI growth (%)	NPV (£)	IRR (%)
1	12.43	4.19	33 014	16.84
2	11.99	2.50	25 410	15.58
3	9.88	3.53	56 350	20.29
4	11.27	3.52	39 474	17.83
5	11.12	3.18	38 538	17.68
6	12.55	3.39	26 514	15.77
7	10.09	3.22	51 015	19.52
8	10.17	4.51	60 340	20.87
9	8.99	4.45	77 943	23.18
10	14.29	2.91	10 641	13.02

200 cycles of each cash flow were recorded. Arguably, this is insufficient a number to ensure that the simulation is absolutely representative of the totality of possible cash flows, but for purposes of illustration 200 will suffice.

Again the mean-variance criterion can be employed in decision making. This time, however, the problem of choice of sample or population standard deviation is effectively avoided, as a large number of cycles will cause the two to equate. Serial correlation between cash flows can also be easily avoided in the simulation exercise (although our simple simulation exercise was not designed to overcome this problem). The problem of skewness is effectively avoided by the use of realistically normal probability distributions for each variable in each case, resulting in a normal distribution of IRRs and NPVs. Hence the following results are satisfactory for our purpose.

	Investment A	Investment B
No. of cycles	200	200
Average IRR	16.89%	18.87%
σ of IRR	0.53%	3.39%
Minimum IRR	15.64%	12.51%
Maximum IRR	18.19%	27.12%
Average NPV	£21 879	£ 47 861
σ of NPV	£ 2 195	£ 23 587
Minimum NPV	£16 779	£ 7 856
Maximum NPV	£27 400	£111 446
Average rental growth/ RPI growth	5.06%	3.56%
Average rental value/ resale capitalisation rate	£52 376	10.89%

The interpretation of the results is as follows.

For Investment A, the average NPV is £21 879. There is a 68.26% probability that the NPV will lie between £21 879 ± £2 195, that is £19 684 and £24 074; a 95.46% probability that the NPV will lie between £21 879 ± (2 × £2 195), that is £17 489 and £26 269; and a 99.74% probability that the NPV will lie between £21 879 ± (3 × £2 195), that is £15 294 and £28 464.

For Investment B, the average NPV is £47 861. There is a 68.26% probability that the NPV will lie between £47 861 ± £23 587, that is £24 274 and £71 448; a 95.46% probability that the NPV will lie between £47 861 ± (2 × £23 587), that is £−687 and £95 035; and a 99.74% probability that the NPV will lie between £47 861 ± (3 × £23 587) that is £−22 900 and £118 622.

Comparison of discrete and simulated results

Investment A

	Discrete mean-variance	Simulation
Average expected IRR (%)	16.90	16.89
σ IRR (%)	0.61	0.53
Coefficient of IRR variation (%)	3.58	3.12
Average expected NPV (£)	21 924	21 879
σ NPV (£)	2 516	2 195
Coefficient of NPV variation (%)	11.48	10.03

Investment B

Average expected IRR (%)	18.817	18.869
σ IRR (%)	4.11	3.39
Coefficient of IRR variation (%)	21.837	17.971
Average expected NPV (£)	48 201	47 861
σ NPV (£)	˙28 687	23 587
Coefficient of NPV	59.52	49.28

Note how the original discrete test overstates risk by a small amount, as a result of the discrete variable values, the effect of the new probabilities, and/or the effect of using the overstated measure of population standard deviation (σp) in the original analysis. The nine cash flows analysed earlier will thus inevitably produce a higher population standard deviation than the 200 used in simulation, all other things being equal; hence the simulation results are to be preferred as being more accurate.

In practice, the discrete mean/variance test, using optimistic, expected and pessimistic values, can hardly be said to be inadequate. The above results show a clear decision on the basis of coefficient of variation measures: the differences between the results of the two approaches are hardly significant. Nonetheless, given that the effort involved in carrying out a simulation need not be greater than alternative less rigorous methods, it is to be recommended.

In conclusion, while the mean-variance criterion allows no clear decision, the coefficient of IRR variation indicates that Investment A is to be preferred by all but the risk-indifferent and risk-seeking investor: while B will probably be more profitable than A, the investor takes on considerably more risk per unit of return.

Figures 8.8 and 8.9 illustrate graphically the relative risks and returns of the two investments.

8.3.8 Portfolio risk

In chapter two we discussed the work of Markowitz and Sharpe in developing modern portfolio theory (MPT). They showed how the combination of two or more investments whose returns fluctuate in different conditions but in opposite directions can reduce risk without at the same time reducing return. Further, the conclusion of MPT must be that a riskier investment may be preferred to a safe investment, as the effect of including that investment may, if it shows inverse correlation with the existing portfolio, be to reduce portfolio risk without paying for that benefit in loss of return.

This may be the case if in our example Investment B were a USA

INVESTMENT A

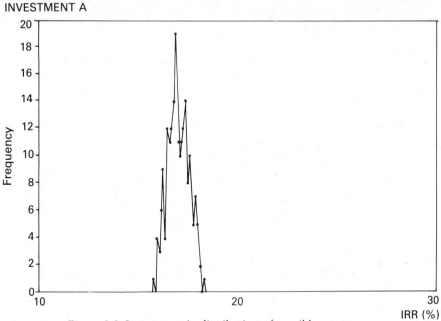

Figure 8.8 Investment A: distribution of possible returns

INVESTMENT B

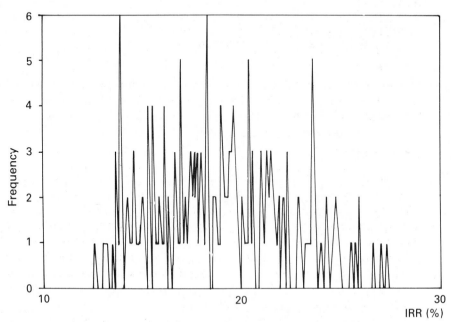

Figure 8.9 Investment B: distribution of possible returns

investment (let us say, Texas). Investment A may be less risky than B. However, if the fund holds only UK real estate, and if USA real estate has a tendency to perform well when UK real estate performs badly, then B may be preferable.

The difficulties of applying this logic are in quantifying the relative attraction of the two investments to the holder of a portfolio and in the assumptions which must be made in order to progress the measurement process.

The capital asset pricing model (CAPM, see chapter two) requires at least one major assumption to be made. The difficulties of measuring the co-variance of a real portfolio and the relative variance of potential new investments are enormous, and the CAPM proceeds by hypothesising that all rational investors hold a market portfolio made up of all investments. This, of course, includes real estate, and must also include all other investment types throughout the world. This need not be an insurmountable objection if it can be shown that relatively small portfolios can be representative of the market. Unfortunately, little or no evidence has been produced to demonstrate this in the context of a portfolio including international real estate.

If, however, we ignore this problem and adduce the return on the market, perhaps by taking the UK stock market as a surrogate market portfolio, then it is necessary to measure β for property investments. The formula

$$R = \text{RFR} + \beta \ (Rp)$$

where R = required return on subject investment
β = measure of relative risk
Rp = market risk premium (return on the market less RFR)

enables us to decide whether an investment is under- or over-priced (see chapter two, page 43). β is a measure of co-variance of the investment's performance against the market. In the example, would we need measures of the expected return on offices in the USA; or in Texas; or in a part of Texas; or in the particular sub-location; or of the particular office?

We also need forecasts of expected returns. Given that reliable forecasts do not exist, we may be tempted (as CAPM requires) to base expectations on past performance. In order to obtain this, we need records of past performance of offices in Texas, shops in the south of England, and so on. We are unlikely to hold records of sufficient scope and reliability for this purpose.

As a result of these problems, it is not proposed to utilise CAPM in a comparative analysis of the two investments, other than by means of an illustration. Let us assume that we are able to derive β for shops in the south of England and for offices in Texas, that the investor holds a UK market non-property portfolio, and that returns on the market have been 18% over the last five years and that the RFR is 9%. If the performance of Texas offices is negatively correlated with the UK stock market, we may find the following betas:

$$\begin{aligned} \text{Texas office} &\quad -0.3 \\ \text{South of England shop} &\quad +0.18 \end{aligned}$$

The required returns are then (R_s and R_t for Investments A and B respectively):

$$\begin{aligned} R_s &= 0.09 + 0.18\,(0.09) \\ &= 10.62\% \\ R_t &= 0.09 - 0.3\,(0.09) \\ &= 6.3\% \end{aligned}$$

Given that expected returns are 16.9% and 18.8% respectively, the probable choice is Investment B, reversing all previous indications.

8.4 SUMMARY

Sensitivity analysis showed that a realistic choice of variable parameters produced a much wider range of returns for Investment B than for Investment A, although the average for B was higher. The conclusion which may be drawn from this is that a higher return is likely for B but at the cost of a higher risk.

Sensitivity analysis produced no simple decision rule, providing the analyst instead with a range of results. We favour this approach in the majority of circumstances: it allows the investor to retain the decision responsibility with the help of the analyst in determining realistic variable parameters.

Risk adjustment techniques, on the other hand, attempt to provide an objective decision, but only by way of subjective risk adjustment. Three methods were presented. On the basis of the risk-adjusted discount rate technique, Investment A produced a higher NPV and a higher margin of return over the risk adjusted rate, and would be preferred. The certainty equivalent technique, offered as a preferable risk-adjustment method, offered an even clearer decision, as the NPV of Investment B became negative and the profitable investment A would have been preferred. The sliced income approach is particularly suited to UK property investment analyses due to the commonality of the upward only rent review at five year intervals, and may be an improvement upon the certainty equivalent technique in some cases. In this case it produces a result which makes a choice between the investments marginal.

The fault of risk-adjustment techniques is the probability that the professional analyst will replace the subjective risk-return indifference of the investor by an apparently objective analysis which is in reality subjective to the analyst. This is unlikely to be acceptable to the sophisticated investor, who may wish to base his decision upon separate measures of risk and return. The measures used in the mean-variance criterion are NPV or IRR for return, and SD of NPV or IRR for risk. Investment A would be preferred if

$$\text{NPV (IRR) A} > \text{NPV (IRR) B}$$
$$\text{and SD A} \leq \text{SD B.}$$

In this case, as is typical, the mean-variance criterion produced no clear decision. The return of B exceeded that of A: but so did its risk. It is impossible to say which is best, as a choice depends upon the investor's risk-aversion. The mean-variance criterion's strict decision rule makes it of little use in many cases.

An attempt to objectify the risk-return trade off is the coefficient of IRR variation, which measures the risk of an investment per unit of return. Strictly speaking this does not improve upon the mean-variance criterion as a decision rule, as the subjective risk-aversion of the individual investor remains to be interpreted. But investors may have little experience of quantifying their own degree of risk-aversion and may prefer to base a decision on a simple comparison of coefficients of IRR variation. A clear decision may emerge for the typical investor (averagely risk-averse): in the comparison of Investments A and B, this was almost certainly true, as B was shown to be around six times as risky per unit of return than was A, and A would therefore have been chosen.

Finally, all of the foregoing analyses may be misleading if the main concern of the investor is the risk of his portfolio, and not of the individual investment. Investment B in the analysis is shown to be much more risky than A; but if it were a USA property and USA real estate investments can be shown to demonstrate a degree of inverse correlation with UK property investments, the effect of including B in a UK property dominated portfolio may be to reduce the overall risk of the portfolio, at the same time improving return by a greater amount than would be expected by buying A. An analysis of this type requires the estimation of betas of individual properties or property types, and there is no clear consensus that this can be achieved in a reliable and useable manner. It remains, however, a persuasive factor, and considerable work in this area is to be expected in the near future.

Chapter Nine

CONCLUSIONS

We began this book by distinguishing between valuation and analysis, the two specific applications of the skill of appraisal. This distinction continued throughout the text and culminated in separate treatment, in chapters seven and eight, of property investment valuation and property investment analysis. In attacking the subject in this way, we reflect the view held by many practising valuers that these are fundamentally different functions, and that as a consequence different models might be appropriate for each.

However, the reader will have noted that there is little variation in the new models we demonstrate for both valuation and analysis. We propose an explicit cash flow model for analysis; and, while we have been careful to make some effort towards an impartial presentation, we have to conclude by proposing an explicit cash flow model for general use in market valuations.

This will be seen as a revolution in market valuation technique which fundamentally alters, for the first time for at least 75 years, the basic valuation model. It appears to replace a tried and tested implicit all-risks yield model by a dangerously subjective explicit cash flow model, forcing the valuer into the hazardous science of forecasting.

We hope to have demonstrated that this is not so. While our examination of market valuation models prior to the appearance of the reverse yield gap (chapter three) shows that, in the context of the investment environment and the expectations of investors, conventional techniques had a logical basis, they were at that time explicit cash flow projections, and were based upon the concept of risk adjusted, opportunity cost based target rates, thereby enabling an investment decision relating property to the alternative gilt to be made. Our recommendation is not, therefore, a revolution; it is a return to pre-reverse yield gap logic. The revolution that radically altered the logical base of conventional valuation techniques was the creeping and gradual effect of inflation, which replaced the explicit cash flow model by a new, growth implicit, all-risks yield technique, riddled (as we show in chapter four) with unforeseen errors, irrationalities and difficulties, but made seemingly innocuous by its familiar appearance.

In addition, we reject the afore-mentioned charge that explicit cash flow valuation models are dangerously subjective and necessitate the use of forecasts. The latter problem is avoided by the analysis of market growth expectations, which we demonstrate in detail in chapter five. This does, nonetheless, leave us with the problem that the target rate or equated yield remains as a subjective choice, and adoption of DCF-based models will create a period of temporary uncertainty where valuers are unused to choosing the appropriate equated yield. But evidence will quickly be collected to facilitate that choice; and we have shown in chapter seven that, within reasonable boundaries, errors in equated yield choice in the analysis/ valuation process for freeholds will be cancelled out by the effect upon implied rental growth and upon the real discount rate. In any case, where (as is typical) the perfect comparable does not exist, the *conventional* model necessitates subjective adjustment. And, as we show in chapter seven, doubling the equated yield in most DCF valuations has much less effect upon the result than doubling the all-risks yield in a conventional valuation, which lacks the former's in-built safety net.

We do not make a case for the adoption of any particular presentation of a DCF-based model. We favour two alternatives: an explicit cash flow projection with (for freeholds and long leaseholds) a cut-off point to simulate re-sale and truncate the cash flow, and a real value/equated yield hybrid, much closer in form to the conventional model. The former is capable of producing a logical solution in all circumstances, subject to care over the constant or equated rent problem (see page 149). It also has the advantage of sharing a common basis as our model for property investment analysis which is not, as far as we can judge, controversial.

The real value hybrid, on the other hand, has the advantage that it is presented in a recognisable 'valuation' format; adjusted slightly (to Wood's design) it presents a basis for real return analysis, likely to be of increasing value in future years (page 199, chapter eight). Our decision to remain on the fence in this respect is based upon our reluctance to fall back upon the educational method we criticise in chapter three (see page 65), a reliance upon 'rules'. It seems to us that a comparison and reconciliation of the explicit DCF and real value models we present in chapters 5 and 6 is the source of a thorough understanding of a framework for property investment appraisal, and we must leave it to the reader to choose his/her own means of presentation based upon what we would hope to be an enhanced perception of underlying theory.

The tests of a valuation model are, we suggest in chapter one, accuracy and logic. Accuracy is not testable; the potential for inaccuracy is therefore perhaps a preferable yardstick. Inaccuracy is best avoided by the application of a logical methodology. Conventional valuations are not logical. It is not logical to value a fixed income at a growth implicit yield; it is not logical to value a leasehold profit rent at a rate of return which is based upon freehold yields.

Neither is it logical that investment worth, especially to a group of purchasers, is believed to be distinguishable from market value. It is not rational for a market to display such inefficiency. If there is inefficiency in sectors of the property market, we are convinced that valuers, influencing market price through the valuation and negotiation process, contribute to that inefficiency. Fundamental within this process is a perceived dichotomy between investment analysis and market valuation: the view that explicit models may be appropriate for analysis, but not for valuation.

The role of the valuer/appraiser is founded upon the two functions of analysis and valuation. One follows the other. As more and more property investment analysis is performed explicitly, the stronger will the motivation become for valuations to be carried out on the same basis. We would like to see the process of change accelerate. When property investment appraisal becomes rational we will not only see an improvement in the quality of valuations: at the same time, we will witness a valuation profession capable of performing comparative investment appraisals, making rational investment decisions and attaining a managerial role. We may even see an improvement in the efficiency of the property investment market.

The adoption of explicit appraisal models will in addition stimulate a drive for improved information in the property investment markets. This process has already started; empirical research in these markets has begun to command a premium.

Much work remains to be done, however. We will wish to know more about investors' criteria for equated yield/target rate choice; their attitude to risk, and whether it is primarily based upon portfolio or single-asset principles; the impact of depreciation upon return and its relationship to rental growth implications; and, among many other areas for research, the existence of any leading indicators for property investment performance.

But information applied within a faulty model is worthless. Only by the adoption of rational appraisal models will decision makers be able to utilise the increasing volume of property market intelligence which will characterise the coming decade.

BIBLIOGRAPHY

AIREA (1984), *The Dictionary of Real Estate Appraisal*, Chicago, American Institute of Real Estate Appraisers.

Baum, A. (1982), The Enigma of the Short Leasehold, *Journal of Valuation* 1: 5–9.

Baum, A. (1983), *Statutory Valuations*, London, RKP.

Baum, A. (1984), The Valuation of Reversionary Freeholds: A Review, *Journal of Valuation* 3: 157–67, 3: 230–47.

Baum, A. (1984b), The All Risks Yield: Exposing the Implicit, *Journal of Valuation* 2: 229–37.

Baum, A. (1985), Premiums on Acquiring Leases, *Rent Review and Lease Renewal* 5: 212–22.

Baum, A. and Butler, D. (1986), The Valuation of Short Leasehold Investments, *Journal of Valuation* 4: 342–53.

Baum, A. and Mackmin, D. (1981), *The Income Approach to Property Valuation* (2e), London, RKP.

Baum, A. and Yu, S.M. (1985), The Valuation of Leaseholds: A Review, *Journal of Valuation* 3: 157–67, 3: 230–47.

Bornand, D. (1985), Conveyancing of Commercial Property Investments, *Solicitors Journal*, August 9 and 16.

Bowcock, P. (1983a), The Valuation of Varying Incomes, *Journal of Valuation* 1: 366–71, 1: 72–6.

Bowcock, P. (1983b), Letter, *Estates Gazette*, 266: 87.

Bowie, N. (1972), Which Way Property Yields?, *Investors Chronicle*, April 7.

Bowie, N. (1982), Depreciation of Investment Properties, *Society of Investment Analysts*, Conference Paper, March 25.

Branch, B. (1985), *Investments: A Practical Approach*, Chicago, Longman.

Brealey, R. and Myers, S. (1984), *Principles of Corporate Finance*, New York, McGraw-Hill.

Brigham, E. (1985), *Financial Management: Theory and Practice* (4e), Chicago, Dryden.

Brown, G. (1985), An Empirical Analysis of Risk and Return in the U.K. Commercial Property Market, unpublished PhD thesis, University of Reading.

Colam, M. (1983), The Single Rate Valuation of Leaseholds, *Journal of Valuation* 2: 14–18.

Crosby, N. (1982), The Investment Method of Valuation: A Real Value Approach, Ryde Memorial Prizewinning Paper, RICS (unpublished).

Crosby, N. (1983), The Investment Method of Valuation: A Real Value Approach, *Journal of Valuation* 1: 341–50, 2: 48–59.

Crosby, N. (1984), Investment Valuation Techniques: The Shape of Things to Come? *The Valuer* 53/7: 196–7.

Crosby, N. (1985), The Application of Equated Yield and Real Value Approaches to the Market Valuation of Commercial Property Investments, unpublished PhD thesis, University of Reading.

Crosby, N. (1986a), Real Value, Rational Model, D.C.F.: A Reply, *Journal of Valuation* 4: 16–20.

Crosby, N. (1986b), The Application of Equated Yield and Real Value Approaches to Market Valuation, *Journal of Valuation* 4: 158–69, 261–74.

Crosby, N. (1987), *A Critical Examination of the Rational Model*, Department of Land Management and Development, University of Reading.

CSO (1983), *Economic Trends* 8: 114, CSO.

Daniels, C. (1981), *UK Commercial and Industrial Property into the 1980's*, London, Economist Intelligence Unit.

Darlow, C. (1983), *Valuation and Investment Appraisal*, London, Estates Gazette.

Davies, T.D. (1908), *Curtis on the Valuation of Land and Houses* (3e), London, Estates Gazette.

Debenham, Tewson and Chinnocks (1983), *Money into Property 1970–1983*, London, Debenham, Tewson and Chinnocks.

Debenham, Tewson and Chinnocks (1984), *Office Rent and Rates*, London, Debenham, Tewson and Chinnocks.

Enever, N. (1977), *The Valuation of Property Investments*, London, Estates Gazette.

Enever, N. (1981), *The Valuation of Property Investments* (2e), London, Estates Gazette.

Fisher, I. (1930), *The Theory of Interest*, Philadelphia, Porcupine Press.

Fraser, W.D. (1977), The Valuation and Analysis of Leasehold Investments in Times of Inflation, *Estates Gazette* 244: 197–201.

Fraser, W.D. (1984a), *Principles of Property Investment and Pricing*, London, Macmillan.

Fraser, W.D. (1984b), Y.P. or D.C.F. – A Question of Comparables, *Estates Gazette* 272; 492–3.

Fraser, W.D. (1985a), *Rational Models or Practical Methods, Journal of Valuation* 3: 253–8.

Fraser, W.D. (1985b), Gilt Yields and Property's Target Return, *Estates Gazette* 273: 1291–4.

Gitman, L.J. and Joehnk, M.D. (1984), *Fundamentals of Investing*, New York, Harper & Row.

Gray, K.J. and Symes, P.D. (1981), *Real Property and Real People*, London, Butterworth.

Greaves, M.J. (1972a), Discounted Cash Flow Techniques and Current Methods of Income Valuation, *Estates Gazette* 223: 2147–55, 223: 2339–45.

Greaves, M.J. (1972b), The Investment Method of Property Valuation and Analysis: an Examination of Some of its Problems, unpublished PhD thesis, University of Reading.

Greaves, M.J. (1985), The Valuation of Reversionary Freeholds: A Reply, *Journal of Valuation* 3: 248–52.

Greenwell, W. and Co. (1976), A Call for New Valuation Methods, *Estates Gazette* 238: 481–4.

Greer, G.E. (1979), *The Real Estate Investment Decision*, Lexington, Lexington Books.

Greer, G.E. and Farrell, M.D. (1984), *Investment Analysis for Real Estate Decisions*, Chicago, The Dryden Press.

Hager, D.P. and Lord, D.J. (1985), *The Property Market, Property Valuations and Property Performance Measurement*, Institute of Actuaries.

Harker, N. (1983), The Valuation of Varying Incomes: 1, *Journal of Valuation* 1: 363–5.

Healey and Baker (1982), *Yield Graph*, London, Healey & Baker, March.

Healey and Baker (1985), *Investment Report*, London, Healey & Baker, March.

Heselgrave, A.A. (1983), Are Investments Worth the Price? *Chartered Surveyor Weekly*, March 10th.

Hillier, F.S. (1963), The Derivation of Probabilistic Information for the Evaluation of Risky Investments, *Management Science*, 9: 443–57.

Hillier Parker Research, *A Forecast of Shop Rents*, annually.

Investors Chronicle/Hillier Parker (1979), *Rent Index*, London, ICHP, May.

Jacob, N. and Pettit, B. (1984), *Investments*, Irwin, Homewood.

Jaffe, A. (1977), Is there a 'New' Internal Rate of Return Literature?

AREUEA Journal 4: 483.

Jones, I.G. (1983), Equivalent Yield Analysis, *Journal of Valuation* 1: 246–52.

Knowles, F.C. and Jenkins, H.R. (1967), Evaluation of Capital Projects by D.C.F., *Chartered Auctioneer and Estate Agent*, July: 304–6.

Lawrence, D.M. and May, H.G. (1943), *Modern Methods of Valuation*, London, Estates Gazette.

Lawrence, D.M., Rees, W.H. and Britton, W. (1962), *Modern Methods of Valuation* (5e), London, Estates Gazette.

Lawrence, D.M., Rees, W.H. and Britton, W.E. (1971), *Modern Methods of Valuation* (6e), London, Estates Gazette.

Legal and General (1982), *Managed Fund Report*, London, Legal and General Assurance Co Ltd.

MacGregor, B.D. *et al.* (1985), *Land Availability for Inner City Development*, Department of Land Management, University of Reading.

McIntosh, A.P.J. (1983), Valuing Leasehold Interests, *Estates Gazette* 265: 939–41.

McIntosh, A.P.J. (1983b), The Rational Approach to Reversionary Leasehold Property Investment Valuations, in *Land Management: New Directions* (Chiddick, D. and Millington, A., eds.), London, Spon.

McIntosh, A.P.J. and Sykes, S.G. (1984), *A Guide to Institutional Property Investment*, London, Macmillan.

Markowitz, H. (1959), *Portfolio Selection – Efficient Diversification of Investments*, New Haven, Conn., Yale University Press.

Marriott, O. (1967), *The Property Boom*, London, Pan.

Marshall, P. (1976), Equated Yield Analysis, *Estates Gazette* 239: 493–7.

Marshall, P. (1979), *Donaldsons Investment Tables*, London, Donaldsons.

Mason, R. (1978), Versatility in Existing Method, *Investment and Management Surveyors Conference*, Nottingham, June.

Miles, J. (1987), Depreciation and Valuation Accuracy, *Journal of Valuation* 5: 125–37.

Millington, A. (1983), Sinking Fund Theory, *Estates Gazette* 266: 595–9.

Neuberger, H.L. and Nicholl, B.M. (1976), The Recent Course of Land and Property Prices and the Factors Underlying it, *Research Report* (4), London, DOE.

Newell, M.J. (1986), The Rate of Return as a Measure of Performance, *Journal of Valuation* 4: 130–42.

Norris, C. (1884), *The Appraiser, Auctioneer, Broker, House and Estate Agent, and Valuer's Pocket Assistant*, London, Crosby Lockwood.

Novi, D.C.S. (1985), Short Leaseholds: The Investment Market and Valuation Methodology, unpublished M.Phil thesis, University of Reading.

Parry Lewis, J. (1980), Investment Valuations, in Trott. A., *Property Valuation Methods: Interim Report*, London, Polytechnic of the South Bank/RICS.

Patrick, M.J. (1983), What Use is Property Performance Analysis?, *Journal of Valuation* 2: 137–41.

Plender, J. (1982), *That's the Way the Money Goes*, London, André Deutsch.

Ratcliff, R. (1965), *Modern Real Estate Valuation*, Madison, Democrat Press.

Reilly, F.K. (1985), *Investment Analysis and Portfolio Management*, Chicago, Dryden.

Richard Ellis (1980), *Property Investment Report*, London.

Richard Ellis (1983), *United Kingdom Property*, London.

R.I.C.S. (1981), *Guidance Notes on the Valuation of Assets* (2e), London, Royal Institution of Chartered Surveyors.

Robinson, J. (1985), Dual Rate D.C.F. Analysis, *Journal of Valuation* 4: 143–57.

Robinson, J. (1987), Cash Flows and Risk Analysis, *Journal of Valuation* 5: 268–9.

Rose, J. (1985), *The Dynamics of Urban Property Development*, London, Spon.

Rutterford, J. (1983), *Introduction to Stock Exchange Investment*, London, Macmillan.

Senior, H.E. (1975), Investment Yields in Perspective, *Estate Gazette* 233: 1115.

Sharpe, W.F. (1985), *Investments* (3e), New Jersey, Prentice.

Smith, S.A. (1924), *Curtis on the Valuation of Land and Houses* (6e), London, Estates Gazette.

Smith, S.A. (1933), *Curtis on the Valuation of Land and Houses* (7e), London, Estates Gazette.

Sykes, S.G. (1981), Property Valuation: A Rational Model, *The Investment Analyst* 61: 20–6.

Sykes, S.G. and McIntosh, A.P.J. (1982), Towards a Standard Property Income Valuation Model: Rationalisation or Stagnation, *Journal of Valuation* 1: 117–35.

Sykes, S.G. (1983a), Valuation Models: Action or Reaction, *Estates Gazette* 267: 1108.

Sykes, S.G. (1983b), The Assessment of Property Risk, *Journal of Valuation* 1: 253–67.

Trott, A. (1980), *Property Valuation Methods: Interim Report*, London, Polytechnic of the South Bank, RICS.

Uthwatt Report (1942), *Report of the Expert Committee on Compensation and Betterment*, Cmd. 6386.

Walls, C. (1977), *Property Shares*, London, W. Greenwell and Co.

Ward, C.W.R. (1979), *Methods of Incorporating Risk in the Analysis of*

Commercial Property Investment, unpublished PhD thesis, University of Reading.

White, P. (1977), The Two Faces of Janus, *Occasional Paper in Estate Management* (9), Reading, College of Estate Management.

Wood, E. (1972), Property Investment – A Real Value Approach, unpublished PhD thesis, University of Reading.

Wood, E. (1973), Positive Valuations: A Real Value Approach to Property Investment, *Estates Gazette* 226: 923–5, 226: 115–17, 226: 1311–13.

Wyatt, A. (1983), Appraisal Techniques in Retail Investment, unpublished conference paper, delivered at Henry Stewart Conference, *The Future of Shop Investment*.

INDEX